Audit Education

Audit professionals are valued members of society and are expected to be both skilled and ethical in their decision-making. The role of the auditor extends far beyond that of counting beans by demanding a social and political awareness, a technical knowledge, ethical principles and relationship skills. In addition, due to the team-oriented nature of the audit approach, auditors require strong team-building and interpersonal skills. This book offers expert descriptions of, and insights into, how such skills and responsibilities can be inculcated in tertiary education and professional training environments. Unlike other books which focus on auditing as a technical process, this volume examines auditing from a teaching and learning perspective. Expert contributors provide authoritative insights into an audit education which is embedded in accounting practice. The book's descriptions of these insights into improving education for future audit professionals may allow the introduction of new and challenging fields of enquiry.

Audit Education will be of great interest to educators in tertiary institutions, trainers in professional firms, and key individuals in accounting professional bodies seeking to ensure their members possess acceptable levels of attainment for admission and continued membership.

This book was originally published as a special issue of *Accounting Education: an international journal.*

Karen A. Van Peursem is Visiting Professor in the School of Accounting & Commercial Law at the Victoria University of Wellington, New Zealand. She has over 30 refereed publications in audit, ethics and public accountability, and is a co-author of a leading New Zealand audit textbook, now in its 6th edition.

Elizabeth A. Monk teaches in the School of Business at the University of Dundee, UK. Her PhD was in audit education and she continues to research in this area. She is also interested in corporate governance in developing countries and in the management of accounting information.

Richard M. S. Wilson is Emeritus Professor of Business Administration & Financial Management in the Business School, and Visiting Professor in the Department of Information Science, at Loughborough University, UK. He is the founding editor of *Accounting Education: an international journal.*

Ralph W. Adler is Professor of Accounting at the University of Otago, New Zealand. He has taught graduate and undergraduate students in the USA and New Zealand for more than 25 years. He is presently the Chairman of the Performance Measurement Association of Australasia.

Audit Education

Edited by
Karen A. Van Peursem, Elizabeth A. Monk, Richard M. S. Wilson and Ralph W. Adler

 Routledge
Taylor & Francis Group

LONDON AND NEW YORK

First published 2012
by Routledge
2 Park Square, Milton Park, Abingdon, Oxfordshire OX14 4RN

Simultaneously published in the USA and Canada
by Routledge
711 Third Avenue, New York, NY 10017

First issued in paperback 2016

Routledge is an imprint of the Taylor & Francis Group, an informa business

British Library Cataloguing in Publication Data
A catalogue record for this book is available from the British Library

ISBN 13: 978-1-138-19285-0 (pbk)
ISBN 13: 978-0-415-69873-3 (hbk)

Typeset in Times New Roman
by Taylor & Francis Books

Disclaimer
The publisher would like to make readers aware that the chapters in this book are referred to as articles as they had been in the special issue. The publisher accepts responsibility for any inconsistencies that may have arisen in the course of preparing this volume for print.

Contents

INTRODUCTION

Audit fulfils an important social and economic role. It adds a certain quality, or 'assurance', to information so as to convince some parties as to the truth of claims made by another. Those providing information seek the auditor's opinion in support of their claims. When that support is either not forthcoming or is misplaced, costs are incurred and disagreements arise. Questions are asked about the auditor's role in disasters that may occur as a result. Audit fees give an indication of these costs and courtrooms tell individual stories of its outcomes.

It follows that audit practice is a sometimes controversial and complex area of accounting. This is recently made apparent by the multitude of company failures and financial institution disasters which have been exposed by the low tide of economic crises. Scandals such as Enron, Parmalat, WorldCom and the Bernie Madoff case epitomise the sometimes unfulfilled ethical obligations of the audit professional. A growing awareness of a governing body's relationship with auditors has also brought the public's attention to the value of having an auditor who can bridge the gap between management and ownership. International auditing standards, and sometimes awkward efforts to come to a consensus on them, also occupy professionals as do the complexities associated with technology and computerisation. The role of the auditor extends far beyond that of counting beans by demanding a social and political awareness, a technical knowledge, ethical principles and relationship skills. Auditor independence, and an awareness of the risks involved in providing such assurance, are a lived experience for the audit professional.

So where does one begin to bring meaning to the audit learner's experience? There is not much time to enculturate them into the professionalism of audit. Audit is usually introduced at a university level as one of the last educational experiences prior to, or sometimes concurrent with, entering the workforce. Work experience in education is reasonably rare and so, while audit is a 'practical' subject in a sense, a real concern is that these students may be thrown into the field without a real chance to assimilate the knowledge they need in order to cope with the pressures they are about to face.

In this context in particular, we are very pleased to be given the opportunity - via this book - to offer ways forward for the audit educator. We are also pleased at the response we received to the *Call for Papers* for this project and now offer to you the results of an array of research and case experiences. We include five research studies which seek answers about how audit education can be improved. These are complemented by two case-based examples focussing on ethical and technical situations drawn from experience and practice, to help educators provide real-world experiences to their students to enable them to assimilate the knowledge which they have learnt in class. Given the constraints in which audit educators operate, insights into improving educational experiences are valuable because they can help sort through the over-whelming range of pedagogical possibility.

We begin with two chapters concerned with the skills and knowledge that could be, or should be, taught at university. Our first chapter looks to the value of generic skills in audit education. Crawford, Helliar and Monk explore the skills which audit and accounting practitioners expect from UK universities and contrast this with thos skills which students and employers expect. Although many of the generic skills deemed important by the various groups were revealed to be the same, this chapter highlights a slight mismatch between academia and practitioners, particularly with regard to where some of the skills should be taught.

Our second chapter creates an interesting parallel in the New Zealand context, focussing on audit skills and experiences expected from tertiary education. Chaffey, Van Peursem and Low uncover practitioners' views with regard to the specific audit knowledge and audit skills required by business. They reveal practitioners' insights on the balance needed between practice and theory and disclose differences among seg-ments of the profession (in particular as to the needs of the small business). They also reveal differences reflecting the professional maturity of the respondents.

From these educational wishlists, our third chapter helps narrow the field. Ballantine and McCourt examine whether and to what extent ethical orientation and gender affect ethical judgement. They find that both male and female students are 'high idealists', with classroom implications arising therefrom. We can also receive some comfort from the view that 'discriminating among students on the basis of ethical orientation [or] gender' would not appear to be necessary in the audit classroom. Their findings echo earlier expressions of needs for students to acquire judgement and decision-making skills.

Our next chapter explores the effectiveness of work-based training for auditors. Marriott, Telford, Davis and Evans reflect on the implications of reduced audit train-ing opportunities in their UK survey of trainees and their mentors. Although work-based training is highly valued, it is found that those employed in smaller firms have less opportunity to benefit from such experiences and are more reliant for their own skill-building on examination-based training. The influence of legislative change is felt in the experiences of these auditors.

This research also illuminates some of the difficulties in bringing real-world experi-ence to the classroom. Our fifth chapter by Drake offers one device for addressing this problem of real-world experience in her use of "living cases" formed from con-temporary news stories and similar reports. Focusing on corporate failure, Drake's chapter also hearkens back to the changing face of audit by showing how the freshness and the realism of using media reports of corporate failure may help engage the stu-dents and encourage the development of the key skills identified by Crawford et al., and Chaffey et al.

Over a decade has passed since Albrecht and Sack (2000) wrote their seminal monograph on the future of accounting education, and the conclusions they reached still ring true today: that we must "add high value to our students as they prepare for careers in a fast-changing business world" (p 59). The changing business world and the changing expectations of graduates' capabilities are perhaps particularly relevant for audit teaching. The need to demonstrate not only subject specific knowledge and skills, but also generic skills required for employment, is a challenge that accounting educators need to address, but technical subjects such as auditing are often harder to build-in this required mix of skills. With this in mind, we finish with two chapters which offer a more concrete example of innovative teaching in two areas of audit education.

Our first teaching resource chapter deals with performing agreed-upon procedures. Debraceny and Farewell present a case study on XBRL filing which is a topical area as regulation surrounding this is voluntary and is still a relatively new area. The case puts the student in the role of the engagement manager, and can be used to encourage students to consider the technical issues of XBRL filing, or it can focus instead on the more managerial processes underpinning this. Culminating in writing up the finding as a report to a client, the case also covers some of the more generic skills associated with client communication.

Our second case, and final chapter, looks at substantive tests of inventory. Clikeman provides an impressively comprehensive set of accounting records and supporting documents to allow students to explore a variety of issues involving inventory testing. In particular it focuses on the types of misstatements that can occur within the inventory. The case materials are flexible and allow educators to introduce a range of issues which can occur in inventory testing.

In the end, all five research studies and the two cases provide insights into an audit education that is embedded in accounting practice. Audit is not usually considered to be 'pure science', knowledge for knowledge's sake: it has its roots and finds its meaning in professional associationism and from the market and the people who engage in that market. The seven chapters presented here explore educational issues, but they also draw from these assumptions and that inextricable link between education and professionalism.

This creates both opportunities and a dilemma. The opportunities are found in the topics, skills, knowledge and experiences which can inform teaching. It is also apparent, and to be made yet more so in the next issue, that audit academics are committed to quality and professionally-relevant learning experiences. We cannot conclude, however, without pointing out that such research also offers up a normative dilemma: Should we prepare our students for current understandings of professional associationism? Should we leave it to the 'profession' to create education's boundaries? Should we benchmark their goals as our own? Or does doing so over-pragmatise the accounting degree?

In response, we can draw from Marriott, Telford, Davies and Evans and from Ballantine and McCourt in particular to suggest that academic research and a tertiary learning environment provide one feature not usually accessible to firms: a degree of objectivity and independence from the firm itself. While we are provided with valuable insights into improving education for future professionals, it may not be out of place to suggest that educators and researchers have another role to play. That is, through education and research can we truly hold up a mirror to professional practice and allow such insights to introduce new and challenging fields of enquiry. We take our cue here from the profession but also from a well-recognised interpretation of the academic's role: "Perspective, as a component of the philosophical approach, calls for the breadth of outlook necessary to grasp the ... full significance of things. Thus the philosopher *'would endeavour to consider any proposition in broad perspective – and not merely from the view of a special pleader – so that he can make well-grounded judgments about it.'"* (Mautz and Sharaf, 1980, p 9).

It is toward providing such insights, insights provided from a carefully considered and slightly distant perspective, that we hope you also find value in the chapters of this book.

Karen A. Van Peursem
Victoria University of Wellington, New Zealand
Elizabeth A. Monk
University of Dundee, UK
Richard M. S. Wilson
Loughborough University, UK
Ralph W. Adler
University of Otago, New Zealand
August, 2011

Reference

Mautz, R.K. & H.A. Sharaf (1980), *The Philosophy of Auditing*, (Sarasota, FL.: American Accounting Association).

Generic Skills in Audit Education

LOUISE CRAWFORD, CHRISTINE HELLIAR and
ELIZABETH A. MONK

University of Dundee, UK

ABSTRACT   *The academic literature and higher education benchmark statements identify groups of skills that are desirable both for students seeking employment and for employers seeking to recruit students. Professional accounting education pronouncements also stipulate skills that are necessary for an individual to possess in order to act as a competent accountant and auditor. Through a questionnaire survey, this research examines: (i) which of these skills audit and accounting practitioners expect UK universities to teach; (ii) which skills audit and accounting academics believe are important for students to acquire; (iii) which skills audit academics believe that employers require; and (iv) which skills audit academics teach in the UK. Institutional theory is used to develop and interpret this research.*

1.   Introduction

In recent years, Higher Education (HE) initiatives and the professional accountancy bodies in the UK and across the world have highlighted the need for all graduates to be employment ready, demonstrating not only subject specific knowledge and skills, but also generic skills required for employment. The National Committee of Inquiry into Higher Education put forward several 'principles' for general education change in the UK. These principles highlighted that: (i) students should participate in their own learning; (ii) learning and teaching should be enhanced; and (iii) learning outcomes should reflect employer requirements, including general or transferable skills (Dearing, 1997). Several studies have been undertaken in the light of the Dearing report to determine the skills that employers expect from a graduate (see, for example, Williams and Owens, 1997; Fallows and Steven, 2000). These studies determine that graduates of HE programmes should exhibit generic skills that will enable them to acquire and retain employment. More recently, the Financial Services Skills Council (FSSC, 2009) highlights that, within the UK, accountancy and finance employers are increasingly relying on HE institutions as training providers and requests:

... more partnership working between employers and HE institutions to deliver the skills required (FSSC, 2009, p. 39).

The professional accountancy bodies have also issued several warnings over the last few decades that university teaching may not be reaching either the needs of students or those of employers (AICPA 1978; Accounting Education Change Commission 1990, 1992), again highlighting a lack of generic skills in undergraduate accounting degree programmes. For example, in 1978 the American Institute of Certified Public Accountants (AICPA) highlighted an 'inadequate emphasis' on communication and interpersonal skills. Further, in 2008 the International Federation of Accountants (IFAC) emphasized the importance of generic skills in its *International Education Standard (IES) 3 Professional Skills and General Education* stating that:

> Appropriate skills enable the professional accountant to make successful use of the knowledge gained through general education. These skills are not always acquired from specific courses devoted to them but, rather, from the total effect of the program of professional accounting education as well as practical experience, and further developed through lifelong learning. ... Relevant skills can give professional accountants a competitive edge in the market place and are useful throughout an individual's career (IFAC, 2008b, paragraphs 8 and 9).

IES3 categorizes these skills as: (i) intellectual; (ii) technical and functional; (iii) personal; (iv) interpersonal and communication; and (v) organizational and business management skills. Acquisition of these skills, according to IES3, is essential for individuals seeking to become professional accountants. Further, in many of the 124 member countries of IFAC, it is only possible to become a qualified auditor after a set period of time as a professional accountant working in audit practice (for example, the UK, Australia and Uganda (IFAC Compliance Programme, 2004–2006)). Thus, the skills listed in IES3 apply equally to professional auditors' education as they do to professional accountants' education. Indeed, IES8 'Competence Requirements for Audit Professionals' prescribes skills for auditors stating that auditing is a '.... structured process that ..... involves the application of analytical skills, professional judgment and professional scepticism' (IFAC, 2008c, para 1). However, the recent financial crisis has called into question the competence of auditors and to the claim that '.... external audit adds credibility to financial statements' (Sikka, 2009, p. 871). The criticism of auditors, especially their auditing of banks, indicates that they are not demonstrating the requisite professional skills and it is, therefore, appropriate to establish whether higher education has a role in developing the requisite skills for professional accountants and auditors.

Using a questionnaire survey of accounting academics and practising chartered accountants (as examples of educators and potential employers, respectively), this research examines 16 generic skills that may be important to the accounting and auditing profession and examines employer and academic views on whether these skills should be taught in UK universities.[1] In particular, the research asks:

(i) Which of these 16 skills do practitioners expect universities to teach?
(ii) Which of these 16 skills do academics believe are important for students to acquire?
(iii) Which skills do academics believe employers require?
(iv) Which skills do audit academics teach?

The research findings are interpreted through the lens of institutional theory.

The paper is structured as follows: Section 2 reviews the extant literature on generic skills both in accounting education in general, and in auditing in particular, and identifies which skills are cited as being important and the teaching methods used to facilitate the development of these generic skills. This section also outlines institutional theory as the framework used to inform and interpret this research. Section 3 details the questionnaire survey and a discussion of the research findings is developed in section 4. The final section of this paper presents the conclusion.

2. Literature Review

2.1. *The nature of generic skills in auditing and accounting education*

Skills that are acquired, or should be acquired, during a programme of undergraduate education can be broadly split between subject specific skills and generic skills. Evidence of this split can be seen in the Quality Assurance Agency (QAA) benchmark statement for Accounting and other subject disciplines in the UK (QAA, 2007). With regard to generic skills, these have also been described as skills that are transferable (i.e. they can be transferred from one job or career to another) and are skills that are required for employability. Other terms used to describe such skills in the literature and educational or professional pronouncements include 'soft', 'key' or 'core' skills (QAA, 2007; Dacko, 2006; Yorke, 2006), as well as 'capabilities' and 'competencies' (IFAC, 2008a). HE course outlines and programme documentation reflect the global acknowledgement that HE should produce students who have mastered both a specific discipline and also:

> A set of achievements—skills, understandings and personal attributes—that makes graduates more likely to gain employment and be successful in their chosen occupations, which benefits themselves, the workforce, the community and the economy (Yorke, 2006, p. 8).

Thus, the term 'generic skill' is often used to describe any skill that is not subject-specific but is desirable for employability purposes.

In the accounting and auditing profession, the acquisition of generic skills is vitally important where practitioners have to compete in a market place that is dominated by advances in information and communications technology. Several studies have highlighted the fact that changes in the use of computer technology in the workplace have meant that more computer literate graduates can do work that was previously restricted only to trained accountants and auditors (Borthick and Clark, 1986; Sangster and Mulligan, 1997; Stoner, 1999; Albrecht and Sack, 2000; Marriott, Selwyn and Marriott, 2003). Indeed, organizations can purchase book-keeping, tax compliance software and audit and risk management software, as well as outsourcing simple compliance work, all of which negates the need to employ professional accountants and auditors. With such advances in technology, the focus of auditors and accountants as compliance workers is shifting and the profession has to develop 'gold-collar' assurance and advisory workers (Howieson, 2003). To succeed as assurance and advisory professionals in various areas of public practice, professional accountants and auditors need to develop skills such as analytical reasoning, communication, negotiating, management, marketing, interpersonal and general business skills (ICAEW, 1996). Howieson (2003) argues that professional accountants must demonstrate broad business skills to ensure that they are competitive and can quickly adapt to changes in the market place, stating that:

> Accountants ... need to have specialist knowledge in a specific industry but they will also have to posses a range of generalist ('generic') skills which enable them to apply their specialist knowledge within the 'big picture' context of a client's/employer's organizations and strategy. (Howieson, 2003, p. 80).

In 1996 The Institute of Chartered Accountants in England and Wales (ICAEW) reported on the challenges facing chartered accountants in the new millennium. The report identified key opportunities for the profession and discussed the broad business and general skills necessary to succeed as a chartered accountant (ICAEW, 1996). The report identified several skills necessary for auditing, including: entrepreneurship and the need to diversify assurance services; team working and team management; general business skills to enable working (and adding value) in different industry sectors; and excellent IT and systems skills. In addition, there was a need to build on a strong reputation for professional ethics as well as develop salesmanship and marketing skills. The ICAEW also made recommendations to the audit profession to 'develop training programmes in the skills necessary to allow members to diversify away from standard audit products' (ICAEW, 1996, p. 22), highlighting the importance of developing staff to meet the changing demands of business.

2.2. *Categorizing generic skills in audit and accounting education*

The QAA Accounting benchmark statement identifies the generic skills and abilities that graduates of accounting programmes should have acquired on top of their respective disciplines (QAA, 2007). These skills are similar to those stipulated by IFAC as being requisite in a programme of professional accounting education, although they are grouped differently (IFAC, 2008b). A review of the skills in IES3 (IFAC, 2008b) shows that many are generic, with the subject specific skills being included under the technical and functional skills heading of IES3. In addition, IES8 prescribes the necessary skills for audit professionals to be applied in an audit environment (IES8, para. 42b) and to be developed at an 'advanced level'[2] in an audit environment (IES8, para. 42a). *IES4 Professional Values, Ethics and Attitudes*, also identifies further skills such as independence and reliability.

Table 1 tabulates the skills in the QAA Accounting benchmark statements, IES3, IES8 and IES4. There are 28 skills and these have been labelled (a) to (bb). A review of Table 1 shows that there is a degree of overlap of the skills identified in the different IESs.[3] These same skills tend to dominate the literature although they may be grouped differently by different authors. For example, Gammie, Gammie and Cargill (2002) develop a business skills module for delivery in undergraduate accounting programmes and synthesize the following 'employability' skills: (i) communication skills (o–u)[4]; (ii) problem-solving skills such as lateral thinking and creativity (a–c); (iii) interpersonal skills including teamwork and the ability to work on one's own (o–u); and (iv) organizational skills such as planning, time-keeping, responsibility and strategic thinking (v–y). Dacko (2006) also categorizes the business skills acknowledged as being important from an examination of the management education literature: decision-making skills (a–c); analytical skills (a–c); leadership skills (x); interpersonal skills (o–u); and communication (oral and written) skills (o–u). There are also clearly overlaps between the Gammie *et al.*'s (2002) and Dacko's (2006) identification and categorizations of generic skills with IESs and the QAA Accounting benchmark statement.

In relation to auditing, Hassall, Dunlop and Lewis (1996) found that skills such as communication (o,t), reasoning (a,b) and problem-solving (b,c) were ranked as being important, and Okike (1999) later identified teamwork (p), client relations (o-u), audit judgment (y) and negotiation (r) as required skills for auditors. However, studies of audit education highlight that practical, critical (b-c), analytical (b-c), judgemental (y) and decision-making skills (e m, and v) are often lacking in accounting graduates

Table 1. Generic skills identified by Professional and Higher Education institutions

Cognitive abilities and generic skills (Accounting benchmark statement, QAA, 2007)	Professional skills and general education (IES3, IFAC 2008b)	Competence requirements for audit professionals (IES8, IFAC 2008c)	Professional values, ethics and attitudes (IES 4, IFAC 2008e)
	Intellectual skills		
(a–c) the ability to locate, extract and analyse data from multiple sources;	(a) the ability to locate, obtain, organize and understand information from human, print and electronic sources;	(a) undertaking appropriate technical research;	
(b,c) critical evaluation of arguments and evidence;	(b) the capacity for inquiry, research, logical and analytical thinking, powers of reasoning, and critical analysis; and	(b,c) identifying and solving problems;	
(b,c) the ability to analyse and draw reasoned conclusions;	(c) the ability to identify and solve unstructured problems which may be in unfamiliar settings.	(b,c) demonstrate capacity for inquiry, abstract logical thought, and critical analysis;	
	Technical and functional skills	(a–c) gathering and evaluating evidence;	
(d) numeracy skills, including manipulating data and appreciating statistical concepts at an appropriate level;	(d) numeracy, mathematical and statistical applications and IT proficiency;		
	(e) decision modelling and risk analysis;		
	(f) measurement;		
	(g) reporting; and		
	(h) compliance with legislative and regulatory requirements	(h) apply relevant audit standards and guidance;	
		(h) evaluate applications of relevant financial reporting standards;	
	Personal skills		
	(i) self-management;		
(j) capacities for independent and self-managed learning;	(j) initiative, influence and self learning;		
	(k) prioritize and organize work to meet tight deadlines;		(k) timeliness
	(l) anticipate and adapt to change;		
	(m) consider professional values ethics and attitudes in decision making; and		(m) ethical dilemma resolution

(Continued)

Table 1. Continued

Cognitive abilities and generic skills (Accounting benchmark statement, QAA, 2007)	Professional skills and general education (IES3, IFAC 2008b)	Competence requirements for audit professionals (IES8, IFAC 2008c)	Professional values, ethics and attitudes (IES 4, IFAC 2008e)
	(n) professional scepticism. Interpersonal and communication skills	(n) demonstrate professional scepticism;	(n) scepticism
(o,p) an ability to work in groups, and other interpersonal skills, including oral as well as written presentation skills	(o) work with others in a consultative process, to withstand and resolve conflict;		
	(p) work in teams;	(p) working in teams effectively;	
	(q) interact with culturally and intellectually diverse people;		
	(r) negotiate acceptable solutions and agreements in professional situations;		
	(s) work effectively in a cross-cultural setting;		
(t) communication skills including the ability to present quantitative and qualitative information, together with analysis, argument and commentary;	(t) present, discuss, report and defend views effectively through formal, informal, written and spoken communication; and	(t) presenting, discussing, and defending views effectively through formal, informal, written, and spoken communication.	
	(u) listen and read effectively, including a sensitivity to cultural and language differences. Organizational and business management skills		
	(v) strategic planning, project management, management of people and resources, and decision making;		
	(w) organize and delegate tasks, to motivate and to develop people;		
	(x) leadership; and		
	(y) professional judgment and discernment.	(y) apply professional judgment; and	
	(z) withstand and resolve conflicts.	(z) conflict resolution;	
			(aa) independence; (bb) reliability.

(Libby, 1991; Fraser, Hatherly and Lin, 1997; Chung and Munroe, 1999; Helliar, Monk, Stevenson and Allison, 2007; Helliar, Monk and Stevenson, 2009).

A number of competency studies have also been carried out by professional organizations over the last two decades, detailing the skills needed for entry-level accountants with particular reference to the audit profession (reviewed in Palmer, Ziegenfuss and Pinkser, 2004). A comparison of these studies found that the key skills required were communication skills (o–u), interpersonal skills (o–u) and problem-solving skills (a–c). Further, it was noted that a crucial skill for auditors was the ability to constantly find and evaluate new information (a,c) (Palmer *et al.*, 2004).

However, it is not clear which skills are seen as being important by students and which are important to employers and this distinction demarks whether the development of skills should be supply-led (emerging from perceived student needs) or demand-led (emerging from perceived employer needs) (McSkimming, 2007). Thus, Table 1 shows the skills that are necessary for accountants and auditors to master; the most effective way of developing these skills is also of relevance.

2.3 *Developing generic skills*

IFAC recognizes that a programme of professional education often includes general and undergraduate accounting education (IFAC, 2008d, para13). However, apart from IES8 requiring 'advanced level' audit skills to be developed in an audit environment, IFAC does not suggest whether skills should be developed at the academic undergraduate level or in post-graduate professional training programmes.

IES4 recommends that participative teaching approaches can be used to facilitate skill development such as: case studies; role-playing; discussion; analysis of real-life business situations; ethical dilemmas and disciplinary pronouncements; and guest speakers with experience of decision-making (IFAC, 2008e). Further, AECC Position Statement No. 2 (1992) recommends that:

> Students' involvement should be promoted by methods such as cases, simulations, and group projects (AECC 1992, p. 250).

These recommendations suggests that the development of generic skills should be student-led when students choose how to learn, are responsible for organizing the material, decide what material to examine and when to study. Interactive teaching methods, such as business games and simulations, may encourage the acquisition of judgement-based skills, for example the formulation of hypotheses, conjectural learning, research skills (a–c) and skills to manipulate and analyse data (b,d), and may help students to develop an active learning philosophy[5] (Bagranoff, 1993; Boyce, 1999; Crawford, Helliar, Monk and Stevenson, 2011; Dowling, Godfrey and Gyles 2003; Oglesbee, Bitner and Wright, 1988).

Teaching methods such as case studies, videos, computerised simulations, virtual factories, and games have all been used in an attempt to improve students' understanding of a variety of accounting and auditing topics, and the development of generic skills, by getting students to participate in their own learning experience (Maltby, 2001; Okike, 1999; McCourt-Larres and Radcliffe, 2000; Helliar, Michaelson, Power and Sinclair, 2000). Case studies are also used by several professional bodies as the method of assessment for the final qualifying examination (see for example the Institute of Chartered Accountants of Scotland (ICAS) and the Chartered Institute of Management Accountants (CIMA) syllabus (ICAS, 2009, CIMA, 2010)); they are reported to facilitate the development of many judgment-based skills (a-d) (Drake, 1999; Davies, 2000). Boyce, Williams

Kelly and Yee (2001) examine teaching methods and note that case studies in auditing often focus on technical issues rather than developing generic skills and suggest that role-play could be used instead to develop communication (o–u) and information gathering skills (a–c).

Clearly generic skills are important for accountant and auditors. However, without an underlying theory to embed skills development within education, the identification of generic skills becomes 'little more that a wish list constructed by interested parties' (Yorke, 2006). Indeed, Yorke goes on to say:

> The Dearing approach to key skills is symptomatic of a widespread failure to underpin key skills with theory. Various lists of skills appear in the literature relating to employment, but they seem to have been produced on an ad hoc basis (Yorke, 2006, p, 11).

The research on which the current paper reports uses an institutional theory framework to explore which generic skills employers think universities should be teaching and compares these with those that academics perceive as being important to employers, and to students. Preliminary arguments are put forward with regard to the potential influences on academics' perceptions of skills that are important in undergraduate education and the extent to which academics' perceptions are reflected in their teaching practice.

2.4 *Theoretical Framework*

Institutional theory is used to develop and interpret the research presented in this paper. Institutions are conceptualised as the assumptions and beliefs of a group or organization of like-minded people. Institutional beliefs are practiced through the routines and habits of the group and, thus, there is an expectation that behaviour should reflect the beliefs of the group (Burns, 2000). However, the degree to which routines are practiced and become unquestioned expected forms of behaviour will depend on internal and external factors that influence these institutions (Burns, 2000; Moll, Burns and Major, 2006).

The academics involved in this research on generic skills are all involved in accounting education and/or research and work in the university sector in the UK and their views arguably should constitute a cohesive institutional set of beliefs. The paper also considers, as a subset of this institutional population, those academics who teach or research auditing to see if their views are different from the overall academic institutional population, and to determine whether the perceptions of this subset on the importance of generic skills constitutes an 'institution' amongst a group of like-minded individuals. The extent to which their beliefs are borne out in practice is investigated by exploring whether academics teach (or would like to teach) the skills which they perceive as being important. Similarities and differences within the population will highlight the extent to which the beliefs and assumptions of employers and academics about the importance of generic skills that should be taught at university have been institutionalized within their respective domains. The views of academics provide an insight into whether skills-development has been institutionalised on the needs of students or the needs of employers reflecting a supply-led or a demand-led emphasis. Factors that may influence these beliefs and assumptions are investigated by exploring differences in academics' perceptions of the importance of generic skills development for meeting student needs compared to employers' needs

3. Research Method

A questionnaire survey was used to explore the perceptions of accounting academics and accounting practitioners about the importance of a set of 16 generic skills. These skills

Table 2. Response rate of all academic respondents

		Number responded rate			
Groups	Total number sent	Total	Questionnaire A	Questionnaire B	Response
Audit academics	142	56	26	30	39%
Accounting education	183	79	42	37	43%
Random	146	55	24	31	38%
All groups	471	190	92	98	40%

Note: This table shows number of total questionnaires sent, number returned and the percentage response rate for each of the three academic groups. Two groups of questionnaires were distributed which were labelled A and B.

were developed from the literature and from the personal experience of the authors, who collectively had 10 years practical experience of auditing, 25 years experience of teaching auditing and 35 years teaching in the HE sector. To confirm relevance, the 16 generic skills were mapped to the QAA Accounting benchmark statement and IES3, IES4 and IES8 in Table 1 as these documents were considered the most applicable in identifying the necessary skills required within a programme of professional accountancy and audit education. The set of 16 generic skills (listed in Tables 2–4) include such skills as critical reasoning, numeracy and oral and written communication skills. Not all the 28 skills (a) to (bb) in Table 1 have been included as some of these were technical skills (f,g,h) and some were professional rather than generic skills (m,n,q,s,aa,bb) or were skills that would be needed by more senior members of the profession rather than recent graduate trainees (v,w,x). Also included in the list of 16 skills that were surveyed are two skills, lateral

Table 3. Practitioners' views on whether universities should encourage the development of generic skills. This table shows whether practitioners think that a range of generic skills should be taught by universities. The table is ordered in order of importance of the skills that universities should teach

	Reference table	Should universities teach this?	
		Yes	No
Analytical skills	(a–c)	290	13
Presentation skills	(t)	286	12
Written communication skills	(t)	270	26
Basic computer skills	(a) (d)	269	30
Information collecting skills	(a)	263	27
Problem-solving	(a–c) (e)	253	29
Planning skills	(k) (v)	252	38
Critical reasoning	(b–c) (m-n) (y) (z)	242	44
Oral communication	(o) (q) (t)	241	52
Time management	(k) (l)	236	56
Self-study/research skills	(a) (i) (j)	232	58
Teamwork	(p) (s)	230	56
Numeracy	(d–f)	226	60
Lateral thinking	(b) (c) (t)	207	78
Listening skills	(u)	200	85
Persistence	(m) (o) (r) (y) (z)	141	135

Table 4. Academics' perception of the importance of generic skills to students after graduation

	All academics			Audit academics		
	Mean	SD	Number	Mean	SD	Number
Analytical skills	1.19	0.67	90	1.19	0.80	26
Written communication skills	1.19	0.65	90	1.27	0.83	26
Oral communication skills	1.23	0.69	90	1.31	0.84	26
Problem-solving	1.36	0.74	89	1.38	0.85	26
Critical reasoning skills	1.38	0.79	90	1.35	0.89	26
Basic computer use (word processing, spreadsheets, e-mail)	1.48	0.78	90	1.38	0.90	26
Listening skills	1.52	0.77	90	1.62	0.98	26
Numeracy	1.52	0.77	90	1.38	0.85	26
Self-study/research skills	1.57	0.80	89	1.48	0.65	25
Time management	1.59	0.83	90	1.62	0.90	26
Presentation skills	1.62	0.79	90	1.69	0.79	26
Planning skills	1.67	0.85	90	1.65	0.94	26
Teamwork	1.72	0.78	89	1.56	0.58	25
Persistence	1.78	0.90	90	1.77	0.99	26
Data/information collecting skills	1.80	0.87	89	1.77	0.95	26
Lateral thinking	1.81	0.84	89	1.85	0.92	26

Note: This table shows all academic responses to the importance of generic skills. The table presents
   the skills ranked in descending order of importance. The responses were on a five-point Likert
   scale where 1 was strongly agree and a 5 was strongly disagree.

thinking and persistence, that do not directly map to the skills in IES3, IES4 or IES8. However, acquisition of these skills is implied as follows: (i) lateral thinking (b,c,t) is using unorthodox or seemingly illogical thinking to solve problems and can be mapped to the problem-solving skills required by IES3 and IES 8 (b,c) and also to communicating and defending results of problem-solving (t); and (ii) persistence (m,o,r,y,z), meaning determination, diligence and perseverance, can be mapped to IES3 personal, interpersonal and communication skills (m, o, r) as well as IES4 and IES8 skills (y,z). Table 2 includes a column showing how the set of 16 generic skills have been mapped to the skills listed in Table 1.

A postal questionnaire was sent to a group of academics selected from the *British Accounting Review Research Register* (Helliar, Gray and Monk, 2002) in December 2002. Those selected came from stratified groups who either: (i) taught auditing or had a research interest in auditing (the Audit Group); (ii) had a research interest in accounting education or in the use of computers in teaching; or (iii) comprised a random sample of other accounting academics in the UK. The questionnaire survey was part of a larger project looking at university teaching more generally with a view to developing a teaching resource to use within an audit module (Monk, 2004; Helliar *et al.*, 2007). Views of the wider academic community were seen as being relevant for two reasons; many academics are fully-qualified accountants with practical audit experience (such as two of the authors), and many of them could already be using innovative teaching methods to encourage the development of generic skills.

For the first two groups, all academics fitting the criteria in the *BAR Research Register* were included, thus no sampling was necessary. For the third group, a list of all remaining academics meeting the criteria in the *BAR Research Register* was compiled and every eighth name was selected to give a comparable sized group. The 2002 edition of the

BAR Research Register contained 1504 names, those who researched or taught audit comprised 142, and those who researched accounting education or IT use comprised 183, leaving 1179 academics. Selecting every eighth name created a random group of 146.

The first mailing was sent out in December 2002 with a follow-up in February 2003. The response rate was favourable, at 40%. This response was split fairly equally between the groups, with the audit sample returning 39%, the accounting education sample (including computers in education) returning 43% and the randomly selected sample returning 38% as detailed in Table 5.

In the autumn of 2003 three professional accounting bodies—the Institute of Chartered Accountants of Scotland (ICAS), the Institute of Chartered Accountants in England & Wales (ICAEW), and the Association of Chartered Certified Accoutants (ACCA)—each kindly provided the postal details of a random sample of roughly 500 of their members. In addition, ICAS provided 400 student members' postal details. In total 1971 questionnaires were posted to accountants and ICAS trainee accountants. Of these, 321 replies were received, resulting in a response rate of 16.2%, which is acceptable for this sort of study.

The questionnaires were six pages long and covered similar questions. Most of the questions were in the form of a five-point Likert scale, with some open-ended questions at the end inviting respondents to note any comments relating to these points.

4. Findings

The practitioner questionnaire asked respondents to indicate whether universities should teach the list of 16 generic skills. Table 3 lists the 16 skills and shows that the majority of practitioners believe that 15 of these skills should be taught at universities, which

Table 5. Academics' perceptions of the importance of generic skills to employers

	All Academics			Audit Academics		
	Mean	SD	Number	Mean	SD	Number
Oral communication skills	1.48	0.92	95	1.41	0.83	29
Analytical skills	1.68	0.86	94	1.59	0.87	29
Written communication skills	1.71	0.98	95	1.69	1.04	29
Teamwork	1.82	0.93	95	1.66	0.81	29
Numeracy	1.86	0.87	95	1.83	0.76	29
Problem-solving	1.89	0.89	93	1.86	0.99	29
Presentation skills	1.99	0.85	94	2.07	0.81	28
Basic computer use (word processing, spreadsheets, email)	1.95	0.89	95	1.93	1.03	29
Critical reasoning skills	2.05	0.95	95	2.03	1.05	29
Time management	2.05	0.94	95	1.97	0.78	29
Planning skills	2.19	0.83	95	2.14	0.83	29
Data/information collecting skills	2.33	0.82	95	2.31	0.97	29
Listening skills	2.41	0.92	95	2.14	0.95	29
Persistence	2.49	0.82	95	2.45	0.74	29
Lateral thinking	2.54	0.95	95	2.55	1.02	29
Self-study/research skills	2.61	0.98	94	2.57	0.96	28

Note: This table shows generic skills ranked in descending order of importance according to all academics' perceptions of their importance to a prospective employer. Means are based on a five-point Likert scale where 1 indicated very important.

indicates an institutional belief amongst this employer group of respondents. The most important skills that practitioners thought should be taught at university were: analytical skills (96% support); presentation skills (96% support); and written communication skills (91% support). However, employers did not demonstrate a common belief about whether universities should teach persistence with only 51% supporting this proposition. This may reflect a belief amongst some practitioners that persistence should be developed at an advanced level in an audit environment (see Table 1, for example skills y,z); indeed IFAC pronouncements such as IES8 may be influencing such practitioner-held beliefs.

The academic respondents were given the same list of 16 generic skills as the practitioners and were asked to indicate the importance of each of these to students after graduation (Table 4). All 16 skills were very highly rated, with mean responses of below three (three being the neutral response). Analytical skills, written skills and oral skills were the highest ranked which was in accordance with the practitioners' requirements. However, presentation skills, ranked second by employers, were ranked much lower (eleventh) by the academics, and oral communication skills were ranked much higher (third) by the academics than the employers (ninth). Despite this difference in ranking, both presentation skills and oral communication skills are categorized together as 'interpersonal and communication' skills in IES3. Therefore, this difference between employers and academics in the ranking of oral skills and presentation skills is not so important; what is important is that interpersonal communication skills are both ranked highly by employers and academics. Overall, there appears to be a similarity between the generic skills that employers want universities to teach (Table 2) and those that academics deem to be important for graduates to possess (Table 3). There was also similarity in ranking of the skill of persistence which was ranked low by both employers (sixteenth) and academics (fourteenth). From an institutional perspective, there is a similarity in beliefs between practitioners and academics and this may be a result of employer expectations influencing the beliefs of academics. Many accounting degrees are accredited by the professional bodies and there are very strong links between the two, thus professional needs may have permeated academia and become institutionalised. Alternatively, both employers' and academics' perceptions may have been influenced by the same external factors, for example, the graduate employability initiatives by such bodies as the Accountancy & Finance Sector Qualification Strategy (FSSC, 2009) and the QAA. Such external factors may also have aligned the views of practitioners and academics over the necessary skills for employability.

Academics were also asked to indicate how important they thought the same list of 16 generic skills was to prospective employers (rather than to the students themselves) to establish whether academics' perceptions of the importance of skills were influenced by employer-needs (demand-led) or student-needs (supply-led) (McSkimming, 2007). Table 4 shows much less agreement over which skills are important to employers where the mean values are higher in Table 4 compared to Table 3, suggesting that academics are less sure about the skills that employers value. Analytical and communication skills are again perceived to be important, but teamwork is viewed as being much more important to prospective employers than to students. This suggests that there is a gap between the skills that academics think are important for students to have and the skills that academics think employers actually want students to have. This may not be surprising as the skills required by employers are likely to change based on changes in market conditions, client profiles and staffing levels, as emphasized in Howieson (2003). That is to say, skills desired by employers may reflect the current demands of the work environment, whereas academics may wish their students to graduate with a complete skills tool kit, adaptable to different career choices in a changeable job market. Arguably, comparison of Table 3 with Table 4 indicates that academics' beliefs about the importance of skills are influenced more by their perceptions of student-needs than employer-needs.

The academics' questionnaire also asked those academics who teach auditing whether they taught any of these 16 skills within their audit courses and the success of teaching these skills. Table 6 shows that almost all of the academics in the audit group teach analytical skills to their students and most believe that they have some success (Table 6). Academics reported that it was more difficult to teach persistence and lateral thinking successfully with nearly 50% perceiving little success in this area. Persistence and lateral thinking may be more closely aligned with IES8's advanced level audit skills (for example, Table 1, skills y and z) and should perhaps be left to be developed in a practical audit environment rather than being taught in undergraduate audit modules.

Comparing Tables 3, 4 and 6, there is clear alignment in academics' ranking of the importance of analytical, written communication and oral communication skills to both students and employers (Table 3 and 4, respectively), although academics perceive that their success in developing oral communication skills is not as high as their teaching of analytical and written communication skills (Table 6). Likewise, there is alignment in the perceived lack of importance of persistence and lateral thinking and few academics indicate that they teach these skills; where they do teach these skills, their success is considered by audit academics to be much lower compared to their teaching of other skills. Persistence and lateral thinking may be especially relevant to audit careers where graduates may need to seek evidence through questioning and analytical reasoning (Table 1, skill b,c,r) (Fraser *et al.*, 1997), and develop moral courage to apply professional judgement (Table 1, skill m,y) and withstand and resolve conflicts (Table 1, skill o,z) (Molyneux, 2008). Overall, it can be argued that academics' beliefs and assumptions are reflected in their teaching routines and behaviours. However, there are some exceptions to this. For example, academic perceptions of the skill of teamwork shows it is ranked highly (fourth) by academics as being important to employers (Table 4), and is

Table 6. Teaching generic skills within the audit course (audit academics)

	Yes some success	Yes little success	Would like to	Not want to	Number
Analytical skills	78.6%	14.3%	3.6%	3.6%	28
Written communication skills	71.4%	17.9%	7.1%	3.6%	28
Teamwork	65.4%	15.4%	7.7%	11.5%	26
Problem-solving	60.0%	24.0%	8.0%	8.0%	25
Self-study/research skills	59.3%	33.3%	0.0%	7.4%	27
Oral communication skills	55.6%	29.6%	3.7%	11.1%	27
Presentation skills	54.2%	16.7%	8.3%	20.8%	24
Critical reasoning skills	50.0%	38.5%	3.8%	7.7%	26
Listening skills	47.6%	28.6%	14.3%	9.5%	21
Planning skills	45.8%	25.0%	4.2%	25.0%	24
Time management	36.4%	36.4%	4.5%	22.7%	22
Basic computer skills	30.0%	0.0%	10.0%	60.0%	20
Information collecting skills	30.0%	1.7%	10.0%	20.0%	23
Numeracy	28.6%	14.3%	0.0%	57.1%	21
Persistence	26.3%	47.4%	0.0%	26.3%	19
Lateral thinking	26.1%	47.8%	13.0%	13.0%	23

Note: Table indicates the percentage of audit academics who teach generic skills. It is ranked in descending order of the skills that are taught successfully.

taught with some perceived success (Table 6). However, this skill is ranked low (thirteenth) by academics in perceived importance to students (Table 3), and low (twelfth) by employers as a skill that should be developed at university (Table 2).

The Audit Group (i.e. those academics who taught on an audit module) responded with a similar profile to the wider academic group in both Tables 3 and 4. Again, all of the skills listed are seen as being important both to students and to employees, but the ranking is slightly different. In Table 3, the audit academics rank teamwork as a desirable skill for students somewhat higher than the overall academic population. Similarly, listening skills are seen as being slightly less important. Looking at the skills seen as important to employers, the audit academics ranked presentation skills as slightly less important and time management as slightly more important that the wider population. Both these tables, however, seem to indicate that academics hold similar views on the importance of generic skills and, thus, the audit academics can be seen to share beliefs and assumptions with the wider academic community.

Table 6, therefore, focuses solely on the audit academics and attempts to ascertain whether belief matches practice by asking what skills are actually taught within an audit module. There were two skills that a majority of audit academics perceived they should not teach: numeracy and basic computer skills (Table 6). Thirty per cent of academic respondents stated that they successfully taught computer skills to their audit students, while 60% did not want to teach this. A similar split was true of numeracy skills, with 28% successfully teaching it and 57% not wanting to teach this. However, Table 4 shows that basic computer skills were ranked highly (fourth) by academics as being important to students and Table 4 shows that numeracy skills were ranked fifth in importance for employers. Nevertheless, the generic skills identified in Table 1 show that numeracy and IT skills are important in undergraduate accounting education (QAA, 2007) and in a programme of professional accounting education (IES3, IFAC, 2008b). However, they are not listed in IES8 as specific skills associated with auditing (IFAC, 2008c), but to be a professional auditor necessitates being a qualified accountant first. It is difficult to explain why a large proportion of audit academics did not want to teach numeracy and basic computer skills without further research, but perhaps it reflects a belief amongst this group that such skills should be taught early in accounting education programmes rather than be the remit of audit training and professional development.

In accordance with the results presented in this paper (per the ranking of skills in Tables 2–6), the literature identifies intellectual (a–c) and interpersonal and communication (o–u) skills as being important skills for trainee auditors (Hassall et al., 1996; Okike, 1999; Palmer et al., 2004). However, the literature also highlights the fact that accounting graduates do not always possess intellectual skills (b–c) (Libby, 1991; Fraser et al., 1997; Chung and Munroe, 1999; Helliar et al., 2000), which contradicts the perception held by academics in this research that they teach these skills with some success (Table 6). The literature also bemoans the fact that accounting graduates often do not possess the skills of judgement (y) and decision-making (m,v). These skills are mapped to the skill of persistence in this research; interestingly employers ranked persistence low as a skill to be developed at university and academics did not want to teach this skill. Thus, it may not be surprising that skills relating to persistence are not possessed by accounting graduates.

5. Conclusion

This study determined a set of 16 generic skills, mapped to both the QAA Accounting benchmark statement and IFAC's International Education Standards and examined whether academics and practitioners believe that these skills should be developed at the undergraduate level and contribute to a programme of professional education.

The practitioners in this study thought that all 16 skills were important, but a ranking of their importance showed that analytical skills, presentation skills and written communication skills were the most important. The academics were asked about which generic skills students should gain at university in general, and were then asked about the skills that employers wanted. In both cases the academics rated the same three skills (analytical, oral and written communication) as the top three, but whereas analytical skills were ranked first when it came to skills most useful for students, academics rated oral communication skills as top when focused on employers. This contrasted to the employers' views which ranked analytical skills as top. Employers also rated presentation skills more highly than the academics who ranked them eleventh in importance for students, but seventh in rank for importance to employers. Overall, the tertiary education institutional view appeared to accord with the requirements of employers, although this slight mis-match may highlight the need for continuing communication between academics and practitioners to align their institutional views and to ensure that accounting graduates are acquiring the necessary skills.

One cohort of academics taking part in the study was that of auditing academics. Auditing is a professionally-focused discipline, as evidenced by IES 8, and audit academics may have institutionalized their views differently from those of their accounting academic counterparts. An analysis of the audit academics' responses showed that there were some skills that they did not want to include in their teaching such as basic IT skills and numeracy: other academics rated numeracy fifth in the list of 16 skills and basic IT skills eighth. This may reflect the more advanced requirements of IES 8 for trainee audit practitioners than those of IES 3 which is focused at a more general professional accounting education. Thus, audit academics have an institutionally different view from other accounting academics.

Overall, both practitioners and academics share similar views on the importance of teaching generic skills, and the extent to which they should be—or are—taught at universities. Thus, they appear to have the same institutional beliefs about the skills necessary to become an accountant and auditor in the twenty-first century. An investigation of the influences on academics and how these reflect the generic skills they deem to be important to teach on an undergraduate degree is an issue that warrants further investigation. Is it external influences such as the professional bodies, IESs or benchmark statements that have moulded academic thinking or is it internal networking between academics that has institutionalized these views? Future research is necessary to examine these findings in more depth to ensure that the accountants and auditors of the future master all the prerequisite generic skills before they qualify as professional accountants and audit practitioners.

Notes

[1] This paper is based on a much larger project which for a Ph.D. thesis (Monk, 2004) and an ICAS monograph (Helliar et al., 2007).

[2] IES8 does not offer further guidance on the meaning of 'advanced level' and the International Accounting Education Standards Board (IAESB) is addressing this in their current consultation of IES8 (IFAC, 2010b).

[3] This has been recognized by the IAESB who are currently redrafting and revising the IESs as detailed in their work plan for 2010-2012 (IFAC, 2010a).

[4] Letters in brackets relate to those skills listed in Table 1.

[5] Active Learning is a method of teaching and learning that gives students an active role in the learning process. Instead of the lecturer presenting the material, the students teach themselves through simulations and the lecturer becomes a facilitator in their learning process (Gibbs, 1992).

References

Accounting Education Change Commission (1990) Objectives of Education for accountants: position statement number one, *Issues in Accounting Education*, 5(1), pp. 307–312.

Accounting Education Change Commission (1992) The first course in accounting: position statement number two, *Issues in Accounting Education*, 7(2), pp. 249–251.

Albrecht, W. S. and Sack, R. J. (2000) *Accounting Education: Charting the Course through a Perilous Future* , Accounting Education Series, 16 (Sarasota: American Accounting Association).

American Institute of Certified Public Accountants (1978) *Commission on Auditors' Responsibilities, Report, Conclusions and Recommendations* (New York: AICPA).

Bagranoff, N. A. (1993) Adopting commercial software in the classroom: a focus on learning, *Journal of Accounting Education*, 11(2), pp. 275–286.

Borthick, A. F. and Clark, R. L. (1986) The role of productive thinking in affecting student learning with microcomputers in accounting education, *The Accounting Review*, 61(1), pp. 43–157.

Boyce, G. (1999) Computer-assisted teaching and learning in accounting: pedagogy or product? *Journal of Accounting Education*, 17(2/3), pp. 91–220.

Boyce, G., Williams, S., Kelly, A. and Yee, H. (2001) Fostering deep and elaborative learning and generic (soft) skill development: the strategic use of case studies in accounting education, *Accounting Education: an international journal*, 10(1), pp. 37–60.

Burns, J. (2000) The dynamics of accounting change: inter-play between new practices, routines, institutions, power and politics, *Accounting, Auditing and Accountability Journal*, 13(5), pp. 566–596.

Chung, J. and Munroe, G. S. (1999) The effects of counter-explanation and source hypothesis on developing audit judgement, *Accounting Education: an international journal*, 8(2), pp. 11–126.

CIMA (2010) The Chartered Institute of Management Accountants. The test of professional competence in management accounting. Available at: http://www.cimaglobal.com/Documents/ImportedDocuments/TOPCIMA2010.pdf (accessed 3 May 2010).

Crawford, L., Helliar, C. V., Monk, E. A. and Stevenson, L. A. (ed.) (2011) SCAM: design of a learning and teaching resource, *Accounting Forum*, 34(1), pp. 61–72.

Crawford, M. and Barr, S. (1998) Integrating IT skills—are green men the answer? 9th Annual CTI-AFM Conference, York.

Dacko, S. G. (2006) Developing the top five skills within an MBA programme: implications for management educators, *The International Journal of Management Education*, 13(2), pp. 21–31.

Davies, M. (2000) Using a computerised case study to teach computer auditing: the reasons, the approach and the student response, *Managerial Auditing Journal*, 15(5), pp. 247–252.

Dowling, C., Godfrey, J. M. and Gyles, N. (2003) Do hybrid flexible delivery teaching methods improve accounting students' learning outcomes? *Accounting Education: an international journal*, 12(4), pp. 373–391.

Dearing, R. (1997) *Report of the National Committee of Inquiry into Higher Education* (London: HMSO).

Drake, J. (1999) Instructional case: the audit of Award Rosette Manufacturers Ltd, *Accounting Education: an international journal*, 8(4), pp. 363–375.

Fallows, S. and Steven, C. (Eds) (2000) *Integrating Key Skills in Higher Education* (London: Kogan Page).

FSSC (2009) *Accountancy and Finance Sector Qualifications Strategy* , Version 1.3 (London: Financial Services Skills Committee).

Fraser, I. A. M., Hatherly, D. J. and Lin, K. Z. (1997) An empirical investigation of the use of analytical review by external auditors, *British Accounting Review*, 29(1), pp. 35–47.

Gammie, B., Gammie, E. and Cargill, E. (2002) Personal skills development in the accounting curriculum, *Accounting Education: an international journal*, 11(1), pp. 63–78.

Gibbs, G. (1992) *Improving the quality of student learning* (Bristol: Technical and Educational Services).

Hardy, C. (1996) Understanding power: bringing about strategic change, *British Journal of Management*, 7, supplement, pp. S3–S16.

Hassall, T., Dunlop, A. and Lewis, S. (1996) Internal audit expectation: exploring professional competence, *Managerial Auditing Journal*, 11(5), pp. 28–36.

Helliar, C. V., Gray, R. H. and Monk, E. A. (2002) *The British Accounting Review Research Register* (London: Academic Press).

Helliar, C. V., Michaelson, R., Power, D. M. and Sinclair, C. D. (2000) Using a portfolio management game (Finesse) to teach finance, *Accounting Education: an international journal*, 9(1), pp. 37–51.

Helliar, C. V., Monk, E. A., Stevenson, L. A. and Allison, C. (2007) *Teaching Audit in an Internet Environment* (Edinburgh: ICAS).

Helliar, C. V., Monk, E. A. and Stevenson, L. A. (2009) The development of trainee auditors' skills in tertiary education, *International Journal of Auditing*, 13(3), pp. 185–202.

Howieson, B. (2003) Accounting practice in the millennium: is accounting education ready to meet the challenge? *British Accounting Review*, 35(2), pp. 69–74.

ICAEW (1996) *Added-value Professionals: Chartered Accountants in 2005, A Consultation Document* (London: ICAEW).

ICAS (ed.) (2009) The Institute of Chartered Accountants of Scotland, *The knowledge and expertise to become the best: Your guide to the ICAS syllabus 2009/10* (Edinburgh: ICAS).

IFAC (2008a) *IAESB Framework for International Education Pronouncements* (New York: IFAC).

IFAC (2008b) *International Education Standards 3. Professional Skills and General Education* (New York: IFAC).

IFAC (2008c) *International Education Standard 8. Competence Requirements for Audit Professionals* (New York: IFAC).

IFAC (2008d) *International Education Standard 2. Content of Professional Accounting Education Programs* (New York: IFAC).

IFAC (2008e) *International Education Standard 4. Professional Values, Ethics and Attitudes* (New York: IFAC).

IFAC (2010a) *IAESB 2010-2012 Strategy and Workplan*, April 2010 (New York: IFAC).

IFAC (2010b) *A Consultation Paper on the Revision of International Education Standard 8: Competence Requirements for Audit Professionals*, March 2010 (New York: IFAC).

IFAC Compliance Programme (2004–2006). Available at: http://www.ifac.org/ComplianceAssessment/published.php (accessed 23 August 2010).

Libby, P. A. (1991) Barriers to using cases in accounting education, *Issues in Accounting Education*, 6(2), pp. 193–213.

Maltby, J. (2001) Second thoughts about 'cases in auditing', *Accounting Education: an international journal*, 10(4), pp. 421–428.

Marriott, N., Selwyn, N. and Marriott, P. (2003) *Information and Communications Technology in UK Accounting Education* (London: Certified Accountants Educational Trust).

McCourt-Larres, P. and Radcliffe, G. W. (2000) Computer-based instruction in a professionally-accredited undergraduate tax course, *Accounting Education: an international journal*, 9(3), pp. 243–257.

McSkimming, C. (2007) An investigation to identify the key strategies Cardonald College can use to improve the employability of its students'. A Report for Cardonald College Strategic Management Group presented at the Scottish Qualification Authority's 'Higher National 2007' conference on 'Employability'.

Moll, J., Burns, J. and Major, M. (2006) Institutional theory, in: Z. Hoque (Ed.) *Methodological Issues in Accounting Research: Theories, Methods and Issues*, pp. 183–205 (London: Spiramus).

Molyneaux, D. (2008) *What do you do now? Ethical issues encountered by Chartered Accountants* (Edinburgh: The Institute of Chartered Accountants of Scotland).

Monk, E. (2004) , Educational theories and teaching methods in audit and accounting education. Unpublished Ph.D. thesis.

Oglesbee, T. W., Bitner, L. N. and Wright, G. B. (1988) Measurement of incremental benefits in computer enhanced instruction, *Issues in Accounting Education*, 3(2), pp. 365–377.

Okike, E. (1999) The Coopers & Lybrand 'Excellence in Audit Education' programme: a note, *Accounting Education: an international journal*, 8(1), pp. 57–65.

Palmer, K. N., Ziegenfuss, D. E. and Pinsker, R. E. (2004) International knowledge, skills, and abilities of auditors/accountants: evidence from recent competency studies, *Managerial Auditing Journal*, 19(7), pp. 889–896.

Quality Assurance Agency for Higher Education (2007) *Honours degree benchmark statements—Accounting* (Mansfield: QAA).

Sangster, A. and Mulligan, C. (1997) Integrating the World Wide Web into an accounting systems course, *Accounting Education; an international journal*, 6(1), pp. 53–62.

Sikka, P. (2009) Financial crisis and the silence of the auditors, *Accounting, Organizations and Society*, 34(6–7), pp. 868–873.

Stoner, G. (1999) IT is part of youth culture, but are accounting undergraduates confident in IT? *Accounting Education: an international journal*, 8(3), pp. 217–327.

Williams, H. and Owen, G. (1997) *Recruitment and utilisation of graduates by small and medium sized enterprises*, Department for Education and Employment Report No 29, (London: DfEE).

Yorke, M. (2006) *Employability in Higher Education: what it is—what it is not* , Learning and Employability Series 1 (York: The Higher Education Academy).

Students' Perceptions of Work-Based Training and Examination-Based Learning Relating to the Professional Competence of Auditors and the Impact of Regulatory Changes on Audit Training in the UK

NEIL MARRIOTT*, BRIAN TELFORD**, MARLENE DAVIES** and
JON EVANS**

*University of Winchester, UK, **University of Glamorgan, UK

ABSTRACT   *The purpose of this paper is to investigate students' perceptions of work-based training and examination-based learning as it relates to the professional competence of auditors. The paper takes as its motivation the fall in the number of accountants registering as qualified auditors in the UK following fundamental changes in the audit environment. Legislation aimed at reducing red tape has resulted in a large number of UK companies taking advantage of an audit exemption, and most of these are clients of small audit firms. This legislative change has had significant pedagogic implications on the experiential learning of audit trainees and the availability of training opportunities for them. The contribution of the paper is to explain the perceived relevance and importance of training opportunities to trainees seeking to obtain audit qualifications. Using data from an on-line questionnaire and focus groups, the study reports that trainees in smaller firms lack opportunities to obtain sufficient audit experience, and there is a lack of synchronization between limited practical experience and classroom tuition provided before taking auditing examinations. The implications are that effective audit training will become restricted to large audit firms the trainees in which often choose different career paths to auditing, thereby limiting the number of qualified auditors in the UK in the future.*

Introduction

It is essential for the future of the auditing profession in the UK that a sufficient number of newly-qualified accountants have the necessary skills to become effective auditors and choose auditing as a career. The Companies Act 2006 (CA 2006) specifies the requirements for conducting statutory audits, and eligibility is restricted to individuals who have been granted an audit qualification—a Recognized Professional Qualification (RPQ)—by a Recognized Qualifying Body (RQB). Obtaining the audit qualification is dependent upon passing the RQB examinations and gaining appropriate work experience. In 2008, only 1,272 newly-qualified accountants were awarded the RPQ in the UK, representing 7.6% of the number of students who qualified in that year (POB, 2008a, 2008b). This low proportion and small number in absolute terms provides the main motivation for the study.

An integral part of gaining the audit qualification is the practical training undertaken while trainees are studying for their professional examinations. For the vast majority of trainees, if they do not obtain audit experience while training, it is unlikely that they will do so once qualified as accountants because the opportunities to obtain audit experience diminishes further. However, the potential for a trainee to gain audit experience in the UK has reduced in recent years mainly due to the audit exemption provision available to companies below a certain size. Initially introduced in 1994, the threshold for exemption was substantially increased in 2004, currently standing at turnover of under £5.6m, a balance sheet value of under £2.8m, and employing less than 50 people on average during the year. As a result, the number of statutory audits undertaken has reduced dramatically with nearly 900 000 companies taking advantage of the exemption (Iwaska, 2008). This has particularly affected smaller audit firms, the clients of which are more likely to meet the exemption threshold requirements. Hence, the availability and range of potential audit experience can depend on the size of firm for which a trainee works. In 2008, for example, 94.4% of UK equity listed companies were audited by the largest nine firms (POB, 2009). Training opportunities will principally be offered by the larger firms which undertake the bulk of the audit work and in which only a small percentage of employees will actually be completing the audit qualification as they have a range of alternative career paths from which to choose.

This paper investigates students' perceptions of work-based training and examination-based learning as it relates to the professional competence of auditors. The aims are to establish the relationship between work-based training and examination-based learning and the trainees' perceptions of their value in preparing them to become auditors.

The paper commences with an overview of the regulatory framework, specifically the requirements for an auditor to gain the audit qualification and the audit exemption provisions. The literature review considers some of the pedagogic imperatives for successful audit training identified by previous research and develops the key questions to be addressed in this research study. The choice of research methods employed is outlined along with a justification for the adoption of a mixed method approach. Unique to this study was a large on-line survey of audit trainees that was endorsed and supported by the professional bodies in the UK. The paper analyses the results from the relevant section of a larger scale study and focuses only on the areas of direct pedagogic interest. The results demonstrate that the separation (or absence) of work-based training and examination-based learning has meant that, for many trainees, examination preparation has become an academic exercise and this may have impacted negatively on examination performance. There is a significant finding in that the size of audit firm has an impact on the level and quality of audit training and experience to which a trainee is exposed. Trainees working for smaller practices are often frustrated by the limited opportunities for work-based audit training. The implications, discussed in the conclusion, are that the restriction of training opportunities could lead to a shortage of auditors in the UK. The conclusion also identifies the scope for further work.

Regulatory Background

There are two regulatory aspects to consider. The first is the requirement for an auditor to have gained the audit qualification and second, the audit exemption provisions. Prior to Companies Act 1989 (CA 1989), all qualified members of four of the UK's six senior professional accounting bodies (the Institute of Chartered Accountants in England and Wales, ICAEW; the Institute of Chartered Accountants of Scotland, ICAS; the Institute of Chartered Accountants in Ireland, ICAI; now known as Chartered Accountants, Ireland; and the Association of Chartered Certified Accountants, ACCA) were deemed to be qualified auditors. However, CA 1989, since replaced by the Companies Act 2006 (CA 2006), specifies the eligibility requirements for conducting statutory audits. Eligibility is restricted to individuals who have been granted an audit qualification by an RQB. Recognition is the function of the Financial Reporting Council (FRC)'s Professional Oversight Board (POB) which currently recognizes six bodies, although only the four Bodies mentioned above have actually awarded the RPQ to its members. The CA 2006 restricts the audit qualification to individuals who have completed at least three years' practical training—of which a part must have been spent in statutory audit work or other audit work similar to statutory audit work (Schedule II, Part 2). Within the regulatory constraint of POB, the bodies design their own practical training requirements for the award of the audit qualification. For example, ICAEW requires a minimum of 48 weeks in statutory audit and work similar to statutory audit work, at least 24 weeks of which must be in statutory audit work.

All RQBs require trainees to pass a suite of examinations in order to gain membership. To apply for the audit qualification, a trainee must also pass a nominated audit paper, for example P7 *Advanced Audit and Assurance* in the case of the RQB, ACCA. The regulations outlining the combination of theoretical and practical training are designed to ensure the quality of competent individuals able to conduct audits.

In some jurisdictions, whether or not a company has its accounts audited is a voluntary decision. This was not the case in the UK until the late twentieth century. Prior to this all companies had to have their accounts audited, and this was seen by many as the price to pay for limited liability. However, in order to reduce the regulatory burden on smaller companies and to take account of the increasing complexity of the auditing regime, the UK government introduced an audit exemption threshold. Since 1994, small companies with an annual turnover of less than £90 000 and a balance sheet total lower than £1.4m, were exempt from having their financial statements audited. In 1997, this turnover threshold for audit exemptions was raised to £350 000, with the requirement for the balance sheet totals remaining the same. In 2000 the turnover threshold was further increased to £1m. The latest increase was for companies with accounting dates ending after March 2004 when the turnover threshold was raised to £5.6m and balance sheet value of less than £2.8m. As a result, the number of statutory audits undertaken has been reducing rapidly: the recent decline in the market can be seen in Table 1. Amendments to the European Union's fourth and seventh Directives give member states the option to increase the audit exemption threshold by a further 20%. In March 2007 the Department of Trade and Industry consulted on plans to implement the Directives, including an increase in the thresholds to £6.5m (turnover) and £3.26m (balance sheet total), but

Table 1. The reduction in statutory audits and registered audit firms

Year ended 31 March	2002	2007
Non-dormant companies filing audited accounts	48%	16%
Number of statutory audits	442 000	217 000
Number of registered audit firms at (31 December)	11 100	8600

Source: 'Statistical Tables on Companies Register Activities 2006–2007', Companies House, and Annual
    Reports to the Secretary of State for Trade & Industry by the Professional Oversight Board

to date no increases have been announced. The Professional Oversight Board (POB, 2008a) noted that the number of registered audit firms had been gradually declining. The overall number of audit firms registered in 2008 (8179) was 25.7% lower than the number in 2003 (11 006).

All of these changes have therefore impacted negatively on the opportunities for trainees to experience audit work. The implications of this are discussed later in the paper.

Acquisition of Audit Expertise

Libby (1995) developed a model to understand the acquisition of audit expertise, as shown in Figure 1:

Libby (1995) identified two aspects of gaining audit expertise: instruction and experience. Instruction can be at an 'educational institution' or via an 'in-house course'. Instruction at an educational institution primarily refers to preparing trainees to pass the professional examinations of their RQB. In-house courses are provided by firms primarily tailored towards a perceived gap in their trainees' practical knowledge. Experience comprises 'Practice' and 'Feedback'. Practice is the execution of specific audit tasks. Feedback on those tasks can be given informally on audit completion or, more formally, through appraisal and mentoring systems.

In this paper 'examination-based learning' refers to instruction at an educational institution and 'work-based training' refers to instruction from in-house courses and experience gained from practice and feedback, as illustrated in Figure 2.

Helliar, Monk and Stevenson (2009) argues that this means of acquiring audit expertise, illustrated by Figure 2 may not work effectively. Trainees were asked if there were any areas of audit work which they consistently found difficult and, rather unsurprisingly, identified 'not knowing why I am doing something' (p. 197). Therefore, the problem of not knowing why an activity is undertaken poses the question as to the relevance of the activity. This incomprehension may arise from the sequence in which trainees acquire audit *experience* as opposed to acquiring knowledge (Helliar, Monk, Stevenson and Allison, 2007), and consequently places an imperative on the relative timing of examination-based learning and work-based training.

The sequencing or timing issues highlighted above could also be related to the difference between 'declarative knowledge' being the knowledge of facts and definitions and 'procedural knowledge', which are the rules or steps needed for performing skilled

	Audit expertise		
Instruction		Experience	
Educational Institution	In-house Course	Practice	Feedback

Figure 1. Audit expertise model. Adapted from Libby (1995, p. 178)

Figure 2. Examination-based learning and work-based training

tasks. Anderson (1982) asserted that the acquisition of declarative knowledge must precede that of procedural knowledge. Bonner and Walker (1994) found that practical experience with feedback, together with some instruction, increased audit understanding and procedural knowledge. However, practice and experience alone does not lead to a development of real understanding of audit. Providing a trainee with an audit manual containing a list of steps to follow with no explanation as to why these steps are appropriate leads to declarative knowledge only. Instead, there is a need to combine prior knowledge with practical application, whereby knowledge is enhanced through practice (Bonner, Libby and Nelson, 1997). The notion that knowledge has to be acquired prior to the practical application and audit experience helps to improve knowledge whilst undertaking the training. Knowledge gained from examination-based learning or in-house courses therefore becomes a precondition to learning from experience.

In addition, the scheduling of the work experience learning phases can be disrupted due to workload pressures and the timescales of the employer relating to the demands from clients. Firms' clients may indirectly be drivers of audit quality through the time spent on the audit and, consequently, limit audit training opportunities. Van Peursem's (2005b) market-based analysis of audit service quality considered the relationship between audit quality and audit 'price', and examined the pressure on audit firms to cut quality by reducing audit time spent and other associated savings. Van Peursem (2005b) further recognized that audit training is part of the 'price' of an audit and hence is subject to competitive pressure in order to reduce such costs. These commercial realities can impact on the amount and quality of work-based training opportunities as clients are reluctant to bear training costs in their audit fees.

Further, the sometimes unique language of auditing, particularly for trainees without practical experience, can lead to a state of ignorance or confusion. In an internal audit context, Van Peursem (2005a) reviewed the work of Burns, Greenspan and Hartwell (1994) and Covaleski, Dirsmith and Rittenberg (2003) who had considered the notion of 'professional mystique'. Such 'mystique' was defined as 'expertise bordering on the sublime over a work ideology that is baffling but essential' (Burns *et al.*, 1994, p. 90).

Van Peursem (2004, p. 380) noted that 'the technical, complex and economically-essential functions traditionally associated with accountants and auditors might, for example, add to their 'mystique'. Again, this suggests the need to explore the link between examination-based learning and work-based training: in particular, their sequencing as RQB examiners may test certain audit concepts that are only known to the privileged few with real work-based audit experience.

Another concern related to sequencing of audit training is that examination-based learning focuses on the theory of auditing whilst practical experience for many trainees centres on audit assurance. Coenenberg, Haller and Marten (1999) recognized that there is a challenge arising from the professions' 'diversification from auditing to assurance services' (p. 369). Elliott (1995) identified the major abilities expected by auditors in connection with those assurance services. They need to: 'gain a much better understanding of users' goals, objectives, ... focus on analysing, interpreting, and evaluating information to enhance the relevance of the information for diverse user purposes; embrace information technology in all of its complex dimensions; adapt quickly to a constantly changing environment.' (pp. 385–386). Elliott (1995) observed that the paramount skill (of an auditor is to): '"learn how to learn" ... prior to entering the profession' (p. 386). This difference between audit theory and audit assurance is potentially where some confusion may lie when trainees are faced with conventional theory-based examination questions.

A review of the above literature further revealed that very little empirical research has been carried out into the acquisition of audit expertise by trainees. An exception in the U.K. is Helliar et al. (2007), but their study was carried out in the pedagogical context of the development of an audit learning package, rather than the broader context of trainees progressing to the audit qualification. In addition, there is a conflict between Anderson (1982), which suggested that the acquisition of declarative knowledge should precede that of procedural knowledge, and Bonner et al. (1997), which suggested that the two should be synchronized.

Regulatory reform has led to a significant reduction in the number of audits conducted in the UK and in the number of firms registered to perform them. The literature indicates that audit expertise is gained successfully through a blend and careful sequencing of examination-based learning and work-based training and the former can be incomprehensible to trainees without the experiential learning of the workplace. In seeking to explain the perceived relevance and importance of training opportunities to trainees seeking to obtain audit qualifications, the first three questions which this study attempts to answer are:

1. Do students feel that work-based training helps prepare them for their work as auditors?
2. Do students feel that examination-based learning helps prepare them for their work as auditors?
3. Do students view work-based training and examination-based learning as linked or separate?

Another key issue that may affect the work-based training and examination-based learning experience is firm size. In a pertinent link between RQB examinations and the debate over the capacity and ability of small audit firms to conduct audits, a recent ACCA examination paper asked students to consider audit quality control. The December 2007 P7 *Advanced Audit & Assurance* paper required students to discuss audit quality control with particular relevance to a small firm of Chartered Certified Accountants. The Examiner's Report (ACCA, 2007) noted some alarming views expressed by some candidates:

... [students] displayed an appalling lack of tact and professionalism in answering the question, seeming to condemn small firms as totally incompetent, and having no ability to produce good quality work at all. Typical comments along these lines included:

- "small firms cannot attract competent staff"
- "small firms have no resources"
- "small firms focus on getting new business and ignore quality controls"

... and the most common suggestion as to how small firms can overcome these alleged "problems" was for small firms to merge with each other and thus avoid being small.

Candidates must appreciate that these types of comments are wholly inappropriate and display a real lack of any kind of commercial awareness.

Whilst some of the comments can be partly explained because students may not have had any experience of auditing in small firms, they do seem to reflect a general malaise regarding the availability of practical audit experience and a perception that audit quality equates with audit services provided by the large firms. This leads to a supplementary, but important, research question:

4. Does the size of audit firm impact on students' experience of work-based training and examination-based learning?

In order to answer the four questions given above, the input of audit trainees regarding their experiences is required. How this was achieved is outlined next.

Research Methods

A mixed method approach was adopted in undertaking this research involving an independently administered on-line anonymous questionnaire survey and a number of focus groups. The questionnaire focused on understanding the views of audit trainees and their training experience. The instrument was structured so that only those who considered themselves an audit trainee would respond. It also contained many 'filters', whereby question choice and design was dependent upon the membership of RQB and stage of training. In addition, some questions were specifically designed for each RQB to ensure terminology appropriate to the individual RQBs, such as 'mentor' or 'supervisor' or 'trainee manager'. Key terms such as 'work-based training' and 'examination-based learning' were defined for respondents in accordance with Figure 2. The questionnaire also contained a series of open-ended questions which gave participants the opportunity to express their views and concerns. In addition to the inclusion of quantitative data from the survey, it is these views that have formed a major element of the analysis section of this paper. An invitation was given to those responding to participate in focus groups that would be the platform for further debate with the researchers. These group discussions facilitated an exploration of some of the issues raised by the survey in some depth.

The online questionnaire survey was administered in August 2007, with the assistance of the RQBs, and 458 trainees and recently-qualified accountants participated. It was felt that the latter, having qualified within the last two years, would have relevant views to express regardless of whether they had gained the audit qualification or not. The number of the total population of audit trainees in the UK was not available, therefore it is not possible to determine the percentage of the audit trainees' or recently-qualified accountants' population responding to the on-line questionnaires. However, the method was a voluntary survey based on the willingness of individuals to participate and, whilst not randomly drawn and hence generalisable, still provided a large amount of data for analysis. The professional bodies involved in the study contacted all their recently-qualified accountants to ask them to participate. In the case of three of the four bodies this was by direct e-mail and web page alerts and, in the fourth, this was by letter. The sampling frame was, therefore, the entire population making up the target group for this study.

As with any survey-based research, there was a possibility of a response bias in the sample. The responses were skewed towards those employed in smaller accounting firms: first year trainees are considered to be relatively under-represented forming only 17% of the sample, second and third year trainees comprised almost two-thirds of the responses, and recently-qualified graduates, 26%. As there is an under-representation of trainees from large accounting firms, the conclusions drawn relate primarily to the practical training arrangements within smaller practices.

After the on-line questionnaires closed, the researchers manually filtered the responses to remove those who were not based in the UK (ascertained from a direct question) or who were clearly not audit trainees (for example, those working in tax departments).

A variable within this survey was the size of the audit firm, which was used as a theme in analysing the responses. In terms of ascertaining the size of the firms in which the trainees were based the questionnaire respondents were asked how many partners there were in the firm for which they work. Firms with one to four partners are described in the results as 'small firms', 5–24 partners as 'medium firms' and 25 or more partners as 'large firms'. This information is reflected in Table 2, along with the age profile of respondents.

Six focus groups were convened. These focus groups were led by the researchers who employed a series of predetermined statements and questions to generate feedback and discussion. The discussion points were based on the questionnaire issues and the response to the survey. Participants were given an opportunity to take part in unstructured discussion on any other pertinent issues that did not arise from the survey.

Results and Analysis

This section sets out the major results obtained from survey respondents and focus group participants. It analyses their perceptions of their audit training experiences whilst briefly considering the impact of such perceptions on their career plans and the consequent supply of future auditors to the profession. For clarity, the responses to the research questions have been grouped in the following eight themes: understanding of theory and concepts and the value of audit training; examination-based learning

Table 2. Age of respondents (trainees and recently-qualified) by firm size

	Firm size (number of partners)			
	Small (1–4)	Medium (5–25)	Large (> 25)	Total
18–24	61	55	64	180
25–30	83	57	74	214
31–40	24	6	5	35
41–50	5	3	0	8
50 +	1	0	0	1
Total	174	121	143	438

and firm size; examination-based learning and audit experience; work-based training in-house and third party courses; synchronization between examination-based learning and work-based training; feedback; firm size as an issue; possible solutions to the firm size issue.

Understanding of Theory and Concepts and the Value of Audit Training

Evidence from the responses indicated that basic auditing concepts and terms might not be understood by trainees early in their careers. One respondent felt that 'technical terms' were not clearly explained—this relates to what Bonner et al. (1997) referred to in terms of knowledge acquisition prior to practical application. Another respondent suggested that:

> Trainees need specific training on 'technical terms' related to auditing before being sent on their first jobs. Managers seem to take for granted that trainees understand technical terms when in fact they do not have any basic knowledge of what, for example, substantive procedures are and why we carry them out. (Trainee, large firm—Questionnaire respondent no. 432.)

Van Peursem (2005b) concluded that training may come at a price that indirectly reduces the profitability of audit. The effect of such commercial realities upon their training environment was outlined by one trainee:

> No structure to training—everything is geared to a fixed budget profit/how the budget reflects on manager's performance rather than on developing a student's understanding of how/what/why to audit. Audit experience also tends to be based on the office politics rather than developing/training students. (Trainee, medium firm—Questionnaire respondent no. 473.)

In an environment of charge out rates, time sheets and tight schedules is it feasible to expect high quality audit training? This central question of whether commercially-motivated professional firms have such an onus to provide a sustainable supply of trained auditors was neatly framed by one small firm trainee:

> (my) firm is ... commercially focused rather than allowing practical resource and time to properly train their students. The responsibility for becoming a competent auditor lies both with the trainee and the training firm. (Trainee, small firm—Questionnaire respondent no. 213.)

In summary, trainees' technical knowledge may fall short of what is required to carry out audits. This is due to incorrect assumptions regarding trainees' prior knowledge on the part their supervisors and to commercial pressures faced by audit firms.

Examination-based Learning and Firm Size

The majority of respondents agreed that examination-based learning helped them in their work as auditors. This provides some reassurance that the RQB examinations have some relevance to the work environment. However, 51% felt that the work-based training was more relevant than the examination-based learning, and this view was more marked amongst respondents from the larger firms. Many respondents felt that the RQB examinations had a large company focus and thus caused a problem for those from smaller firms. This is possibly because respondents from large firms are more likely to have received exposure to large company audits.

With the perceived view that RQB examinations are large firm focused, it is not surprising that learning providers were accused of focusing their attention on students from the larger firms.

Exam based lectures were all large firm orientated ... it was impossible to apply knowledge
from the classroom to the smaller firms I dealt with each day. (Trainee, medium firm—Questionnaire respondent no. 429.)

Agreement with the statement that 'examination-based tuition helped them to do their
work' was more prevalent where the audit experience gained enabled the trainees to apply
directly their own experiences to scenarios set in the examination questions.

To summarize, examination-based learning is felt by trainees to be of value in their audit
training. However, there is some disagreement from small firm respondents due to the perceived large firm and large company focus of the examinations set by the RQBs.

Examination-based Learning and Audit Experience

With their limited availability of audit experience, some trainees felt that the majority of
their auditing knowledge came via their examination-based learning. Indeed, one trainee
asserted that all his knowledge about auditing came from his professional studies:

I have learned all my auditing knowledge from studying for my exams. (Trainee, small firm—
Questionnaire respondent no. 14.)

Such a dearth of audit experience led to problems in successfully passing the professional audit examinations for some trainees:

My first two attempts at my final audit paper were when I was working out of practice...were
more difficult when I wasn't in an audit environment. I do believe it helped that I was back to
conducting audits on a regular basis. (Trainee, medium firm—Questionnaire respondent no. 62.)

Further, audit experience needs to happen at the same time as examination-based learning:

I joined my present employer (with) no (previous) audit experience I ... find I am continually
playing "catch up"—learning how to apply the exam-based knowledge I have into the practical audit work which I am expected to perform. (Trainee, large firm—Questionnaire respondent no. 190.)

The above comments suggest a need to combine examination-based learning with practical experience. This reaffirms Bonner *et al.'s* (1997) views on the need for combined
knowledge and practice.

Audit experience appears to aid preparation for professional studies. One trainee felt
that practical audit aided the level of understanding, appreciation and knowledge when
it came to sitting the audit examination papers:

I found that once I started auditing in a practical work environment, it helped me a lot to
understand my studies towards the auditing paper. (Trainee, medium firm—Questionnaire
respondent no. 186.)

Although this view may appear to contradict Andersen's (1982) argument that declarative knowledge should precede procedural knowledge, it does indicate the value of practical audit experience, albeit as an aid to studying professional audit examinations as
suggested by Bonner *et al.* (1997).

Some trainees expressed a degree of cynicism over the role of RQBs, the merit of their
examinations and the focus of certain tuition providers. Consequently the usefulness of the
examinations in their role as trainee auditors was questioned:

Most training was exam-focussed during trainee contract. Exam training is not particularly
tailored to actual auditing. (Trainee, medium firm—Questionnaire respondent no. 250.)

Libby's (1995) audit experience model showed that gaining audit expertise was an inter-action between instruction and experience. This model was further developed in Figure 2 showing the integrated relationship between work-based training and examination-based learning. The ramifications when this 'circle of knowledge' is incomplete were expressed by several survey and focus group respondents:

> The exams should be more relevant to your job—i.e. they don't teach you about any SORPs, SAR, FSA rules, etc and small firms have limited access to such training. (Trainee, large firm—Questionnaire respondent no. 252.)

> I think the focus from (my RQB) is just ... more academic rather than practical and I think so long as you sign up to a college, sit the courses, then you're fine, but in terms of the experience I don't ... I can't relate to it, I can't match the (RQB) ... with the current experience. (Trainee, Focus Group.)

To summarize, the lack of practical audit experience for some trainees results in their acquiring the majority of their knowledge from their examination-based learning. Some then find it difficult to pass the examinations because of a lack of understanding caused by that absence of practical experience. As a result, trainees might view audit examin-ations as purely an academic exercise unrelated to practice.

Work-based Training: In-house and Third Party Courses

In-house courses are where firms or groups of firms provide generic or tailored courses for their trainees. For example, a firm may provide training on a new auditing standard or some specific training related to the audit of a particular client or industry sector. There is broad agreement that in-house training courses helped the respondents to do their job as trainee auditors. High quality, tailored in-house training was seen as being particularly useful to the trainee auditor.

> The practical audit training I received has been very high quality. I feel I have been well-equipped with the skills I need to work as an effective team member on an audit engagement. (Trainee, large firm—Questionnaire respondent no. 247.)

However, trainees working for large accounting firms tended to agree more than those at smaller firms. The amount of such training available to the trainees in larger firms may explain the differing response to the number of training days attended (see Table 3). This training is divided between in-house provision by firms themselves and provision by third party training organizations.

Trainees with large firms receive a substantial number of in-house training days, in con-trast to trainees with small and medium firms. Over 43% receive 20 or more in-house train-ing days as opposed to less than 19% for small and medium firm trainees. Small firms often use third party organizations for their training. However, the amount of training given is still relatively insignificant, with more than 70% receiving less than five days' third party training. The contrasting experience and views of students in different size firms is dis-cussed later.

Synchronization between examination-based learning and work-based training. Respondents reported that, where the work-based training and examination-based learning were not synchronized, the examination preparation became an academic exercise which may adversely impact on examination performance. It was strongly supported that passing an examination was no substitute for practical experience. This reinforces Bonner and

Table 3. Approximately how many work-based audit training days have you attended since the start of your training contract?

	Small	Medium	Large	Total
(a) In house. $\chi^2 = 66.957$ Sig ≤ 0.000 (significant at 1% level)				
0 days	35.0%	28.1%	6.5%	23.5%
1–5 days	31.9%	31.6%	18.8%	27.4%
6–10 days	11.3%	11.4%	13.8%	12.1%
11–20 days	5.6%	10.5%	17.4%	10.9%
> 20 days	16.3%	18.4%	43.5%	26.0%
Total	100.0%	100.0%	100.0%	100.0%
(b) Third party. $\chi^2 = 10.528$ Sig ≤ 0.230 (not significant)				
	Small	Medium	Large	Total
0 days	44.6%	41.4%	38.8%	44.6%
1–5 days	25.9%	30.3%	33.0%	29.3%
6–10 days	12.2%	13.1%	8.7%	11.4%
11–20 days	7.9%	6.1%	1.9%	5.6%
> 20 days	9.4%	9.1%	17.5%	11.7%
Total	100.0%	100.0%	100.0%	100.0%

Walker's (1994) views on the value of practice and experience, together with instruction and feedback.

An employing firm might withhold a trainee from attempting some examinations until he/she has spent a period of time gaining practical experience. Others attempt to provide practical experience in tandem with the examination-based learning. The objective is to ensure that examinations are not theoretical exercises and to encourage trainees to draw on their practical experience and apply this knowledge and understanding to examination scenarios. The research findings show evidence of limited links between examination preparation for audit and practical experience in smaller firms as there is less audit work available from which trainees can gain experience. The level and extent of experience can therefore be dependent on the size of the firm and consequently the number of audit clients, their size and the range of audit work available. The focus groups indicated that the lack of audit experience is a real issue and one which is set to deteriorate due to the proposed further increases in the audit turnover threshold and the resultant significant decrease in the number of audit clients. It was felt by trainees that passing an auditing examination alone did not prepare a trainee for conducting an audit.

> The timing of the audit training is very poor. The [examination-based] training that we are receiving is on audit issues that we have already had to face in our working experiences. The training should come first and not after. (Trainee, medium firm—Questionnaire respondent no. 449.)

The relevance of practical training to examination preparation divided respondents. Only half of respondents, 51%, agreed with the statement 'work-based training helped to prepare for my professional examinations'. This result was not significantly different depending on firm size. This lack of consensus reflected concerns over the synchronization between examination and work-based audit experience. Sometimes this experience was not obtained until after the examinations and thus negated any benefit. In contrast, some respondents preferred the practical experience first as an aid to their examination studies, for example:

> I just remember the first time I saw like a letter of representation and a management letter and I was like "Oh my God, we learnt about that! I didn't realize it was a real thing! . . . if only I'd realized!"—they hadn't just made it all up just for an examination. (Trainee, Focus Group.)

Again, these views appear to contradict Andersen (1982) who asserted that declarative (in this application, examination-based) knowledge should precede procedural (practical) knowledge However, the need for both and the dissonance that may occur when one element is missing or out of sequence can be seen, again supporting the discussion by Bonner *et al.* (1997).

Where examination-based learning and work-based training are synchronized, significant benefits accrue to trainees, not only in preparation for their examinations but more significantly in facilitating their practical audit training:

> I like the way that my experience matches (my studies) . . . whilst doing the audit paper I've been working in audit, planning audits. I could relate the two and it's helped me with my exams and my exams have helped me with my experience. (Trainee, Focus Group.)

Therefore, where a trainee does experience synchronization of work-based training and examination-based learning, it is of benefit not only to the individual but to the execution of audit tasks on behalf of the firm. If the examination syllabus is structured in such a manner as to mirror the progress of the trainees through their training contact, it will inevitably be useful in terms of the additional responsibilities that they undertake at much the same time on actual audits.

Conversely, some trainees expressed some disquiet as to the usefulness of examination-based learning and its link to work-based training as it sometimes failed to live up to expectations. In these instances, trainees find themselves being re-trained by the audit firm through either training courses or practical experience, their examination-based learning having been of little practical use. Some trainees expressed a degree of cynicism about the value of examination-based learning and suggested they were able to complete the examinations without necessarily having the ability to apply that knowledge in a practical manner.

> . . . it is quite possible to pass all the exams (having been crammed by talented tutors) and be unable to apply this in a practical way. (Trainee, medium firm—Questionnaire respondent no. 305.)

Another factor is the appropriateness of the audit examination papers set by the RQBs. Such papers, particularly for the larger RQBs, are set for an international audience; although some attempt is made to tailor the papers where there are regional differences in the regulatory and economic environments. Standard papers are set for all students regardless of the size of firm in which the students may be employed. It could be argued that this leads to a 'lowest common denominator' approach which does not always reflect the work-based experience of individual trainees. For example, it is rare for questions to be set on financial services clients, but some trainees may gain the majority of their experience auditing these companies.

> Work-based training . . . has been very useful. In terms of exams . . . I find it worrying that the (RQB) just focus on getting through the exams rather than ensuring your experience matches the paper. Because . . . the college focuses on getting through the exam, but in practice they don't know how to prepare an audit; they don't know what an audit test is. (Trainee, Focus Group.)

Consequently, contrasting views were expressed by respondents regarding the link between work-based training and examination-based learning. Some could clearly identify the link and their audit training and examination performance benefited commensurately.

Others struggled to appreciate the link between the two and expressed, at times, a sceptical view of the RQB examination structure and content with particular reference to their auditing studies and experience.

This trainee found the inappropriate sequencing of work experience and training to be a cause for concern supporting the findings of Helliar *et al.* (2009) and Van Peursem (2004; 2005a).

> The timing of the audit training is very poor. The training that we are receiving is on audit issues that we have already had to face in our working experiences. The training should come first and not after. (Trainee, medium firm—Questionnaire respondent no. 323.)

Feedback

Concomitant with the less than satisfactory quality of the practical experience obtained was the lack of availability of trained audit staff to provide feedback on practical training. A commonly held view amongst trainees was that partners and managers were not able to find sufficient time to brief them prior to, or indeed during, an assignment, and therefore, it was difficult to find meaningful work which assisted them in building up their knowledge, whether in audit or non-audit work. This view was re-iterated by two respondents:

> ... those on audit experience tend to be left to work by themselves and consequently are not trusted with any 'important' work and often end up photocopying and sending faxes, filing, etc. (Trainee, large firm—Questionnaire respondent no. 397.)

> ... there's so many deadlines it's just complete one job, finish it, start another one, finish it.... They don't have time to really go in-depth where my weaknesses lie and how they can improve on the next job. (Trainee, Focus Group.)

This resonates with Van Peursem's (2005b) points relating to the commercial realities of audit training. Conversely, when partners or managers were able to offer assistance it was greatly valued. A parallel study into the views of audit trainees considers the role and worth of mentors in enhancing the audit training experience (POB, 2008b).

To summarize, the general consensus indicates that work-based training is a positive activity but dependant on the areas of audit giving the appropriate experience to the trainees. However, whether this is received is often dictated by the industrial sector and firm size, as discussed next.

Firm Size as an Issue

The trainees at small firms often felt that the progression of their practical experience did not mirror the examination syllabus. Some trainees expressed frustration at the drawbacks of working for a small firm and the examination focus of the professional bodies – in terms of practical experience at their firm and the approach of tuition providers.

> I work in a small firm that's not willing to invest in training that just relies on on-the-job training and my (RQB) studies; the (RQB) is just exam focused, it doesn't rely on the practical side of training. (Trainee, Focus Group.)

The 'teach yourself' approach is another feature of working for a small firm, as evidenced by this respondent:

> My firm is a small two partner firm which takes the attitude of "teach yourself". This is not a practical way of training and gives the trainee no real basis for how to tackle technical audit problems. (Trainee, small firm—Questionnaire respondent no. 429.)

In contrast, trainees employed by large firms tend to receive training which co-ordinates the timing of examinations and practical experience to give them the best opportunity to develop their audit knowledge and experience.

Respondents who were trainees from large firms spoke highly about the quality and suitability of in-house training received. Large firms are able to provide various types of in-house training. This not only incorporated technical audit training but also the development of softer skills. Trainees often get the opportunity to talk about their audit training issues and share experiences, thus embedding the knowledge they have gained.

This difference is reflected in the response from one trainee with experience at both small and large firms who was able to discriminate clearly between the qualities of experience gained:

> I started working in a small audit firm, then transferred to a large firm, the difference in practical audit training I received was significant. The larger firm invested more time in training and helped me to understand the purpose of the audit, risks, why we perform certain procedures, etc., whereas the smaller firm had been more 'get the job done' orientated). (Trainee, large firm—Questionnaire respondent no. 247.)

Whilst there was general agreement that work-based training helped trainee auditors do their job (Table 4), there was a distinct contrast between small and large firm trainees. Whilst 74.8% of the large firm trainees agreed with the statement, surprisingly few (55.2%) of the small firm trainees concurred. This is consistent with qualitative findings from the focus groups and may suggest that the quality of work-based training was perceived to be sub-standard or irrelevant, or may reflect the general malaise of small firm audit trainees.

The qualitative evidence indicates that some trainee respondents from smaller firms felt that the examinations were a theoretical exercise, far removed from their experiences at work, indicating that they often fail to see the link between what the theory and practice is meant to convey.

Solutions to Firm Size Issue

As mentioned previously, commercial imperatives may reduce the availability and quality of in-house training received by small firm trainees. Four solutions offered by the survey participants to the practical problems facing small firms and their trainees are discussed below.

Co-operation between small firms. Often small firms and, by implication, their trainees are 'in the same boat' regarding the cost of appropriate in-house training. The firms could co-operate with other similar firms to provide the opportunity for varied, high quality training.

> Provision of work-based training would be of great benefit, but given our lack of experience in audit an in-house training programme is unlikely to be appropriate. However, because we are a small firm, we are unlikely to have enough trainees to warrant a third party training provider to come to us. Perhaps some joint training days with other small firms in the area would be the answer. (Trainee, medium firm—Questionnaire respondent no. 304.)

Responsibility and role of the RQBs and tuition providers. The RQBs arguably have a role to play where they could provide better support and supervision for small to medium audit firms. A suggestion from one respondent referred to continuous assessment, and the onus on tuition providers not to neglect their small firm tutees:

Table 4. My work-based training helped me to do my job as a trainee auditor. $\chi^2 = 22.321$ Sig ≤ 0.004 (significant at 1% level)

	Small	Medium	Large	Total
Strongly disagree	5.8%	3.3%	3.6%	4.4%
Disagree	8.7%	15.0%	5.0%	9.3%
Neutral	30.2%	18.3%	16.5%	22.5%
Agree	40.7%	49.2%	51.8%	46.6%
Strongly agree	14.5%	14.2%	23.0%	14.5%
Total	100.0%	100.0%	100.0%	100.0%

> Smaller training firms should be subject to continuous assessment to ensure that trainees are actually being trained and not just used for cheap labour! More supervision is definitely required to help trainees get a better training. Lecturers need to give a small company perspective to students and not just give examples on how to tackle audits of large corporations. (Trainee, small firm—Questionnaire respondent no. 429.)

Improved mentoring and supervision. A parallel study will consider the role of mentoring and supervision in the audit profession, but one trainee identified its key role in improving audit practical training:

> Throughout the majority of my training I have been left to deal with audits completely on my own with little or no guidance from more senior staff. (Trainee, small firm—Questionnaire respondent no. 429.)

Secondments.. Another option suggested is that of the possibility of introducing a system of inter-firm secondments.

> I still do enjoy auditing, but I'm not involved in as much audit as I'd like to be. I'm not getting the exposure as much as someone in a bigger firm. So I think if the (RQB) could maybe have a network system where trainees get the opportunity to work in bigger firms and work on other audits then maybe. (Trainee, Focus Group.)

Overall, there is a consensus in this research that the size of firm has an impact on the level and quality of audit training and experience to which a trainee is exposed. While there are exceptions, there is a general perception and, at times, frustration amongst 'small firm' trainees regarding the limited opportunities for work-based audit training.

Conclusion

The changed environment for audit in the UK, brought about by the introduction of the audit exemption provisions for smaller companies, has impacted upon the acquisition of audit expertise by audit trainees. The concluding section of the paper begins by re-visiting the research questions in the light of the evidence gained from the analysis of the perceptions of audit trainees, before drawing some wider implications. In reaching these conclusions it is important to recognize that the sample of data on which they are based is biased towards smaller audit firms and any analysis and results have the caveat that, for larger firms, these conclusions may be different. Since the sample was not random, it cannot be said to be representative of all trainees in the UK, hence, care must be taken to avoid making any inference beyond those trainees who chose to participate in the study.

The first question asked: 'Do students feel that work-based training helps prepare them for their work as auditors?'

It appears that the in-house element of work-based training helps trainees to do their job as trainee auditors. Practical day-to-day relevant audit experience is highly valued by trainees. However, the feedback element of their experience, though valued when provided well, is often deficient where partners or managers are unable to find the time to provide such feedback properly.

The second question asked: 'Do students feel that examination-based learning helps prepare them for their work as auditors?'

Trainees' acquisition of understanding of the theory and concepts of auditing is often unstructured, partly due to the commercial realities of the training environment. The more structured element of trainees' acquisition of audit expertise, instruction through an educational institution by way of examination-based learning, does help trainees in their work as auditors. However, this is seen as less relevant and valuable than the range of work-based training offered—in-house training, practical experience with feedback. Where trainees have little opportunity to gain practical experience, the majority of their audit expertise necessarily comes from their examination-based learning. This lack of practical experience can make the audit examinations difficult for trainees to pass.

The third question asked: 'Do students view work-based training and examination-based learning as linked or separate?'

A lack of synchronization between examination-based learning and work-based training can undermine the acquisition of audit expertise. Trainees may struggle with examination topics which they have not yet encountered as part of their practical experience or, conversely, they may not understand an audit task which they are called upon to perform because they have not yet studied that particular audit theory or technique. Trainees endorsed the fact that specific examination-based learning is still required to prepare them for their work as auditors. The respondents reported that, where the practical experience and examination-based learning were not linked, the examination preparation became an academic exercise which impacted on examination performance. It was strongly supported that passing an examination was no substitute for on–the-job experience. This is reinforced by Bonner and Walker's (1994) views on the value of practical experience with feedback. When trainees were asked if work-based training and examination-based learning were linked or separated, contrasting views were expressed by respondents. Some could clearly identify the link and their audit training and examination performance benefited consummately. Others struggled to appreciate the link between the two and, at times, expressed a cynical view of the RQB examination structure and content with particular reference to their auditing studies and experience.

Finally, the fourth question asked: 'Does the size of firm impact on students' experience of work-based training and examination-based learning?'

All aspects of trainees' acquisition of audit expertise are often better in larger firms. Trainees in larger firms are likely to attend more in-house courses and receive better quality feedback on their audit practice. They have far more opportunity to work on audits. Their examination-based learning is more likely to be timed to coincide with their progression onto the execution of more complex audit tasks. There is a consensus that the size of firm has an impact on the level and quality of audit training and experience to which a trainee is exposed. While there are exceptions, there is a general perception and, at times, frustration, amongst small firm trainees regarding the limited opportunities for work-based audit training.

The introduction and expansion of the audit exemption threshold for small companies in the UK have resulted in a substantial decline in the number of accountants awarded the qualification required to enable them to sign audit opinions. While this significant environmental change has had far-reaching effects, this paper indicates that another contributing factor is the link between work-based training and examination-based learning that discourages many trainees from pursuing a career in auditing. The analysis of the results of a large-scale and professionally-supported questionnaire-based survey of audit trainees and their mentors supplemented with focus group interviews found that students feel work-based training to be a positive activity. However, this is dependent on the areas of auditing being available to provide appropriate experience, which is dependent on both the industry sector and accounting firm size.

Given the substantial reduction in the opportunities to obtain the necessary audit experience to enable an audit qualification to be gained, the future of the auditing profession in the UK is changing rapidly. The demand for audit services has reduced significantly and the supply of trained auditors will respond to the market dynamics as the organizations that supply them are driven by commercial objectives. It is, therefore, imperative that the audit training that takes place does so in accordance with known and tested pedagogic principles. This paper has demonstrated that work-based audit training has to be timed to coincide with the appropriate stage of the examination-based learning for it to be meaningful and effective. Unfortunately for many audit trainees, especially those working for smaller accounting practices, there is an inadequate amount of suitable audit work available, resulting in a reliance on examination-based learning becoming a purely academic exercise. Many accounting trainees who train with large firms of accountants where audit work is relatively plentiful often chose careers in non-audit areas and are, therefore, lost to the audit profession at a time when their skills and services are in increasingly short supply.

Whist this paper has identified the combination of examination-based learning and work-based training as being desirable, further work is required to support this view. It was outside the scope and methods of this study to determine the strength of this relationship. Quantitative analysis that enables variables such as performance in audit examinations and the correlation with the amount of relevant work-based training is required to substantiate the precise nature of any relationship. In addition, this future work can consider whether or not those performing well in their audit examinations also chose to enter the auditing profession.

Acknowledgements

The authors are grateful to the trainees who took part in the research and to the Professional Oversight Board for releasing the data for academic purposes with certain caveats. The authors are also indebted to the suggestions for improvement contained in the reviews of two anonymous referees and to the assistance one of the Guest Editors.

References

ACCA (2007) *Paper P7 Advanced Audit and Assurance, Examiner's Report* , December 2007 (London: ACCA).

Anderson, J. R. (1982) Acquisition of cognitive skill, *Psychological Review*, 89(4), pp. 369–460.

Bonner, S. E., Libby, R. and Nelson, M. W. (1997) Audit category knowledge as a precondition to learning from experience, *Accounting, Organizations and Society*, 22(5), pp. 387–410.

Bonner, S. E. and Walker, P. L. (1994) The effects of instruction and experience on the acquisition on auditing knowledge, *The Accounting Review*, 69(1), pp. 157–178.

Burns, D. C., Greenspan, J. W. and Hartwell, C. (1994) The state of professionalism in internal auditing, *The Accounting Historian's Journal*, 21(2), pp. 85–116.

Coenenberg, A. G., Haller, A. and Marten, K. (1999) Accounting education for professionals in Germany—current state and new challenges, *Journal of Accounting Education*, 17(4), pp. 367–390.

Covaleski, M. A., Dirsmith, M. W. and Rittenberg, L. (2003) Jurisdictional disputes over professional work: the institutionalization of the global knowledge expert, *Accounting, Organizations and Society*, 28(4), pp. 323–355.

Elliot, R. K. (1995) The future of assurance services: implications for academia, *Accounting Horizons*, 9(4), pp. 118–127.

Helliar, C., Monk, E., Stevenson, L. and Allison, C. (2007) *The Development of an Audit Learning Package* (Edinburgh: Institute of Chartered Accountants of Scotland).

Helliar, C. V., Monk, E. A. and Stevenson, L. A. (2009) The development of trainee auditors' skills in tertiary education, *International Journal of Auditing*, 13(3), pp. 185–202.

Iwasaka, J (2008) Responding to audit exemption: the UK experience, *The Accountant*, Spring, pp. 36–40.

Libby, R. (1995) The role of knowledge and memory in audit judgement, in: R. H. Ashton and A. H. Ashton (Eds) *Judgement and Decision Making Research in Accounting and Auditing*, pp. 176–206 (Cambridge, MA, Cambridge University Press).

Professional Oversight Board (POB) (2009) *Key Facts and Trends in the Accountancy Profession* (London: Financial Reporting Council).

Professional Oversight Board (POB) (2008a) *Key Facts and Trends in the Accountancy Profession* (London: Financial Reporting Council).

Professional Oversight Board (POB) (2008b) *Report on Practical Training for Auditors* (London: Financial Reporting Council).

Van Peursem, K. A. (2004) Internal auditors' role and authority, *Managerial Auditing Journal*, 19(3), pp. 378–393.

Van Peursem, K. A. (2005a) Conversations with internal auditors: the power of ambiguity, *Managerial Auditing Journal*, 20(5), pp. 489–512.

Van Peursem, K. A. (2005b) Audit challenges: dilemmas for the auditor in a global economy, *Asian Academy of Management Journal of Accounting and Finance*, 1, pp. 53–66. Available at: http://web.usm.my/journal//aamjaf/vol1_2005.html

Audit Education for Future Professionals: Perceptions of New Zealand Auditors

JENNA CHAFFEY, KAREN A. VAN PEURSEM and MARY LOW

University of Waikato, New Zealand

ABSTRACT   *Audit professionals are charged with gathering evidence and expressing their opinions on the financial claims made by others. In New Zealand, as elsewhere, these opinions are relied upon for a myriad of decisions as to the economic position and operations of an organisation. The educational experience that future professionals receive in their tertiary study is important because it lays the pedagogical foundation for this role. The aim of this study is to evaluate those teaching practices, subjects and techniques that might be of value to future audit professionals. The analysis is uniquely from the perspective of the professional members who are most likely to benefit from students' experiences. The literature is used to identify relevant questions, and a survey of 360 professional auditors in New Zealand yielded a 36.4% response rate. A triangulated analysis of comments and scaled questions reveals that these professionals are concerned with communication, small business engagements and the relationships between, for example, risk and planning and independence and ethics. Findings also confirm the value of experiential and practice-informed learning and direct us to a few topics that may accommodate non-traditional teaching methods. Conclusions consider implications for teaching and future research.*

Introduction and Background

Audit professionals are charged with gathering evidence and expressing their opinions on the financial claims made by others. In New Zealand, as elsewhere, these opinions are relied upon by a wide range of stakeholders and for a myriad of financial decisions as to the economic position and operations of an organisation. The educational experience that future professionals receive in their tertiary study is important, therefore, because it lays the pedagogical foundation for this role (e.g. see Johnson, Baird, Caster, Dilla, Earley and Louwers, 2003, p. 262; Okike, 1999).

Audit courses and teaching modules[1] combine information on an array of audit- and accounting-related subjects. Instructors in audit and developers of audit educational programs draw on such diverse disciplines as law, accounting, systems and ethics for material that serves the future needs of audit professionals. Instructors of audit are also tasked with helping students prepare for their evolving roles in satisfying both professional and public expectations of due care (see Awayiga, Onomuh and Tsamenyi, 2010; Johnson et al., 2003; Scheiwe and Radich, 1997). Developers of audit curricula are thus challenged to find the right balance between teaching facts, nurturing skills and raising professional conscientiousness (Johnson et al., 2003, p. 263). Coming to an understanding of what professional and experienced auditors see as being important can lend guidance to such teaching challenges as deciding what material is most important and identifying the best methods by which to encourage learning. Research that can support educators in this challenge would seem to comprise a real contribution.

Despite the complex nature and diverse topics in audit curricula, many tertiary accounting programs offer only one short module in audit. Furthermore, and creating challenges for the educator, there is no clear consensus as to what should be taught or what teaching methods should be employed in doing so (Carr, Chua and Perera, 2006; Van Peursem and Julian, 2006). The primary teaching method—at least in New Zealand and of which there is some evidence overseas—is the somewhat maligned textbook-based large lecture class approach (Johnson et al., 2003; NZICA, 2010a). It would be important to know, therefore, how educators may be able to improve audit education in the brief time they have with such students

Accounting professional bodies, institutions and accountancy firms have made it clear that they have an interest in what is taught to their future members and employees (e.g. Okike, 1999 on the UK and US professions; Carr et al., 2006 on New Zealand). All too often, however, professionals are bypassed in research. It is far more common to seek the views of inexperienced students to find answers to such questions (Carr et al., 2006; Becket and Brookes, 2006, p. 136). A study that seeks the views of professionals may, therefore, contribute to understandings of what is important for audit education from an 'outcome' perspective.

The aim of this study is to evaluate those teaching practices, subjects and techniques that might be of value to future audit professionals. The contribution is in coming to an understanding of how this important external stakeholder views such matters, how their views may vary and why, and to consider the implications of these findings for education and research.

New Zealand audit graduates are first exposed to audit within the second or third year of university (tertiary) study. Advanced material is also required (under 2010 requirements) for provisional membership into the primary New Zealand professional association, the New Zealand Institute of Chartered Accountants (NZICA). From this foundation, and often prior to completing professional examinations, students then enter the workforce. If their first work experience is in a professional firm, it is reasonably common to be assigned to audit as an introduction to accounting practice. Such students will be therefore exposed to audit very early in their career (e.g. see Hellier, Monk and Stevenson, 2009), and therefore, tertiary modules may comprise students' only pre-experience exposure to auditing.

This is a challenging task. Studies in audit education reveal the difficulty of resourcing quality programs (Awayiga et al., 2009), the limitations of non-critical programs (Sikka, Haslam, Kyriacou and Agrizzi, 2007) and the challenge in keeping up with current developments in audit education (Johnson *et al.*, 2003). Johnson *et al.*, (2003) find that most auditing curricula offer only one audit module. Few bring technology into the classroom or incorporate higher-order learning activities. While some innovations have been introduced in selective institutions, offerings in audit education remain limited generally (e.g. Johnson *et al.*, 2003; Adair, Marden and McCartney, 2002).

Moreover, there is little agreement as to what comprises 'good' audit education. While some demand less theory (Johnson *et al.*, 2003), others call for more (Sikka *et al.*). Some argue for the importance of a decision-making environment in the classroom (Knechel, 2000), others look to structured frameworks (Wright and Kaufman, 1994). The Bedford Committee of the American Accounting Association (Dennis, 2003; AAA 1986) highlighted the gap between what accountants do and what accounting education teaches. Overall, these findings point to the need for a study such as ours, which attempts to evaluate those aspects of an audit module that are more or less relevant to practitioners.

As to New Zealand in particular, there is little research precedent in audit education practice. Prior studies include a longitudinal survey of students' preferences in accounting generally (Tan and Laswad, 2007). A general survey of accounting alumni finds that neither 'audit' education nor work experience take a high priority (Carr *et al.*, 2006). Audit education in New Zealand is, therefore, something about which we know too little. This study contributes to that which educators should know about what professionals think should be taught in tertiary audit education.

The following sets out the scope of this investigation followed by an analysis of how the educational literature informs the survey. The research methods are then detailed followed by the findings to the study. A discussion and conclusion interpret these findings and considers educational implications, closing with suggestions for future research.

Scope

The fieldwork is confined to New Zealand practitioners. The implications are global, however. New Zealand has now adopted both international accounting and international auditing standards, bringing its practices into the global network. There are also international firm and firm policy associations as most audits in New Zealand are conducted by the 'big four' accounting firms. Finally NZICA is part of a global network of professional accounting bodies with reciprocal memberships among the most recognised of these including the Institute of Chartered Accountants in England and Wales (ICAEW), the American Institute of Certified Public Accountants (AICPA), the Canadian Institute of Chartered Accountants (CICA) and the Institute of Chartered Accountants in Australia (ICAA) among others (NZICA, 2010b). In all, the tertiary curriculum found in New Zealand is firmly grounded in the same principles as those in the UK, the USA and other western nations (e.g. see Lothian and Marrian, 1992; Birkett, 1993; and Carr and Matthews, 2004).

Yet the distinctions provided by a New Zealand study are valuable as well. In a small society (four million in population) it is possible to survey a very wide range of locations and firms, providing the potential for an unusually extensive picture within the context. Furthermore, New Zealand professionals are commonly posted overseas for training, secondment or as part of their decision to have an 'OE' (overseas experience), giving them an unusually wide and deep range of international experience. Their responses are, therefore, likely to reflect both this common background and distinctly international and non-insular views of what the profession may require.

This paper reports on a constructive, not critical, study. While there is also a critical literature about the use of technology as 'legitimization' (e.g. Robson, Humphrey, Khalifa

43

and Jones, 2007), exploring this topic is outside the scope of this paper. In an effort to keep the questionnaire to a size to encourage a reasonable response rate, the many topics, skills and learning activities emerging from the literature have been reduced to 70 questions in total plus an open-ended question. This has led to some 'combinations' (such as 'hands-on computer work' and 'working papers') which is inevitable considering the volume of topics and skills that could be raised. Where possible 'similar' issues are combined (as, for example, 'psychology' and 'sociology'), or activities are introduced to several questions (such as with 'hands-on computer work, or 'reviewing') so as to be able to measure related patterns. The value of these topics, knowledge bases and skills are thus formed from the literature and professional expectations, and take form in the questions raised.

Academic Content

The audit education literature, and its links to specific survey questions, is now reviewed. The purpose is to demonstrate how this literature inspired all of the 70 survey questions used in the survey. The survey is divided into two parts, the first of which focuses on audit 'topics, skills and disciplinary knowledge' so as to evaluate the knowledge and abilities that might be expected of new graduates. The second part focuses on evaluating traditional (lecture) and non-traditional delivery methods.

Topics, Skills and Disciplinary Knowledge

Audit history, the auditor's role, judgement, risk, professionalism, ethics, regulation, practice, communication and technology issues feature prominently in this literature. Each of these is addressed in turn, implications for professional education are discussed and particular questions (indicated in 'parentheses') are referred to, so as to indicate where these issues are addressed in the survey (see Table 1).

Audit history is seen to be an important topic to which students should be exposed. Understanding the context of a subject allows a contextualisation of practices and assumptions, thereby introducing relevance to a subject. History explains the rationales by which the understanding of a profession, its practices and its interests are formed (e.g. see Sangster, 2010; Quick, 2005). This is no less so in the case of auditing where it is said that 'principles, structures and tendencies ... [may] become clearer when viewed in their historical context' (Quick, 2005, p. 317). Questions pertaining to 'history' are included in the survey therefore, asking about its relevance to students generally and particularly as to the professionals' interest in audit (10, 11).

Decision-making is often raised in this literature and under a wide range of nomenclature including 'audit judgement', 'analysis', 'logic' and 'critical thinking'. It is an important topic in audit (e.g. Cohen, Krishnamoorthy and Wright, 2008; Nelson, Ratliff, Steinhoff and Mitchell, 2003; Knechel, 2000) and refers to the auditor's ability to apply or to select evidential matter from the field and to translate that 'matter' into informed decisions (Pratt and Van Peursem, 1993). Critical thinking, judgement and decision-making skills are fundamental to effective audit outcomes (e.g. Hellier *et al.*, 2009). Decision-making skills, therefore, underpin a number of survey questions posed to these audit professionals including those related to audit applications generally (38), sampling (40), systems (37) and, indirectly, to why audits can fail (13).

Understanding risk is seen to be important as well. Discussions around the risk of an audit client, clients' control systems and client fraud permeate the literature. Survey questions as to whether to accept an engagement and how to reduce its risk are important (e.g.

Table 1. Audit topics and skills

Audit topic	Related issues	Survey questionnumbers
History	Context, past practices	10, 11
Decision-making	Audit judgement, analysis, logic, critical thinking	13, 37, 38, 40
Risk	Audit client risk, control and systems risks, client fraud, acceptance risk, business and industry risk, liability risk, evidence and judgement, risk analysis, materiality and tolerable limits	19, 21, 26, 31, 35
Regulation	Standards, law and regulation, courts, code, legislation, statutory requirements	22, 23, 64
Profession	Associations, professional identity, institution, firm, professional expectations, professional obligations, rules and sanctions	16, 17, 18, 55, 60
Professional ethics	Ethical behaviour, moral development, defining issues test, ethical judgement, ethical codes, ethical rules, ethical principles	14, 15, 18, 38, 50, 54, 55, 62
Practical knowledge and skills	Core competencies, rudimentary tools of audit practice, practical knowledge, skills, planning, working paper preparation, sampling, testing, test design	12, 25, 27, 28, 32, 33, 34, 36, 39, 51, 42, 43, 44, 53,
Communication	Teamwork, written skills, negotiation skills, verbal skills	29, 33, 34, 43, 44, 50, 51, 52, 62
Computer literacy	Technology, computer skills, internal control systems, audit program design, audit programs, monitoring system controls, virtual audit, networks	24, 56, 57, 58
Knowledge	Other disciplines, humanities, philosophy, law, professional life	54, 63, 64, 66, 67, 68, 69, 70

Earley and Philips, 2008; Gramling and Karapanos, 2008; Jennings, 2004). Some authors refer to the risk of failing to identify weak controls, business or industry susceptibilities and risky clients generally (e.g. Arens and Elder, 2006; Vinten, 2004; Jennings, 2004). Survey questions thus touch on these issues as well, in particular as to liability risk (19), risk elements (20), evidence and judgement relationships (21), and the implications of client fraud (26). Skills which may enable the graduate to address risk issues are subject to enquiry in asking about the ability to perform a risk analysis (31) or to determine materiality and tolerable limits (35). Knowledge and, in particular, skills in developing reasoned alternatives are clearly valued in this literature. Whether they are valued in the (New Zealand) field is yet to be seen.

Audit professionals do not operate within a vacuum, but within a legal and regulatory context (Hellier *et al.*, 2009). International standards of auditing, with some modifications, are imposed on New Zealand organisations. Under New Zealand company legislation, the audit client must provide all documents and records to the auditor (Companies Act 1993, Section 194–201). Also under New Zealand law, the contents of the audit report is regulated (Financial Reporting Act, 1993, Sections 15–16) and accounting standards are mandatory (Regulations (Disallowance) Act 1989; Financial Reporting Act, 1993). Similar requirements are found in UK and Australian regulation under, for example, the Financial Reporting Council and the Auditing Practices Board (see for discussion Ministry of Economic Development, 2005). These represent important sources of information for auditors, and questions arise as to whether such standards and law should be taught are addressed in questions 22, 23 and 64.

Professional associations are also a powerful source of influence on audit practice (e.g. Mataira and Van Peursem, 2010). What is unknown, however, is how much of this is expected to be 'understood' by the time graduating students begin their professional careers. Audit education research gives some indication as to the importance of associational understandings, but guidance from the literature remains vague. Mayer-Sommer and Loeb (1981) refer to 'professional identity', while Wright and Kauffman (1994) speak about the value of teaching with regard to the institutional (firm or professional) environment. In response, we ask how important it is to introduce tertiary students to professions generally, their own profession, professional expectations, rules, obligations and sanctions (16, 17, 18 and 55 as to related activities). We also ask whether students should be engaged with professional journals (60), an activity that may bring current events, professional actions and professional culture to their attention.

The subject of professional ethics forms another source of discussion around the profession and professional learning (e.g. Hellier *et al.*, 2009; Fleming, Lightner and Romanus, 2009; Johnson et al., 2009; Boylan, 2008). An extensive literature informs as to relationships between demographics and professional ethical behaviour, educational programs, recommended teaching methods (including case and drama) and moral development (see Van Peursem and Julian, 2006 for a review). In particular, the use of Rest's (1979) Defining Issues Test (DIT) cited in Massey and Thorne (2006) has been extensively taken up in this literature (see Massey and Thorne, 2006). The DIT is an instrument used in experimental studies of, for example, accounting students to evaluate the impact of educational interventions on their moral development; so, and with respect to our study, it is the 'learning activities' as well as the 'topics' and 'skills' which are important. For that reason, our survey includes questions on ethics 'topics' (14, 15, 18), 'skills' (38), and delivery methods by which such skills can be enhanced (50, 54, 55 and 62).

There is some expectation in the literature that acquiring practical knowledge and skills are also part of the tertiary sector's responsibility. Hellier *et al.* (2009) refer to 'core competencies' and Fischman (2007) to rudimentary tools of audit practice. Topics and skills that emerge from these discussions include the ability to plan, complete working papers, sample and test (e.g. Hellier *et al.*, 2009; Gramling and Karapanos, 2008; Cohen *et al.*, 2008; Fischman, 2007 Johnson *et al.*, 2003). These are reflected in questions as to audit process generally (12, 42, 53), and to these specific elements of the audit process (27, 28, 32, 33, 34, 41, 43, 44). As the ability to understand, design and conduct tests also form part of these discussions, they are also raised in the survey (25, 39, 36).

'Communication' is a relatively new interest in this field, but its importance is affirmed by new audit standards concerned with its conduct and effectiveness.[2] The literature is starting to reinforce an interest in professional communication skills (e.g. Hellier *et al.*, 2009; Murthy and Kerr, 2004; Johnson et al., 2003). The ability to communicate and work in a team is seen to be an important learning outcome. Communication issues are introduced by enquiring as to respondents' views about the skills needed for working with a team (29) and working with clients (30). Written communication skills are also part of the questionnaire (33, 34, 43 and 44). Some learning activities also implicate communication skill development (50 on presenting, 51 on debates, 52 on visits, and 62 on role playing) We ask, therefore, about the value of a number of skills and activities in particular, which would develop a student's communication abilities for audit purposes.

Technology and computer literacy skills are important for auditors in two respects. Auditors must be sufficiently conversant with the client's internal control systems so as to be able to make relevant enquiries, design audit programs and monitor system controls (Masli, Peters, Richardson and Sanchez, 2010; Taylor and Dzuranin, 2010; Broad, Matthews and Shephard, 2003). In another respect, technology and computer literacy skills are important because they are needed to carry out the practical aspects of an audit. Since today's audits are conducted in a 'virtual' environment, auditors must be conversant with complex networked systems of their own firm's (and sometimes a client's) system (e.g. see Retzlaff, 2006; Murthy and Kerr, 2004; Broad *et al.*, 2003). It is relevant, therefore, to incorporate questions about the sorts of systems knowledge that professionals would need for this purpose (24) as well as whether and how students should be exposed to this knowledge in their tertiary experiences (56, 57 and 58).

Finally, there is a need for professional auditors to be conversant with a broad knowledge base such as accounting, law and the humanities (Awayiga *et al.*, 2009, pp. 2–5; Johnson *et al.*, 2003, pp. 262–263). We address this issue by recognising them in the closing questions to the survey. In particular, we ask about financial and management accounting (63), law (64), general management (54), marketing (66), economics and finance (67), philosophy and ethics (68), communication (69) and psychology or sociology (70). An understanding of these preferences may contribute to an understanding of their value to professional life.

Learning Activities

Learning activities are repeatedly reflected upon in this literature. In this context we take 'activities' to refer to the classroom exercises and delivery methods by which audit content is conveyed, shared and absorbed. Traditional learning activities (in particular, large-group lectures) tend to be unidirectional in which a 'knowledgeable' instructor conveys 'facts' to the 'unknowing' student. While widely employed[3] possibly because lectures absorb fewer teaching resources, such experiences may offer little in terms of creating a learning environment in which students can contribute to their own learning. The educator has some room for choice in the way lectures are conveyed, however, and we attempt to address three of these alternatives in questions about the instructor's background ('academic' or 'practitioner'), the type of content ('facts' or 'applications') and in the style of exposition ('face-to-face' at fixed times or computerised in flexible times) (47–49).

Non-traditional learning activities offer other possibilities. 'Non-traditional' refers here to that combination of events and activities which encourage student involvement, self-reflection and active engagement with audit problems (see Table 2).

We are particularly interested in activities that can be incorporated into an otherwise 'traditional' educational programme (Questions 47–62). Non-traditional learning activities may be a challenge to develop, but their benefits are acknowledged. Fischman (2007), for example, claims that audit educators have a specific responsibility to introduce their students to the basic tools which they will need to deal with practice challenges. Support for experiential (life-imitating) learning in the audit classroom is popular in this literature (Hellier *et al.*, 2009; Van Peursem and Julian, 2006; Ferguson, Richardson and Wines, 2000; Knechel, 2000).

A frequently-cited non-traditional activity is the use of cases (e.g. Braun and Stallworth, 2009; BeMiller, Lindberg and Wirtz, 2009; Earley and Philips, 2008) (50, 48(b) in the survey). Those supporting case-based teaching point to its virtues in enabling students to apply principles learned from texts or lecture to practice-based situations (e.g. Hellier *et al*, 2009; Dennis, 2003; Maltby, 2001; Hassall, Dunlop and Lewis, 1996). Cases are also said to create deeper learning experiences which can help students to integrate the

Table 2. Non-traditional learning activities for auditors. Neither textbook-based learning nor lectures are incorporated into the Likert scale questions for reasons set out in the narrative.

Learning activity	Survey question numbers
Case-based learning: using case studies, real-life situations, case analysis in-class	48(b), 50
Role playing, using drama and acting out scenarios	51, 62
Communication-based activities	50, 51
Guest speakers	47(b)
Working directly with computers, hands-on exercises and work, using generalized audit software	56, 57, 58
Use of videos in class	54

lessons which they have absorbed from other fields. Cases tend to inspire holistic under-standings of practice (Cohen et al., 2008) and if well-designed and appropriately directed (Siddiqui, Nasreen and Choudhury-Lema, 2009; Dennis, 2003), case study analyses enable students to engage in a sort of self-reflection not likely to be nurtured by text- and lecture-based lessons alone.

Other non-traditional learning activities find space in this literature as well. Role-playing and drama come recommended (e.g. Maltby, 2001) (51, 62). Techniques which encourage teamwork and communication skills are advised (Hellier *et al.*, 2009; Johnson et al., 2003) (50, 51). The use of guest speakers receives some attention (Fischman, 2007; Johnson *et al.*, 2003) (47(b)) and videos (Hellier *et al.*, 2009; Johnson *et al.*, 2003) (54) can serve to bring practice into the classroom.

Providing hands-on experience with computers is said to have its advocates (e.g. Broad *et al.*, 2003; Johnson *et al.*, 2003) (56, 57, 58). Audit software use for the classroom, first recommended in the 1980s (Vasarhelyi and Lin, 1985) attracts more recent supporters as well (Nieschwitz, Pany and Zhang, 2002; Groomer and Heintz, 1999). Overall, it is apparent that, while traditional learning activities may be less resource-intensive, they may also deprive the student of valued forms of learning. Our interest in non-traditional activities is particularly pertinent therefore because knowledge about them helps contribute to class-room applications. Non-traditional activities are thus brought into the survey in questions 50–62 (Table 2).

Each year accounting firms invest capital in professional training. From their perspective at least, having better-educated graduates, gives firms and clients a firmer foundation in audit professionalism (Hellier *et al.*, 2009). While professionals are not the only stake-holders (Johnson *et al.*, 2003, p. 262–263), they may be in the unique position of antici-pating the sorts of skills and knowledge which these students will need from their tertiary learning experiences.

Methods

A post-positivist methodological approach was applied in the project, incorporating assumptions that research is generally value-free and observable (Grimmer and Hansen 2005). The survey, while incorporating a qualitative element, allows for generalisations to be made from its quantitative (Likert scale) results as well (Bryman, 2004), providing a basis for triangulation.

The population surveyed consists of currently-active professional auditors in New Zealand. There are 31 674 members of NZICA (late 2009) and approximately 30% of them work within firms of chartered accountants (NZICA, 2009, p. 1). The population of interest, therefore, is active members (i.e. the 9500 or so who conduct audit and assurance services). There is no formal database distinguishing these members from others, so we used nation-wide telephone *Yellow Pages* sources to identify firms and individuals within firms. Of the over 1000 firms found, 350 were selected on a systematic random and cluster basis (ensuring that large and small, urban and rural firms are represented) and questionnaires were posted.

A survey should reflect the population (Cresswell, 2003) and, in this case, we sought demographic information about our respondents to enable us to analyse differences as well as similarities. We sought information on their experience, location, gender, firm type and position (e.g. see Koch, Moyes and Williams, 2006; Garavan, O'Hanlon and O'Brien, 2004 for precedent).

The second section of the questionnaire asked what audit topics and graduate skills are wanted. Questions here use a five-point Likert scale (e.g. see Emerald Group Publishing Ltd, 2009). Section three give two-choice alternatives on broader curriculum management issues: the educator, presentation type and material content. We acknowledge some limitation in restricting our questions in this category, but offer three reasons for doing so. Given cost constraints, together with high accounting enrolments, it is unlikely that providers will have many options to change whole structures. In addition, such questions may be more ably handled by educators (experienced in educational management) than practitioners. Finally, and as an exploratory vehicle, our results—taken together—may contribute to broader teaching implications, implications which will be explored through our multicollinearity and qualitative analysis. The questionnaire, in its final section, incorporates questions about small group activities and disciplinary knowledge bases (see Appendix I).

A pilot was completed by three practicing auditors to ensure that the questions were relevant and clear to the typical respondent (Hair, Money, Page and Samouel, 2007). To obtain the highest response possible, and to reduce non-response bias, a follow-up was conducted five weeks after the initial posting. An Excel database was used to arrange the data, and SPSS was applied for statistical tests (e.g. see Hair *et al.*, 2007).

Respondent 'comments' are analysed as follows. One of the authors categorised the qualitative responses into 'themes' and a second author reviewed the classifications. Only those themes commented upon by three or more different respondents are raised in the analysis.

Descriptive (quantitative) statistics reveal general patterns of preference and dispersion. The Chi-square (for dichotomous variables in the LECTURE EXPERIENCES section) and Kruskal-Wallis tests (for the remaining ordinal data questions) reveal patterns as to the characteristics of the respondents. A Pearson analysis of correlation rounds out the statistical analysis to suggest where responses might be 'moving together'. Inferences, to the extent reasonable, are made by collating the conclusions from each of these sources.

The possibility of non-response bias is tested by comparing 'early' and 'late' (follow up) respondent results on selected questions. While the Kruskal-Wallis (and Chi-square for categorical data) tests identify some significant differences among the respondent groups, they do not distinguish how they lie within the categories, so a scan of the cross-tab results provides us with answers to some of these questions. The results are set out below.

Results

Our results are organised by survey section: AUDIT TOPICS, AUDIT SKILLS, LECTURE EXPERIENCES, LEARNING ACTIVITIES and DISCIPLINARY KNOWL-EDGE. Both qualitative data (from the comments) and quantitative data (from the closed-ended questions) are evaluated, beginning with respondent demographics.

Respondents

A total of 162 questionnaires were returned: 130 useable, 15 uncompleted from firms not conducting audit, and 17 returned for missing addresses (see Table 3). Given that audits are primarily performed by major firms, non-respondents likely include firms the members of which do not engage in audit and would not be within our population of interest. The response, while exhibiting a technical response rate of 36.4%, is therefore likely to be higher as a proportion of the population of firms in which experienced, active auditors are to be found.

Of the usable responses, 79 were 'on time' and 51 were 'late'. As requested in the covering letter (see Appendix I), the questionnaires were completed by experienced audit staff (where available) in nearly all cases; only six of the 130 returned were completed by staff with less than two years' experience. The respondents have wide experience, most within 'financial statement audit'. The respondents include a large proportion of small firm owners, have a variety of educational experiences, and represent a reasonable gender balance (Table 3). More than half (72) have over 10 years of audit experience, again indicating the quality of the respondents. The results comprise, therefore, a reasonable representation of the experienced professional auditor in New Zealand.

Multiple answers from a single respondent are treated as 'missing data' and excluded (e.g. Rodeghier, 1996). Non-response bias tests 12 questions chosen systematically (the first three of each category, T10, T11, T12, S29, S30, S31, L47, L48, L49, D50, D51 and D52) and Chi square tests are run to determine differences. Of the Chi square tests, only one result shows significance above 90%, which is likely in any case given the number of tests (12). A Multinomial Regression run to determine if 'lateness' predicts response did not draw 'lateness' into predictor variables. It was concluded, therefore, that non-response bias was not significant to the results.

Qualitative Results

Table 4 summarises open-ended comments.

Several themes emerge, and the first relates to the importance of a professional's communication skills and public persona. Six different respondents raise this point.

Another theme is as to the value of small business audit skills with comments pointing to the many small non-profit and sole trader clients typical in New Zealand practice. Two further points are to do with the DISCIPLINARY KNOWLEDGE, but produce contradictory findings. Some respondents believe an 'audit' or 'technical' base is important (eight comments) and others point to the value of a 'broad disciplinary base' (four comments). This is early evidence of what we found to be two distinct views within our survey respondent group.

In the category of NON-TRADITIONAL LEARNING, we found eight commentators mentioning the value of practical exercises and seven the importance of learning 'within [the] practice'. Both highlight these respondents' interest in experiential learning and non- traditional learning activities. No theme emerged as to a best LECTURE EXPERIENCE. These results are incorporated into our Discussion and Conclusion.

Table 3. Respondent statistics

Profile of respondents	Frequency	Percentage %	Profile of respondents	Frequency	Percentage %
Audit experience (years)			Other tertiary major?		
Up to 2 years	6	4.6	Yes[d]	13	11.9
Between 2-5 years	19	14.6	No	104	88.1
Between 5–10 years	33	25.4			
More than 10 years	72	55.4	Number of audit courses		
Total	130	100	None	15	11.6
Primarily function			One-half	8	6.2
Firm partner or owner			One	70	54.3
Director or senior manager	76	58.5	Two or more	25	19.4
Manager	31	23.9	Not recalled	11	8.5
Senior	15	11.5	Total	129	100
Junior	6	4.6			
Other[a]	2	1.5	Gender		
Total	130	100	Male	90	69.2
Audit experience (activities)			Female	40	30.8
Financial statement audits	104	83.9	Total	130	100
Internal or performance audits	3	2.4			
Reviews, advisory, compilations	5	4.0	Organisation type		
All types	11	8.9	International accounting firm	31	24.4
Other[b]	1	.8	Mid-size accounting firm	7	5.5
Totals	130	100	Small accounting firm	66	52.0
Degree type			Sole trader	17	13.4
Four-year degree (or equivalent)	64	49.2	Corporate sector	1	.8
Three-year degree	49	37.7	Government sector	3	2.4
Non-degree tertiary qualification[e]	10	7.7	Other[c]	2	1.6
Post-graduate qualification	7	5.4	Total	127	100
Total	130	100			

[a]Other functions: Intermediate auditor

[b]Other audit types: real estate trust accounts, charitable bodies, computer audit, business process risk assessment, election expense audits, design sets and train audit software

[c]Other organisation: type not stated

[d]Other major: Dip HR, Dip Business studies, History, Marketing, Economics, Neuroscience, BA in Chinese and Japanese, Law, Bachelor of arts, Commerce, Mathematics, Politics, Management

[e]Non-tertiary qualifications—ACCA, NZICA, ACA.

Audit Topics and Knowledge

Descriptive statistics (see Table 5) indicate a preference for teaching AUDIT TOPICS that require judgement (risk, planning, evidence, materiality, and opinions), practical skills (audit process and standards) and ethics.

This places extensive demands on what is usually a short curriculum. Of least interest are topics in history and public expectations. Topics on which respondents most 'disagreed' with each other (indicated by larger standard deviations) include those of liability, public expectations and again history and background. As before, two distinct views

Table 4. Qualitative comment summary[a]

Comment theme	Resp #	Section	Example
Importance of communication skills and personality	3, 5, 27, 51, 75, 105	AUDIT SKILLS	'What is critical in auditing is being able to explain things to the client about what can be quite complex matters and keeping things simple so no confusion can arise' (75).
Importance of having a sound background in audit foundations	5, 12, 27, 43, 66, 82, 102, 106,	DISCPL. KNOWL.	'It is important in the audit profession to have a good foundation in auditing theories. This should be emphasised in the undergraduate program supported by business cases under an experiential learning approach' (66)
Importance of small audits	9,14,75	AUDIT TOPIC	'The ability to scale their knowledge of audit from university to suit the actual client—all clients aren't Enron. Does training cover typical client in small practice, i.e. the churches, rugby clubs and kindergartens?' (14)
Importance of in-field learning experiences	10, 43, 63, 82, 94, 99, 106	NON-TRADIT LEARN.	'Most of the audit process[es] are best learnt on the job rather than during study'(99)
Importance of practical-applied lessons	48, 51, 66, 78, 96, 105, 27, 1119	NON-TRADIT LEARN.	'A number of graduates in the accounting/audit profession have a good knowledge of the theory of auditing but lack the ability to apply that knowledge in a practical situation' (27)
Importance of a sound academic base	10, 12, 14, 106	DISCPL. KNOWL	'Auditing requires a wide set of transferable skills, therefore I do not believe that courses at uni need to be specific to audit as long as the student can demonstrate the ability to learn and apply knowledge and work in a team' (106).

[a]A more detailed schedule of qualitative responses is available from the corresponding author.

emerged. All questions in this category are ordinal, so a Kruskal-Wallis statistic determined differences by respondent category (see Table 6).

A number of findings show a correspondence between respondents' personal experience and their particular educational preferences. Respondents' with 3-year degrees (64 or 49.2% of the total) and non-degree qualifications placed greater weight on procedural audit steps (Q12) than those with four-year and honours degrees. These respondents may have had less formal experience in situations which introduce concepts and theories. In all, seven questions where 'years of experience' is found to be related to a response, the more experienced respondents chose the risk-based topics (audit failure, liability, risk model, fraud, independence) (Table 6). Partners placed greater weight on matters of risk (Q18, Q19 and Q14), perhaps a response to dealing with the courtroom consequences of risk more than their less-experienced juniors.

Table 5. Descriptive statistics: audit topics

Question no.	Topics	n	Mean	SD
20	Risk and its elements for audit planning	130	4.4846	0.7385
12	The steps in the audit process	127	4.4331	0.8027
22	Auditing standards	130	4.3769	7802
21	The meaning of evidence and audit judgement	128	4.3437	0.7678
23	Accounting standards	130	4.2846	0.7996
14	General ethical principles and the idea of independence	130	4.2846	0.8381
27	The meaning of audit opinions	130	4.2231	0.7601
13	Why audits can fail	128	4.1797	0.7678
15	Specific ethical codes and rules	129	4.1628	0.7885
25	Differences between tests of controls and tests of balances	129	4.0930	0.7649
26	The implications of client fraud	129	3.9845	0.8568
24	Accounting systems principles	128	3.8281	0.8613
16	The local profession, its rules and expectations	130	3.6769	0.8911
28	The meaning of other types of report opinions	127	3.6693	0.8457
19	Liability auditors may face in the courtroom	130	3.6615	1.089
18	Obligations and sanctions imposed by the profession	129	3.6434	0.9747
11	Why different people want or demand audit	129	3.5426	1.045
17	Professions in general and expectations of professionals	130	3.2923	0.9996
10	The history of audit and how it came to be as it is now	129	2.5116	1.133

Likert scale ranking: 1, not important to 5, vital.

Senior managers attribute greater value to lessons they would use in their management capacities: audit demand (Q11), standards (Q23), codes and rules (Q15). Those with 'all types' of experience place value on market demands, professions in general, and systems principles (Q11, Q17, Q24); that is, general knowledge bases. Small firm respondents, who may struggle with meeting multiple technical and legal requirements, attribute value to lessons on ethical codes, liabilities, professions, obligations and sanctions (Q15, Q19, Q17 and Q18). Such preferences indicate how (and together, perhaps why) differences of opinion *within* the professional association may occur.

Audit Skills

The AUDIT SKILLS group of questions yielded patterns as indicated in Table 7.

The most-preferred, and agreed, skill is as to developing a student's communication skills (Q30), a finding consistent with the qualitative commentary. Other preferences lean toward skills to do with either practical elements (preparing working papers and audit plans) or judgement-based procedures (audit dilemmas, risk analyses, test design, materiality determinations, results evaluations). Skills of least interest are to do with more standardised procedures: designing a statistical sample and preparing letters. Patterns in 'audit skills' and 'respondent characteristics' are revealed in Table 8.

Those with the greatest experience (more than 10 years) attribute greater value to preparing engagement and management letters (Q33, Q34), a role perhaps not given to new staff; and the judgement-demanding process of determining materiality (Q35). 'Senior managers' place greater weight on graduates' teamwork skills (Q29), skills they would themselves be supervising. Those with 'all types' of audit experience show interest in

Table 6. Audit topics related to respondent characteristics: Kruskal-Wallis

Q No.	Audit topics	B1 Experience years		B2 Function		B3 Experience type		B4 Firm type		B5 Education years		B7 Audit course background		B8 Gender	
		Value	Sig	Value	Sig	Value	Sig	Value	Sig	Value	Sig	Value	Sig	Value	Sig
10	History	2.876	0.579	1.564	0.815	4.447	0.349	8.008	0.091[a]	10.874	0.028[a]	3.840	0.428	5.542	0.236
11	Demand	6.953	0.138	10.58	0.032[a]	9.451	0.051[a]	1.141	0.888	4.241	0.374	9.648	0.047[a]	4.407	0.354
12	Audit steps	4.695	0.320	2.672	0.614	1.978	0.740	7.837	0.098[a]	8.355	0.079[a]	1.252	0.869	5.106	0.277
13	Audit failure	6.459	0.091[a]	4.732	0.193	1.018	0.797	.886	0.829	.273	0.965	2.950	0.399	4.245	0.236
14	Independence	8.802	0.066[a]	10.19	0.038[a]	4.770	0.189	2.217	0.696	7.629	0.106	2.888	0.577	2.952	0.566
15	Ethics codes	3.284	0.350	7.082	0.069[a]	2.230	0.526	6.502	0.090[a]	3.050	0.384	3.901	0.272	3.402	0.334
16	Prof. rules	6.687	0.153	11.77	0.019[a]	6.643	0.156	6.029	0.197	3.849	0.427	1.668	0.796	2.646	0.619
17	Professions	4.195	0.380	4.386	0.356	11.21	0.024[a]	9.649	0.047[a]	2.172	0.704	7.431	0.115	3.256	0.516
18	Sanctions/obl	5.434	0.246	12.25	0.016[a]	5.945	0.203	8.853	0.065[a]	2.457	0.652	1.957	0.744	1.456	0.834
19	Liability/courts	8.533	0.074[a]	13.83	0.008[a]	3.649	0.456	10.09	0.039[a]	4.933	0.294	5.664	0.226	0.551	0.968
20	Risk/planning	7.858	0.097[a]	5.280	0.260	60.51	0.109	4.357	0.360	3.889	0.421	5.246	0.263	10.67	0.899
21	Evidence/Jdgjdg	3.003	0.391	3.540	0.316	.489	0.921	2.560	0.465	1.611	0.657	1.253	0.740	1.167	0.761
22	Audit stnds	7.983	0.092[a]	6.756	0.149	1.613	0.807	5.755	0.218	1.714	0.788	3.510	0.476	4.166	0.384
23	Accnt. stnds	7.125	0.1259	12.77	0.012[a]	2.454	0.653	1.262	0.868	1.237	0.872	4.117	0.390	3.512	0.476
24	Systems	3.114	0.539	1.945	0.746	7.867	0.097[a]	4.850	0.303	1.372	0.849	2.823	0.588	3.456	0.485
25	Tests: types	7.969	0.047[a]	1.174	0.759	.692	0.875	2.200	0.532	5.217	0.157	1.567	0.667	2.419	0.490
26	Client fraud	7.931	0.094[a]	6.100	0.192	6.808	0.146	4.217	0.377	1.840	0.765	2.763	0.598	5.353	0.253
27	Audit opinions	5.364	0.147	4.578	0.205	2.026	0.567	1.256	0.740	1.711	0.634	2.768	0.429	1.607	0.658
28	Opinions (other)	1.524	0.677	2.889	0.409	2.454	0.484	5.894	0.117	3.566	0.312	12.30	0.006[a]	2.648	0.449

[a]Significant results at 90% confidence or above.

Table 7. Descriptive statistics: Audit skills

Q no.	Skills	n	Mean	SD
30	Communicate with clients	130	4.346	0.746
43	Prepare audit working papers	128	4.180	0.8734
38	Apply principles of audit judgement to audit dilemmas	126	4.087	0.8857
31	Perform a risk analysis of a client	129	4.078	0.8349
36	Design tests of controls	128	4.016	0.7097
32	Develop a detailed audit plan	128	4.000	0.8511
35	Determine materiality and tolerable misstatement	129	3.868	0.7642
40	Evaluate the results of an audit sample	128	3.867	0.7357
46	Conduct a going concern analysis	129	3.853	0.9023
41	Perform a bank reconciliation	128	3.828	0.9729
29	Work with a team	129	3.791	0.9656
37	Evaluate a computerised accounting and control system	127	3.638	0.8607
45	Conduct a subsequent events analysis	129	3.628	0.8203
42	Conduct a small audit independently	128	3.617	0.9232
34	Design and prepare a letter to management	127	3.598	0.9020
44	Prepare the audit report	128	3.516	1.065
33	Design and prepare an engagement letter	127	3.315	0.9735
39	Design a statistical audit sample	129	3.217	0.8000

teaching students how to develop an audit plan (Q31), a preference that, in a pattern that emerged before, aligns with their own current experiences and needs.

Sole practitioners place less value on teamwork skills (Q29) but, together with small firms, more on computerisation and system skills (Q37). Those with three-year degrees or less attribute greater value to lessons on preparing working papers (Q43), bank reconciliations (Q41) and system evaluations (Q37). Overall, this reveals a preference for a reasonably pedantic range of skills by respondents from small firms; a call for teamwork skills by those managing teams; and a preference for planning skills by those more likely to have been involved in a wide range of engagements. There also seems to be a strong interest in providing audit graduates with the skills to engage immediately with their tasks, however those tasks are perceived, on coming into a firm.

Lecture Experiences

Responses for the three questions on lecture experiences are summarised in Table 9.

Respondents prefer the 'visiting professional' lecturer in a 'face-to-face' format, with some preference for 'case studies' over more structured learning. Respondents with non-degree qualifications distinguish themselves in preferring 'case studies' (Q48). Although there is a general preference for the traditional over computerised lectures format (Q49), those with three-year degrees were more evenly split between the personal and the computerised style. Respondents who had taken two or more audit courses prefer an experienced academic; others prefer the 'visiting professional' although less so as their own audit experience increases. Other patterns follow in the Correlations section below.

Non-traditional Learning Activities

Descriptive statistics on non-traditional learning activities can be found in Table 10.

Table 8. Audit skills related to respondent characteristics: Kruskal-Wallis

		B1 Experience Years		B2 Function		B3 Experience type		B4 Firm type		B5 Education years		B7 Audit course background		B8 Gender	
Q No.	Audit skills: engage in or prepare a	Value	Sig	Value	Sig	Value	Sig	Value	Sig	Value	Sig	Value	Sig	Value	Sig
29	Teamwork	6.429	0.169	1.94	0.018[a]	2.779	0.596	11.08	0.026[a]	2.611	0.625	1.571	0.814	7.558	0.109
30	Communicate	0.493	0.974	0.395	0.983	2.165	0.706	2.077	0.722	2.636	0.620	2.582	0.630	1.961	0.743
31	Risk analysis	3.825	0.430	2.254	0.689	6.434	0.092[a]	4.969	0.290	4.488	0.344	0.321	0.988	1.312	0.859
32	Audit plan	4.610	0.330	3.347	0.501	3.486	0.323	3.950	0.413	6.749	0.150	4.657	0.324	.558	0.968
33	Engag. letter	8.917	0.063[a]	2.656	0.617	1.753	0.781	5.849	0.211	8.182	0.085[a]	1.881	0.758	3.377	0.497
34	Mngt letter	7.881	0.096[a]	3.318	0.506	1.433	0.839	6.494	0.165	5.612	0.230	0.777	0.941	7.159	0.128
35	Materiality	10.24	0.017[a]	1.557	0.669	4.172	0.243	6.384	0.094[a]	5.640	0.130	3.080	0.380	2.707	0.439
36	Control tests	5.607	0.132	4.413	0.220	3.972	0.265	3.057	0.383	4.168	0.244	2.301	0.512	0.769	0.857
37	System eval	4.660	0.324	1.712	0.789	3.174	0.529	9.40	0.052[a]	4.725	0.317	8.544	0.074[a]	3.762	0.439
38	Apply jdgment	6.548	0.162	3.834	0.429	1.607	0.658	0.802	0.938	5.240	0.264	0.095	0.999	5.605	0.231
39	Statist sample	7.625	0.106	1.856	0.762	5.843	0.211	30200	0.555	6.317	0.177	4.263	0.372	5.800	0.215
40	Sample analysis	2.954	0.399	1.688	0.640	2.214	0.529	0.660	0.883	6.012	0.111	1.125	0.771	1.912	0.591
41	Bank reconcil	3.539	0.316	4.984	0.173	2.434	0.487	2.039	0.564	2.070	0.558	7.483	0.058[a]	5.207	0.157
42	SME audit	2.736	0.603	2.606	0.626	4.377	0.357	2.633	0.621	0.193	0.996	1.251	0.870	0.261	0.992
43	Wkng papers	0.807	0.848	1.642	0.650	2.388	0.496	2.871	0.412	12.79	0.005[a]	7.672	0.053[a]	0.075	0.995
44	Audit report	7.189	0.126	1.291	0.863	1.700	0.791	8.787	0.067	4.690	0.321	1.761	0.780	2.436	0.656
45	Subse events	5.539	0.136	4.562	0.207	5.778	0.123	3.944	0.268	2.914	0.405	4.542	0.209	0.760	0.859
46	Going conc	2.489	0.477	5.841	0.120	2.972	0.396	3.026	0.388	5.204	0.157	2.612	0.455	0.042	0.998

[a]Significant results at 90% confidence or above.

Table 9. Lecture experiences related to respondent types and audit topics: Chi square

Q no.	Lecture experience categories[a]	B1 Years experience		B2 Function		B3 Experience type		B4 Firm type		B5 Education years		B7 Course history value		B8 Gender	
		Value	Sig	Value	Sig	Value	Sig	Value	Sig	Value	Sig	Value	Sig	Value	Sig
47	Presenter	1.76	0.938	c	1.87	0.985		c	15.28	0.018[d]	22.05	0.005[d]	1.13	0.570	
48	Content	1.49	0.683	1.18	0.947	2.89	0.576	6.99	0.429	7.11	0.069[d]	6.239	0.182	c	
49	Exposition:	c		3.28	0.658	10.37	0.035[d]	5.68	0.578	6.34	0.096[d]	6.16	0.188	1.17	0.279

Q no.	Audit topic categories[b]	T11 Why		T16 ProfG		T17 ProfS		T19 Liab	
		Value	Sig	Value	Sig	Value	Sig	Value	Sig
47	Presenter								
48	Content								
49	Exposition	11.1	0.026	9.92	0.042	7.94	0.094	9.39	0.052

[a]Presenter (academic or practitioner); content (facts or applications); exposition (face-to-face/fixed time, or computerised/flexitime).
[b]Results for 'Audit topic categories' only show the four results with 90% confidence level or above of 19 possible.
[c]Cell count <5.
[d]Significant to 90% confidence level.

Table 10. Descriptive statistics: Non-traditional learning activities

Q no.	Small group activities	*n*	Mean	SD
53	Going over audit processes and procedures	127	4.000	0.7766
55	Going over standards, rules and regulations	129	3.884	8256
58	Hands-on computer work with analytical review problems	128	3.836	0.8942
57	Hands-on computer work with risk and materiality problems	128	3.797	0.9167
56	Hands-on computer work with working paper programs	127	3.669	1.0240
51	Debates on current, topical issues	127	3.378	0.9166
50	Student presentations of audit cases	125	3.144	0.9563
60	Reviewing professional journal articles	125	3.048	0.8877
52	Visiting and audit office	125	2.920	1.0671
59	Reviewing law cases	128	2.914	0.9559
61	Reviewing research about audit	124	2.750	0.8983
54	Watching videos or CD	123	2.732	0.9150
62	Drama: acting out the auditor's role	125	2.664	1.0772

As indicated by the means, preferences are not as strong generally in this category. Compliance and practice elements (processes, procedures, standards, rules and regulations) and hands-on computer work of all kinds top the range. Of least interest, and with the largest variation, is the use of 'drama' (Q62). Visiting offices (Q52) and some working paper programs (Q56) are somewhat controversial. Differences by respondent types are highlighted in Table 11.

This is the only category in which significant differences exist in the 'gender' category, occurring with respect to 'debates' (Q51) (which the men prefer) and 'review procedures' (Q53) (preferred by women). The former is one of the communication skills of interest, the latter a more technical skill. Gender studies may be of interest for further research, but the few distinctions found here do not suggest any fundamental differences.

Non-managers with extensive experience show a preference for teaching the standards, rules, regulations and audit research (Q55, Q60). Audit managers reveal low preference for lessons on law cases or professional articles (Q59, Q60). As they are not the 'owners' in their firms, it may be that they have less interest in the liabilities that arise from ownership. Those with 'international firm experience' reveal both 'high' and 'low' scores for the use of 'drama' (Q62), and neither small firms nor sole traders value it as a learning device. In a pattern now repeated, it is seen that respondents seek out learning activities that are associated with their own particular experience.

Disciplinary Knowledge

The last section of the survey questions the disciplinary knowledge to which future auditors should be exposed. Descriptive results can be found in Table 12.

Topics on 'accounting' rank first and the strength of respondents' preferences for it (indicated by the mean) appears to be well above preferences for other disciplines; although the second-ranked choice, 'communication', is also of interest. Law, philosophy, management, economics and psychology/sociology follow on with marketing the discipline of least interest. Distinctions between respondent groups may help explain these rankings (see Table 13).

Those with more years of experience show a greater preference for psychology or sociology (Q70) and economics/finance (Q67). Knowledge of 'law' (Q64) is preferred by partners and managers, less so by directors and junior staff. These results, yet again, reflect

Table 11. Non-traditional learning activities related to respondent characteristics: Kruskal-Wallis

Small group learning activities	B1 Experience Years		B2 Function		B3 Experience type		B4 Firm type		B5 Education years		B7 Audit course background		B8 Gender	
	Value	Sig	Value	Sig	Value	Sig	Value	Sig	Value	Sig	Value	Sig	Value	Sig
50 Presentations	6.759	0.149	7.646	0.105	6.005	0.199	1.858	0.762	8.286	0.082[a]	3.521	0.475	9.460	0.051[a]
51 Debates	3.962	0.411	6.501	0.165	4.517	0.341	5.408	0.248	10.09	0.039[a]	3.181	0.528	13.64	0.009[a]
52 Office visit	3.183	0.528	1.019	0.97	3.753	0.440	0.229	0.994	0.419	0.981	4.220	0.377	1.658	0.798
53 Review proc	7.452	0.114	5.972	0.201	2.287	0.683	4.155	0.385	3.548	0.471	0.948	0.918	9.862	0.043[a]
54 Videos/ DVD	2.085	0.720	0.878	0.928	2.008	0.734	2.449	0.654	8.896	0.064[a]	2.647	0.618	5.796	0.215
55 Review stds	7.574	0.056[a]	7.187	0.066	3.415	0.332	4.584	0.205	6.098	0.107	2.190	0.534	4.968	0.174
56 IT: work paper	4.757	0.313	3.904	0.419	1.280	0.865	2.308	0.679	6.255	0.181	7.875	0.096[a]	2.626	0.622
57 IT: risk/mtlty	0.775	0.942	2.865	0.581	4.460	0.347	4.028	0.402	6.338	0.175	8.862	0.065[a]	5.232	0.264
58 IT: analysis rev	1.112	0.892	2.039	0.729	1.877	0.758	3.340	0.503	5.484	0.241	10.62	0.031[a]	0.932	0.920
59 Review law	6.445	0.168	7.836	0.098[a]	1.450	0.835	5.868	0.209	6.209	0.184	5.705	0.222	4.677	0.322
60 Review jour	8.465	0.076[a]	11.96	0.018[a]	3.658	0.454	5.293	0.259	3.677	0.451	1.733	0.785	3.414	0.491
61 Review resch	3.834	0.429	3.967	0.410	1.136	0.889	5.987	0.200	1.873	0.759	5.606	0.231	2.189	0.701
62 Drama	4.759	0.313	3.362	0.499	2.225	0.695	11.39	0.023[a]	2.170	0.705	6.696	0.153	3.724	0.445

[a]Significant results at 90% confidence or above.

Table 12. Descriptive statistics: Disciplinary knowledge

Q no.	Other topics	n	Mean	SD
63	Financial and management accounting	119	4.135	0.9199
69	Communication	129	3.830	0.9025
64	Law	124	3.331	0.9519
68	Philosophy and ethics	127	3.165	1.037
65	General management	125	3.072	0.8996
67	Economics	126	3.032	0.9290
70	Psychology or sociology	126	2.341	1.005
66	Marketing	126	2.238	0.9502

interests that accord with respondents' own current experiences. There is some preference for 'management' (Q65) and 'psychology/sociology' (Q70) by those engaged in multiple assurance engagements, perhaps reflecting the variety of client and engagement with which they deal. The greatest interest in 'philosophy/ethics' (Q68) comes from respondents with three-year degrees, a finding which is difficult to interpret on its own but of interest if related to their educational experience and potentially worthy of future study.

Correlations

Correlation tests for multicollinearity (see Table 14[4]) point to some interesting patterns.

In particular, the results reveal how respondents reveal 'patterns' of thinking. We can deduce that, for example, the source of standards (Audit Q22 or Accounting Q23) matters less than the fact that knowledge of them is similarly seen as being important (or unimportant, depending on the respondent). Letter writing skills (Q33 and Q34 and Q34 and Q44) move together irrespective of the purpose of the letter; review functions are similarly correlated (Q59 and Q60 and Q60 and Q61) irrespective of that which is being reviewed; and hands-on computer experience—rated as important generally—is not distinguished by its content (Q57 and Q56; Q58 and Q56; and Q57 and Q58).

Other patterns relate to correlations found among audit concepts associated with the planning process. The first of these is between Risk (Q20) and Evidence (Q21). Both are recognised audit planning concepts. Risk relates to the probability of audit failure due to the susceptibilities of a client, the client's systems, or because audit practices fail to reveal misstatements. Evidence has to do with how the auditor evaluates these susceptibilities and reduces them through the collection of relevant evidential matter (Pratt and Van Peursem, 1993). That is, the greater the 'risk' associated with an audit, the greater is the need for the sort of 'evidence' that would reveal the problem. That these respondents associate one with the other speaks to their own assimilation of these ideas, their bearing on the audit process, and their interest in ensuring that such associations are addressed in tertiary study.

An analogous pattern is found in the correlation between Risk (Q31) and Planning (Q32). Determining audit 'risk' is an accepted part of the modern planning process. Risk determinations provide guidance as to what evidential matter will be relevant; and planning follows for that evidence which is, as a result, relevant. There is a direct relationship; the auditor must plan for the resources before accessing and assessing evidential matter that responds to the risk. Furthermore, a risk assessment that reveals a high potential for audit failure would be best conducted at the planning stage so that decisions could be made prior to proceeding with the engagement. To associate 'risk' and 'planning' makes sense in terms of the audit process, therefore, and the respondents appear to have absorbed this understanding into their own thinking and preferences.

Table 13. Disciplinary knowledge related to respondent characteristics: Kruskal-Wallis

Q No.	Other courses advised for audit students	B1 Experience Years		B2 Function		B3 Experience type		B4 Firm type		B5 Education years		B7 Audit course background		B8 Gender	
		Value	Sig	Value	Sig	Value	Sig	Value	Sig	Value	Sig	Value	Sig	Value	Sig
63	Fincl & mngt Accounting	1.773	0.777	3.863	0.425	4.543	0.337	3.995	0.407	3.158	0.532	.333	0.988	1.906	0.753
64	Law	7.620	0.107	9.588	0.048[a]	6.692	0.153	5.879	0.208	2.324	0.676	5.159	0.271	1.315	0.859
65	Management	2.810	0.590	3.853	0.426	17.66	0.001[a]	1.553	0.817	5.993	0.200	3.790	0.435	2.896	0.575
66	Marketing	3.552	0.470	3.524	0.474	5.539	0.136	3.313	0.507	5.112	0.276	7.514	0.111	2.442	0.655
67	Econ/finance	7.425	0.115	3.257	0.516	4.537	0.338	14.59	0.006[a]	5.161	0.271	1.804	0.772	1.774	0.777
68	Philos/ethics	2.433	0.657	6.494	0.165	6.085	0.193	3.729	0.444	10.34	0.035[a]	4.095	0.393	3.002	0.557
69	Commun.	4.612	0.329	2.159	0.707	2.906	0.574	3.260	0.515	3.864	0.425	3.576	0.466	10.49	0.902
70	Psych/sociol	8.225	0.084[a]	2.003	0.735	13.88	0.008[a]	4.228	0.376	1.151	0.886	8.013	0.091[a]	4.790	0.310

[a]Significant results at 90% confidence or above.

Table 14. Pearson two-tailed correlations

First variable	Correlate variable	Pearson statistic	First variable	Correlate variable	Pearson statistic
AUDIT TOPICS			NON-TRADITIONAL LEARNING ACTIVITIES		
Q14Ind	Q15Ethic	0.672	Q57CmpRM	Q56CmpWP	0.770
Q20Risk	Q21Evid	0.697	Q58ComAR	Q56CmpWP	0.803
Q23StdsC	Q22StdsU	0.796	Q57CmpRM	Q58ComAR	0.833
			Q59RevL	Q60RevJ	0.606
AUDIT SKILLS			Q60RevJ	Q61RevR	0.600
Q31Risk	Q32Plan	0.577			
Q33LetE	Q34LetM	0.630			
Q34LetM	Q44LetR	0.558			

Correlations above 0.550 at 99% significance or above only selected, conducted within sections of the survey with ordinal data.

The correlation between independence (Q14) and ethics (Q15) is also powerful (67.2%, Table 14). A value of employing an external audit is to do with their skills but also, of course, with their 'independence'. An unbiased attitude toward the outcome of the audit investigation is a well-recognised attribute of an auditor. That these respondents recognise 'independence' and 'ethics' together signals to us that they enjoy a comprehension of this concept and that they want their graduates to benefit from a similar understanding.

The discovery of such correlations is useful to us because they provide some indication as to the source and foundation of respondents' views about audit education. In particular, their recognition of relationships between risk, evidence and planning; and of independence and ethics speaks to a deeper understanding of professional identity and their interest in ensuring that new staff are aware of these values.

Finally, a few correlations between lecture experience type and audit topics are significant (Table 15). In particular, a presentation format may serve to convey information about the local profession or why there is a demand for audit (T16, T11). Alternatively, online lectures may be sufficient for topics on professions generally, or for court case descriptions (T17, T19). Although not highly significant, the latter alludes to the possibility that students can pick up this material without the formal lecture structure. No other lecture experience is found to be significantly related to audit topics.

Discussion

The purpose of this research was to determine the value of tertiary-taught audit educational topics, knowledge, skills and learning activities as perceived by New Zealand audit professionals. The interest is in teasing out those practices which, when applied to audit modules, might best serve future audit professionals. The results have international implications given the wide reach of the International Federation of Accountants (IFAC) and its International Standards on Auditing (ISAs) (IFAC, 2010). The expectations of audit professionals are one benchmark by which educators can expect to be held to account.

A total of 130 usable responses were received from a survey of experienced auditors. The results point to findings which conform to expectations of the literature in some respects, and which reveal new insights in others. The importance of nurturing skills in judgement and critical thinking is prominent in the literature (Adair *et al.*, 2002; Knechel, 2000; Hellier *et al.*, 2009) and also emerges from our results. Furthermore, our analysis refines an understanding of how the relationship between the planning process and those decisions which are integral to planning are an important application of these expectations.

Other issues are less exercised in the literature but emerge from these findings. Communication skills are one example. Unlike most other topics, the ability to work with clients is given prominence by all participant types.

The interests of small firm respondents are another distinctive element. The following commentary illustrates:

> ... the ability to scale their knowledge of audit from university to suit the actual client—all clients aren't Enron. Does training cover typical clients in a small practice i.e. the churches, rugby clubs and kindergartens?

> There is a general lack of appreciation of the thousands of non for profit group[s] who need CAs to audit them ..., yet the ICANZ [sic] pretends they don't exist. I do some 50 of them in a relatively small community. Most of my peers refuse to do them to any extent.

> The new standards introduced have caused a lot of grief for small to medium-sized firms, clubs, and societies, auditors need to explain the difference between a review which is what most clubs and societies need and a full audit. The implications to a number of these clubs and societies have been confusion, added costs and stress trying to stay within their rules and regulations set out by their club and society as well as meeting ICANZ [sic] rules and IFRS.

Small firm professional members struggle to keep up with changing regulations. Quite reasonably, therefore, they want new staff to be able to engage with this material for all different types of engagements. Yet, tertiary educators are in a better position to prepare students *conceptually* rather than *specifically*. So perhaps the lesson to take away from this is, while possibly specific to a small or regional office, the needs of small-to-medium firms may call for supplementary training to prepare new staff for the variety of situations which they are likely to encounter.

Other issues are more prominent in the literature than in the minds of these respondents. There is the matter of regulation, law, standards and other 'rules' of practice with regularity over the years (Hellier *et al.*, 2009; Arens and Elder; 2006; Gavin, Hicks and Scheiner, 1987; Elam and Engle, 1985; Robertson and Smith, 1973). While these are of interest generally to our respondents, what emerge are distinctions as *to whom* they may be of interest. Those most concerned with regulation and law are the highly-exposed owner and partners. Implications are that it may be difficult for educators to meet such specific expectations in tertiary design, though using case studies to apply concepts to different situations is one way forward.

Small firm respondents also demonstrate a greater interest in skills and procedures, possibly a reflection on their own limited training budgets for new staff (that is, let the tertiary sector 'train' students) and their involvement in the sorts of businesses that would require such services. As noted earlier, distinctions in respondents' preferences appear to align with their personal experiences and roles. Managers look for students with knowledge of the standards and reviewing skills; senior managers—often in charge of teams—look for good team members. Respondents who are senior in their firms are interested in staff who can converse on a wide range of topics and those with vast experience in years seek a widely-disciplined, judgement-and-history-informed and ethically-driven form of tertiary education. So while these interests are all consistent with a literature seeking a multi-faceted auditor in the larger sense (e.g. Van Peursem and Julian, 2006; Johnson *et al.*, 2003; Fleming *et al.*, 2009), they vary individually. This creates such a challenge for educators because audit curricula are restricted and tend to be minimally resourced.

Undergraduate education in audit is unlikely to have the time or abilities to appeal to all elements of professional interests.

There are other direct implications for teaching. Our Lecture Experience results reveal that there may be a place for online teaching. These professionals indicate that it may be an acceptable, or even preferred, format for fact-based topics such as professional rules, standards, court precedents and regulation. Once technical capabilities for online learning are made available, it would seem that this alternative to the large-group lecture could produce cost savings at little loss to education quality.

Conclusion

A contribution of the study on which this paper reports is in revealing subtle understandings of where differences lie among (New Zealand) professional accountants and the implications thereof. Knowing the source of such distinctions may be of value in understanding particular markets for audit and for selecting that most relevant from the vast range of possible material. One implication, for example, is that smaller communities may benefit from hiring graduates who have been exposed to the practical skills and compliance requirements of the local environment. Providers serving a corporate community may focus on teamwork, marketing, communication and decision-making skills in audit. Case work could add recent and local cases without having to change major elements of the curriculum. While it is unrealistic to expect that tertiary educators can respond to each professional interest, they may be able to tailor the class to elements of the local environment.

There are other contributions. The call for 'practical' exposure to case and computer-based audit practices remind us that some types of classroom structure can directly serve professional interests. Methods employing experiential learning activities are widely viewed as being valuable by our respondents and they are consistent with prior research (Fergusen et al., 2000; Fischman, 2007; Johnson et al., 2003; Braun and Stallworth, 2009; Ballou and Heitger, 2008).

Our results also point to the value attributed to core understandings of what a profession is: its values and the role and attitudes expected of professionals. A course dominated by lecture or compliance lessons alone would not seem to serve these identity-creating needs. Clearly, there is a call for students to experience complex audit dilemmas in their undergraduate education so that they have an opportunity to understand that they are not just technicians, but that they have ethical and professional responsibilities. The use of non-traditional activities—although resource-intensive—seems to 'matter', particularly on some topics. Knowing what those topics are—such as the relationship between ethics and planning, and between risk and materiality—provides the educator with an opportunity to select elements of the curriculum to which more resource-intensive methods could be usefully applied. By so doing, they may be able to achieve greater educational value for cost.

In concluding, we also note some of the limitations of the study. Each respondent is audit-experienced to a different degree and may not be able to contribute the same level of practice knowledge, although we have taken this into consideration in our analysis. Nor are these respondents likely to bring pedagogical experience to their preferences, hence we did not attempt to elicit from them preferences about curriculum management. Nonetheless, in drawing together 'patterns of preferences', we believe implications for educational management can be drawn. So for example, providing programs that are managed in order to integrate multiple concepts into learning environments would acknowledge these respondents' preferences for integrated 'risk' and 'materiality' concepts.

Another limitation of a survey of preferences is the concern that these respondents, in particular, will not have cost constraints in mind in stating their opinions. Clearly, accounting education departments have such constraints and cannot ignore them. To address this concern, the survey covering letter (and instructions to the respondents) asked that respondents keep such resource constraints in mind. Also, we clarified that most modules would *have* to include some form of large-group lecture (a realistic situation in New Zealand and probably elsewhere). We also asked the respondents to 'assume that it is not possible' for all of the topics to be covered to the same degree in an audit curriculum; and we asked them to choose from the full range of preference options (on the scale from 1 to 5). Finally, and while we used a Likert scale for the topics, skills and activities to compare preferences, we kept our analysis of 'lecture presentation' separate from this material. Thus, the analysis considers *relative* interests in coming to an understanding of respondents' priorities.

Arising from these findings are several potential areas for further research. Engagements conducted by smaller firms are one example. Unlike larger firms, smaller firms have to bring in expertise for most audits (Van Peursem and Wells, 2000). Studies that explore the vertical integration needs of these smaller firms may be useful. A rich area of further study could further explore, say in other locations or contexts, how understandings and preferences of audit professionals vary by experience. Understanding the source of their experience-formed views may assist in targeting audit curricula to the local market.

Audit research could usefully turn its attention to auditor communication even as recent standards have been extended to do so. The communication skills of graduates are clearly important to these respondents, yet the field itself is under-researched. Studies into communication practices would serve the profession and educators in coming to an understanding of what may be important to convey.

Notes

[1]New Zealand professional standards require students to take material sufficient to comprise an entire course in their tertiary study; though trends and some practices overseas would incorporate audit 'modules' only. For consistency purposes, this paper will use the word module to refer to tertiary audit education.

[2]See, for example, ISA (NZ) 210 Agreeing the terms of audit engagements; ISA (NZ) 260 Communication with those charged with governance; ISA (NZ) 265 Communicating deficiencies in internal control to those charged with governance and management; ISA (NZ) 580 Written representations and the many instances in which communications are required such as to do when looking or discovering instances of fraud (ISA (NZ) 240 The auditor's responsibilities relating to fraud in an audit of financial statements) or other illegal acts (ISA (NZ) 250 Consideration of laws and regulations in an audit of financial statements). All of these are either new in 2006–2010 or have been revised to include communication issues.

[3]A section of the survey addresses the 'large lecture' format, but not in a way that directly compares it to non-traditional methods.

[4]An example of the correlation matrix can be found in Appendix II.

References

Adair, L., Marden, R. and McCartney, M. (2002) Topical coverage in internal auditing: academic vs practitioner perceptions, *Accounting Education: an international journal*, 11(4), pp. 311–329.

American Accounting Association (1986) The Bedford Report Future Accounting Education: Preparing for the expanding profession. Available at http://aaahq.org/AECC/pdf/future/faculty.pdf (accessed 11 June 2009).

Arens, A. and Elder, R. (2006) Perspectives on audit education after Sarbanes Oxley, *Issues in Accounting Education*, 21(4), pp. 345–362.

Awayiga, J. Y., Onumah, J. M. and Tsamenyi, M. (2010) Knowledge and skills development of accounting graduates: the perceptions of graduates and employers in Ghana, *Accounting education: an international journal*, 19(1), pp. 139–158.

Ballou, B. and Heitger, D. (2008) Kofenya: the role of accounting information in managing the risks of a new business, *Issues in Accounting Education*, 23(2), pp. 211–228.

Becket, N. and Brookes, M. (2006) Evaluating quality management in university departments, *Quality Assurance in Education*, 14(2), pp. 123–142.

BeMiller, S., Lindberg, D. and Wirtz, R. (2009) Sky Scientific, INC: an auditing minefield, *Issues in Accounting Education*, 24(2), pp. 219–236.

Birkett, W. P. (1993) *Competency-Based Standards for Professional Accountants in Australia and New Zealand,* Education Discussion Paper, Australian Society of Certified Practising Accountants, The Institute of Chartered Accountants in Australia and New Zealand Society of Accountants, Sydney, Link Publishing.

Boylan, S. (2008) A classroom exercise on unconscious bias in financial reporting and auditing, *Issues in Accounting Education*, 23(2), pp. 229–245.

Broad, M. J., Matthews, M. and Shephard, K. (2003) Audit and control of the use of the Internet for learning and teaching: issues for stakeholders in higher education, *Managerial Auditing Journal*, 18(3), pp. 244–253.

Braun, R. and Stallworth, L. (2009) If you need love get a puppy: a case study on professional scepticism and auditor independence, *Issues in Accounting Education*, 24(2), pp. 237–252.

Bryman, A. (2004) *Social Research Methods, 2nd edition* (New York: Oxford University Press Inc.).

Carr, S. and Matthews, M. R. (2004) Accounting curriculum change and iterative programme development: a case study, *Accounting Education: an international journal*, 13(Supplement 1), pp. 91–116.

Carr, S., Chua, F. and Perera, H. (2006) University accounting curricula: the perceptions of an alumni group, *Accounting Education: an international journal*, 15(4), pp. 359–376.

Cohen, J., Krishnamoorthy, G. and Wright, A. (2008) Waste Is Our Business, Inc.: The importance of non-financial information in the audit planning process, *Journal of Accounting Education*, 26(3), pp. 166–178.

Cresswell, J. W. (2003) *Research Design: Qualitative, Quantitative, and Mixed Methods Approaches,* 2nd edition (California: Sage Publications: Thousand Oaks).

Dennis, I. (2003) OK in practice—and theory, *Accounting Education*, 12(4), pp. 415–426.

Earley, C. and Phillips, F. (2008) Assessing audit and business risks at Toy Central Corporation, *Issues in Accounting Education*, 23(2), pp. 299–307.

Elam, R. and Engle, T. (1985) The status of collegiate auditing education, *Issues in Accounting Education*, 3(12), pp. 97–108.

Emerald Group Publishing Ltd (2009) *How to use surveys effectively.* Available at http://info.emeraldinsight.com.ezproxy.waikato.ac.nz/research/guides/surveys.htm?part=5 (accessed 11 June 2009).

Ferguson, C., Richardson, G. and Wines, G. (2000) The effect of formal studies and work experience, *Accounting Horizons*, 14(2), pp. 137–168.

Fischman, M. (2007) Teaching for the accounting profession: CPAs and PhD, *The CPA Journal*, 77(6), p. 12. Available at: http://www.nysscpa.org/cpajournal/2007/607/perspectives/plz.htm (accessed 11 June 2009).

Fleming, D., Lightner, S. and Romanus, R. (2009) The effect of professional context on accounting students' moral reasoning, *Issues in Accounting Education*, 24(1), pp. 13–30.

Garavan, T., O'Hanlon, D. and O'Brien, F. (2004) Career advancement of hotel management since graduation: a comparative study, *Personal Review*, 35(3), pp. 252–280.

Gavin, T., Hicks, R. and Scheiner, J. (1987) Auditors common law liability: what we should be telling our students, *Journal of Accounting Education*, 5(1), pp. 1–12.

Gramling, A. and Karapanos, V. (2008) Auditor independence: a focus on the SEC independence rules, *Issues in Accounting Education*, 23(2), pp. 247–260.

Grimmer, M. and Hanson, M. (2005) The mix of qualitative and quantitative research in major marketing journals, 1993–2002, *European Journal of Marketing*, 41(1–2), pp. 58–70.

Groomer, S. M. and Heintz, J. A. (1999) Using flowcharts to teach audit reports: an update, *Journal of Accounting Education*, 17(4), pp. 391–405.

Hair, J. F., Money, A. H., Page, M. and Samouel, P. (2007) *Research methods for business* (Chichester, West Sussex, UK: John Wiley and Sons Ltd).

Hassall, T., Dunlop, A. and Lewis, S. (1996) Internal audit education: exploring professional competence, *Managerial Auditing Journal*, 11(5), pp. 28–36.

Helliar, C., Monk, E. and Stevenson, L. (2009) The development of trainee auditor's skills in tertiary education, *International Journal of Auditing*, 13(3), pp. 185–202.

International Federation of Accountants (2010) International Auditing and Assurance Standards Board. Available at http://www.ifac.org/IAASB/ (accessed 11 June 2009).

Jennings, M. (2004) Incorporating ethics and professionalism into accounting education and research: a discussion of the voids and advocacy for training in seminal works in business ethics, *Issues in Accounting Education*, 19(1), pp. 7–26.

Johnson, E. N., Baird, J., Caster, P., Dilla, W. N., Earley, C. E. and Louwers, T. J. (2003) Challenges to audit education for the 21st century: a survey of curricula, course content, and delivery methods, *Issues in Accounting Education*, 18(3), pp. 241–263.

Knechel, W. (2000) Behavioural research in auditing and its impact on audit education, *Issues in Accounting Education*, 15(4), pp. 695–712.

Koch, B., Moyes, G. and Williams, P. (2006) The effects of age and gender upon the perceptions of accounting professionals concerning their job satisfaction and work-related attributes, *Managerial Auditing Journal*, 21(5), pp. 536–561.

Lothian, N. and Marrian, I. F. Y. (ed.) (1992) New Zealand Society of Accountants International Review of Admission Policy (Wellington: NZSA).

Maltby, J. (2001) Second thoughts about cases in auditing, *Accounting Education: an international journal*, 10(4), pp. 421–428.

Masli, A., Peters, G. F., Richardson, V. J. and Sanchez, J. M. (2010) Examining the potential benefits of internal control monitoring technology, *The Accounting Review*, 85(3), pp. 1001–1033.

Massey, D. W. and Thorne, L. (2006) The impact of task information feedback on ethical reasoning, *Behavioral Research in Accounting*, 18(1), pp. 103–116.

Mataira, K. and Van Peursem, K. A. (2010) An examination of disciplinary culture: two professional accounting associations in New Zealand, *Accounting Forum*, 34(2), pp. 109–122.

Mayer-Sommer, A. and Loeb, S. (1981) Fostering more successful professional socialisation among accounting students, *The Accounting Review*, 56(1), pp. 125–136.

Ministry of Economic Development (MED) (2005) Position statement. Available at www.med.govt.nz/buslt/bus_pol/bus_law/corporate-governance/financial-report (accessed 23 February 2005).

Murthy, U. S. and Kerr, D. S. (2004) Comparing audit team effectiveness via alternative modes of computer-mediated communication, *Auditing: A Journal of Practice and Theory*, 23(1), pp. 8.

Nelson, I. T., Ratliff, R. L., Steinhoff, G. and Mitchell, G. J. (2003) Teaching logic to auditing standards: can training in logic reduce audit judgment errors? *Journal of Accounting Education*, 21(3), pp. 215–237.

New Zealand Institute of Chartered Accountants (NZICA) (2010a) Notes from the 2010 Conference on New Zealand Audit, Auckland, 15 June, available from the authors.

New Zealand Institute of Chartered Accountants (NZICA) (2010b) Recognition of Overseas Qualifications and Study. Available at http://www.nzica.com/AM/template.cfm?Section=Recognition_of_Overseas_Study (accessed 29 June 2010).

New Zealand Institute of Chartered Accountants (NZICA) (2009) Membership Statistics Available at http://annualreport2009.nzica.com/People/MembershipStats.aspx (accessed 11 June 2009).

Nieschwitz, R., Pany, K. and Zhang, J. (2002) Auditing with technology: using generalized audit software in the classroom, *Journal of Accounting Education*, 20(4), pp. 307–329.

Okike, E. (1999) The Coopers and Lybrand 'Excellence in Audit Education' programme: a note, *Accounting Education: an international journal*, 8(1), pp. 57–65.

Pratt, M. J. and Van Peursem, K. A. (1993) Towards a conceptual framework for auditing, *Accounting Education*, 2(1), pp. 11–32.

Quick, R. (2005) The formation and early development of German audit firms, *Accounting, Business and Financial History*, 15(3), pp. 317–343.

Retzlaff, R. (2006) Audits and inspections: improving efficiency with technology, *Professional Safety*, 51(12), pp. 42–45.

Robertson, J. and Smith, C. (1973) Auditing and professionalism at the graduate level, *The Accounting Review*, 48(3), pp. 599–602.

Robson, K., Humphrey, C., Khalifa, R. and Jones, J. (2007) Transforming audit technologies: business risk audit methodologies and the audit field, *Accounting, Organizations and Society*, 32(4/5), pp. 409–438.

Rodeghier, M. (1996) *Surveys with Confidence: A Practical Guide to Survey Research Using SPSS* (SPSS Inc: Chicago, Illinois).

Sangster, A. (2010) Using accounting history and Luca Pacioli to put relevance back into the teaching of double entry, *Accounting, Business and Financial History*, 20(1), pp. 23–29.

Scheiwe, D. and Radich, R. (1997) A programme to address emerging problems in auditing education in Australian universities, *Accounting Education: an international journal*, 6(1), pp. 25–37.

Siddiqui, J., Nasreen, T. and Choudhury-Lema, A. (2009) The audit expectations gap and the role of audit education: the case of an emerging economy, *Managerial Auditing Journal*, 24(6), pp. 564–583.

Sikka, P., Haslam, C., Kyriacou, O. and Agrizzi, D. (2007) Professionalizing claims and the state of UK professional accounting education: some evidence, *Accounting Education: an international journal*, 16(1), pp. 3–21.

Tan, L. M. and Laswad, F. (2007) Understanding students' choice of academic majors: a longitudinal analysis, *Accounting Education: an international journal*, 18(3), pp. 233–253.

Taylor, E. Z. and Dzuranin, A. C. (2010) Interactive financial reporting: an introduction to eXtensible Business Reporting Language (XBRL), *Issues in Accounting Education*, 25(1), pp. 71–83.

Van Peursem, K. A. and Julian, A. (2006) Ethics research: an accounting educator's perspective, *Australian Accounting Review*, 16(38), pp. 13–29.

Van Peursem, K. A. and Wells, P. K. (2000) Contracting services in SMEs: a case of New Zealand professional accounting firms, *International Small Business Journal*, 19(1), pp. 68–82.

Vasarhelyi, M. A. and Lin, W. T. (1985) EDP auditing instruction using an interactive generalized audit software, *Journal of Accounting Education*, 3(2), pp. 79–89.

Vinten, G. (2004) The future of UK internal audit education: secularisation and submergence? *Managerial Auditing Journal*, 19(5), pp. 580–596.

Wright, G. B. and Kauffman, N. L. (1994) Internationalizing audit education, *Accounting Education: an international journal*, 3(2), pp. 155–165.

Statutes Cited

New Zealand Companies Act (1993) Wellington.
New Zealand Regulations (Disallowance) Act (1993) Wellington.
New Zealand Financial Reporting Act (1993) Wellington.

Appendix I: Questionnaire and Covering Letter

SECTION 1: YOUR BACKGROUND (Please place an 'x' in the appropriate box(es))

1. What is your audit and/or assurance service experience in years?

Up to 2 years	☐
Between 2–5 years	☐
Between 5–10 years	☐
More than 10 years	☐

2. In what capacity do you *primarily* function as an auditor: As a

Firm partner or owner	☐
Director or Senior Manager	☐
Manager	☐
Senior	☐
Junior	☐
Other (please specify) _____	☐

3. In what type of engagement is your *primary* audit/assurance experience?

Financial statement audits	☐
Internal or performance audits	☐
Reviews, Advisory Services and/or Compilations	☐
All types	☐
Other: Please specify_____	☐

4. In what type of organisation have you *primarily* applied your audit experience?

International accounting firm	☐
Mid-size accounting firm (more than 10 partners)	☐
Small accounting firm (2–10 partners)	☐
Sole trader	☐
Corporate Sector	☐
Government Sector	☐

Other (please specify) _____ ☐

5.   What type of tertiary qualification(s) do you have?

Four-year degree (or three-year degree plus one-year diploma)   ☐
Three-year degree   ☐
Non-degree tertiary qualification: Please specify_____   ☐
Do you have a post-graduate qualification (e.g. master's or honours)?   ☐

6.   If your tertiary major (speciality) was in other than accounting or accounting & finance, please specify what that was:

_____

7.   How many audit courses did you take during your tertiary years?

None   ☐
One-half (i.e. combined with tax or other courses)   ☐
One   ☐
Two or more   ☐
I do not remember   ☐

8.   Gender: Male   ☐   Female   ☐

SECTION 2: AUDIT EDUCATION PRACTICES

Place an 'x' in the appropriate box to classify the importance of each of the topics or methods listed below to the future audit professional. Assume that it is not possible for all topics and understandings to be achieved to the same degree in undergraduate, and please select from as full a range of options (1) to (5) as you deem appropriate so that we can understand your priorities.

(1)   Not important (2) of minor importance (3) of some importance (4) very important (5) vital

It is important that the student of audit   (1)   (2)   (3)   (4)   (5)   No opinion

AUDIT TOPICS: **... understand ...**

10   The history of audit and how it came to be as it is now
11   Why different people want or demand audit
12   The steps in the audit process
13   Why audits can fail
14   General ethical principles and the idea of independence
15   Specific ethical codes and rules
16   The local profession, its rules and expectations
17   Professions in general and expectations of professionals
18   Obligations and sanctions imposed by the profession
19   Liability auditors may face in the courtroom
20   Risk and its elements for audit planning
21   The meaning of evidence and audit judgement
22   Auditing standards
23   Accounting standards
24   Accounting systems principles
25   Differences between tests of controls and tests of balances
26   The implications of client fraud
27   The meaning of audit opinions

28   The meaning of other types of report opinions
     AUDIT **SKILLS:**   ... **Be able to** ...
29   Work with a team
30   Communicate with clients
31   Perform a risk analysis of a client
32   Develop a detailed audit plan
33   Design and prepare an engagement letter
34   Design and prepare a letter to management
35   Determine materiality and tolerable misstatement
36   Design tests of controls
37   Evaluate a computerised accounting and control system
38   Apply principles of audit judgement to audit dilemmas
39   Design a statistical audit sample
40   Evaluate the results of an audit sample
41   Perform a bank reconciliation
42   Conduct a small audit independently
43   Prepare audit working papers
44   Prepare the audit report
45   Conduct a subsequent events analysis
46   Conduct a going concern analysis

SECTION 3: LECTURE EXPERIENCE

Lectures: Assume that cost constraints mean that the lecture format must be used as part of an audit course. For each of the three questions below, place an 'x' in the appropriate box to indicate which one of each two choices might be best suited to teaching future audit professionals

                                                                            (a)   (b)
47   Lectures are given by either:
     (a) a person experienced in education, research with some audit
experience or   □   □
     (b) visiting professionals all of whom are currently in audit practice □   □
48   Lecture material *primarily* covers either:
     (a) the details of standards, regulation, processes and concepts or   □   □
     (b) case studies that apply judgement to audit situations   □   □
49   Lectures are given either:
     (a) face-to-face by a lecturer who is present or   □   □
     (b) computerised (online) lectures observed by student in their own time □   □
                                    (1)   (2)   (3)   (4)   (5)   No opinion

How important are each of the following small group learning activities?
50   Student presentations of audit cases
51   Debates on current, topical issues
52   Visiting an audit office
53   Going over audit processes and procedures
54   Watching videos or CDs
55   Going over standards, rules and regulations
56   Hands-on computer work with working paper programs
57   Hands-on computer work with risk and materiality problems
58   Hands-on computer work with analytical review problems

59   Reviewing law cases
60   Reviewing professional journal articles
61   Reviewing research about audit
62   Drama: acting out the auditor role

SECTION 4 (b): DISCIPLINE KNOWLEDGE

How important are the following other courses in preparing the audit professional?

63   Financial and management accounting
64   Law
65   General Management
66   Marketing
67   Economics and Finance
68   Philosophy and Ethics
69   Communication
70   Psychology or Sociology
     Other? Please specify _____

SECTION 4 (a): LEARNING ACTIVITIES

SECTION 5: FURTHER COMMENTS

Are there any comments or recommendations that you would like to add?

COVERING LETTER (sent on university letter-head)

COVER LETTER
(University letterhead)
27 July 2009
Please give this packet to a professional within your firm who has **audit experience.**

Dear Participant,

I am a fourth year student from the University of Waikato conducting research on audit education. I wish to identify topics and educational methods which could be, or have been, of greatest benefit to experienced auditors such as you in professional practice. I am therefore seeking your expert opinion so that I can formulate an analysis of best-practice for audit educators (assuming cost constraints).

I have tried to keep the survey as brief as possible so as not to take up too much of your valuable time. A follow-up will be conducted to obtain as much field knowledge as possible.

Your participation in the research is voluntary, and please be assured that any responses will be treated with confidentiality. At no time during this survey will you be individually identified and you are not required to provide your name. If you have any questions or concerns about this study, please contact Professor Karen Van Peursem at   or Ms Jenna Chaffey at

Instructions: Please return by email to Alternatively, the file can be emailed back as an attachment when you have completed the questionnaire.

If you wish to receive a summarised copy of the results of the survey please tick this box and include a business card (or address): ☐

I appreciate your participation in this survey.

Kind regards,

Jenna Chaffey, WMS Student, Affiliate Student Member NZICA

Appendix II. Example of correlation data

Correlations		B1Yrs	B2Fctn	B3Expe	B4Firm	B5Edu	B7Pap	B8Gend
B1Yrs	Pearson correlation	1.000	−0.647[a]	0.083	0.066	0.139	0.069	−0.256[a]
	Sig. (2-tailed)	0	0.357	0.460	0.115	0.437	0.003	
	n	130.000	130	124	127	130	129	130
B2Fctn	Pearson correlation	−0.647[a]	1.000	−0.089	−0.071	−0.108	−0.047	0.325[a]
	Sig. (2-tailed)	0	0.327	0.426	0.220	0.600	0	
	n	130	130.000	124	127	130	129	130
B3Expe	Pearson correlation	0.083	−0.089	1.000	−0.010	−0.069	0.093	−0.074
	Sig. (2-tailed)	0.357	0.327	0.914	0.445	0.306	0.415	
	n	124	124	124.000	123	124	123	124
B4Firm	Pearson correlation	0.066	−0.071	−0.010	1.000	0.100	−0.013	−0.018
	Sig. (2-tailed)	0.460	0.426	0.914	0.264	0.887	0.844	
	n	127	127	123	127.000	127	126	127
B5Edu	Pearson correlation	0.139	−.108	−0.069	0.100	1.000	−0.058	−0.002
	Sig. (2-tailed)	0.115	0.220	0.445	0.264	0.516	0.984	
	n	130	130	124	127	130.000	129	130
B7Pap	Pearson correlation	0.069	−0.047	0.093	−0.013	−0.058	1.000	−0.028
	Sig. (2-tailed)	0.437	0.600	0.306	0.887	0.516	0.751	
	n	129	129	123	126	129	129.000	129
B8Gend	Pearson correlation	−0.256[a]	0.325[a]	−0.074	−0.018	−0.002	−0.028	1.000
	Sig. (2-tailed)	0.003	0	0.415	0.844	0.984	0.751	
	n	130	130	124	127	130	129	130.000

[a]Correlation is significant at the 0.01 level (2-tailed).

The Impact of Ethical Orientation and Gender on Final Year Undergraduate Auditing Students' Ethical Judgments

JOAN BALLANTINE* and PATRICIA MCCOURT**

*University of Ulster, UK, **Queen's University, Belfast, UK

ABSTRACT   *This study considers the possibility of auditing students' ethical judgment being affected by two factors, namely ethical orientation and gender. While tests revealed that more idealistic students judged some unethical situations more strictly than did less idealistic students, overall no significant relationship was found between ethical orientation and ethical judgment. The study also reported no significant relationship between gender and ethical judgment. Furthermore, males were as likely as females to be classified as high idealists. Overall, the findings from the current study inform auditing educators that discriminating among students on the basis of ethical orientation and gender may not assist in stimulating students' discussion and resolution of ethical dilemmas.*

Introduction

If statutory audit is to make a positive contribution to the efficient operation of global capital markets, then the external auditor's honesty, integrity and ability to perform an audit without bias need to be beyond doubt. To this end, the auditor must always maintain a high level of moral reasoning when undertaking his professional duties. Moreover, never has the case for ethical awareness among auditors been stronger than it is currently in the wake of so many financial scandals and amid an atmosphere of general mistrust of corporate dealings by the public at large. If, in the aftermath of these highly publicized corporate scandals, we as educators are to assist in rebuilding public confidence in the auditing profession and help dispel the mistrust directed at accountants in general, and at auditors in particular, then we must engender an awareness of ethical issues among our students.

The obvious source to provide direction on ethical issues in the UK is the Ethical Standards produced by the Auditing Practices Board (APB) under the auspices of the Financial Reporting Council (FRC).[1] In line with most professions, the FRC, through its constituent bodies, defines, and enforces a code of professional conduct, in the form of Ethical Standards, among audit members. However, even the most broadly framed professional code of conduct cannot anticipate the circumstances of every ethical dilemma with which a member may be faced. This is particularly the case in the modern business world with its increasingly sophisticated corporate structures, evermore complex financial instruments and rapid technological innovation. Therefore, it is incumbent upon professional auditing educators to augment ethical code instruction with a more general discussion on moral reasoning and ethical judgment. In so doing, auditing students should be encouraged to consider the circumstances of and possible courses arising from action of ethical dilemmas for which guidelines, statute or legal precedents do not exist. The expectation is, of course, that when these students finally enter the world as accounting graduates, their undergraduate ethics experience will assist them in taking the appropriate course of action when faced with an ethical dilemma.

If students' ethical judgment is to be influenced to any degree by classroom-based ethics instruction it would be helpful to gain insights into the factors which help form students' ethical judgment. A number of theoretical models have been proposed by psychologists to identify these factors and explain their contribution to differences in moral outlook and ethical development (see for example, Hogan, 1973; Kohlberg, 1982; Rest, 1986). The current study applies one such model by Forsyth (1980) to examine the ethical orientation of a group of final year undergraduate auditing students to determine whether ethical orientation is one such factor which has a significant influence on ethical judgment. The study also draws on Gilligan's (1982) thesis and gender socialization theory, both of which purport that females, on account of their caring nature, act more ethically than do males, to investigate if gender is another significant determinant of ethical judgment. This theory has become particularly relevant given the fact that the whistleblowers in the two main corporate disasters and scandals of recent years, i.e. Enron and WorldCom, were both women.

In recent years, a number of empirical studies have been carried out on the impact of ethical orientation and gender on the ethical decision-making process (see for example, Hartikainen and Torstila, 2004; Marques and Azevedo-Pereira, 2009). However, little work in this area has been undertaken in a UK context, even less so from an auditing perspective. This study addresses this deficiency and extends this research by examining ethical orientation and gender ethics among auditing students enrolled in a UK university. In particular, it considers whether ethical orientation, as defined by Forsyth (1980), and gender have a significant influence on ethical judgment in audit scenarios. This focus on auditing rather than accounting is particularly apposite since audit professionals are valued members of society who are expected to be, *inter alia*, skilled ethical decision-makers. It is anticipated that the results of this research should contribute to the development of ethical audit instruction at tertiary level which, in turn, should influence professional auditors' ability to reason morally long after their training.

In respect of ethical orientation, the first of the two possible determinants of ethical judgment analysed in the study, the findings indicate that, overall, the relationship between ethical orientation and ethical judgment is not significant. Therefore, it would appear that students' ethical judgment, in the context of auditing dilemmas, is not significantly affected by their ethical orientation. In addition, the findings from the current study report that there are also no statistically significant gender differences in ethical judgment among final year undergraduate auditing students. The conclusion to be drawn from these findings is that undergraduate classroom ethics instruction need not be tailored to take account of differences in ethical orientation and gender.

The paper addresses its research objective in the following manner. First, a literature review with respect to the topics of ethical orientation and gender is provided. Second, the research methodology applied in the current study is set out. Third, the results of the tests carried out are analysed and discussed. Fourth, conclusions are drawn and further work identified.

Ethical Orientation and Gender Difference

Views on what constitutes ethical or unethical behaviour differ. Sharp (1898), at the turn of the nineteenth century, attributed the lack of consensus which may exist in moral reasoning to individual differences in people's personal ethical system. Ethical ideology, alternatively known as ethical orientation (Radtke, 2004), are terms used to describe an individual's approach to ethical judgment. Ethical orientation comprises two dimensions, namely adherence to a moral code and concern for the welfare of others (Schlenker and Forsyth, 1977). The first of these is the concept of relativism, namely the extent to which an individual adheres to a rules-based moral code when reaching a decision on an ethical question. At one extreme, an absolutist complies with a pre-determined moral protocol regardless of the consequences. This is akin to a Kantian deontological approach. At the other end of the relativism spectrum, the relativist pays no regard to a deontological code, but is guided in his ethical decision making by the circumstances of the moral dilemma.

The second dimension which affects an individual's ethical orientation, according to Schlenker and Forsyth (1977), is idealism. In the extreme, idealism takes on a utilitarian mantel with the idealist's ethical decision being determined by undertaking the right action to produce good consequences. At the other end of the continuum from the idealist is the opposing view that both good and bad consequences may ensue from an ethical decision and that, under the circumstances, both are acceptable (Forsyth, 1980).

Rather than simply classifying individuals as being either relativistic or idealistic, Forsyth (1980) brings the concepts of relativism and idealism together to produce a '2 × 2 matrix' or taxonomy of ethical orientations. This matrix of ethical orientations is set out in Table 1. The taxonomy, thus devised by Forsyth (1980), provides a means of categorising individuals into one of four ethical orientations. 'The inclusion into one of these [four] groups is determined by whether a person espouses idealistic or non-idealistic values and believes moral rules are universal or relative' (Forsyth, 1980, p. 176). In order to operationalize his taxonomy, Forsyth (1980) developed the Ethics Position Questionnaire (EPQ) to assess individuals' personal moral philosophy and classify them into one of the four ethical orientations, i.e. situationist, subjectivist, absolutist or exceptionist. The EPQ comprises 20 statements pertaining to relativism and idealism which require respondents to indicate their agreement using a Likert scale with 'completely agree' and 'completely disagree' as anchors. The relativism subscale contains statements such as 'Whether a lie is judged to be moral or immoral depends upon the circumstances surrounding the action' and 'There are no ethical principles that are so important that they should be part of any code of ethics.' In contrast, the idealism statements are phrased to measure the respondent's perspective on positive and negative consequences with assertions such as 'People should make certain that their actions never intentionally harm another even to a small degree' and 'The existence of potential harm to others is always wrong, irrespective of the benefits to be gained.' A high score on the relativism subscale of the EPQ indicates that the respondent embraces an ethical orientation,

Table 1. Taxonomy of ethical orientation[a]

Idealism	Relativism	
	High	Low
High	Situationists They reject moral rules and instead review the circumstances of a given situation to determine the appropriate action. The action results in good consequences for everyone.	Absolutists They are of the opinion that universal moral rules should be applied to a given situation to achieve the best possible outcome.
Low	Subjectivists They reject moral rules and apply their own personal values and perspectives to a given situation. While the objective is to ensure that good consequences are achieved for almost everyone, bad consequences for some are acceptable.	Exceptionists They are guided by moral judgements but only in a pragmatic way and are willing to accept exceptions to these rules even if bad consequences ensue.

[a]Adapted from Forsyth (1980).

which rejects universal moral absolutes whereas a high score on the *idealism* subscale suggests that the respondent espouses a more altruistic personal moral philosophy which reflects a concern for the welfare of others (Forsyth, Nye and Kelly, 1988).

The subject of ethical orientation, as defined by Forsyth (1980), and its influence on ethical judgment has been addressed in a number of studies. Barnett, Bass and Brown (1994) investigated the relationship between ethical orientations and ethical judgment among business students and reported that absolutists were the most ethical while subjectivists were the most lenient. This finding coincided with that of Tansey, Brown, Hyman and Dawson (1994) who also reported that, among life insurance agents, absolutists were the strictest in terms of their ethical judgment and subjectivists were the most lenient. Barnett, Bass, Brown and Herbert's (1998) finding in a later study carried out among marketing professionals supported their earlier findings among business students in that absolutists were found to be the most ethical and subjectivists the least so. They also reported significant differences between absolutists and exceptionists in terms of strict ethical judgment. Bass, Barnett and Brown's (1998) findings among sales managers correspond to those of the aforementioned studies in this area in that they reported a significant difference in ethical judgment with absolutists being stricter than both subjectivists and exceptionists. However, as was the case with Barnett *et al.* (1998), no significant difference in ethical judgment was reported between absolutists and situationists. Most recently, however, research carried out by Marques and Azevedo-Pereira (2009) among Portuguese chartered accountants indicated that ethical judgments did not differ significantly depending on ethical orientation. Their conclusion, unlike that of the aforementioned studies in this area, was that ethical ideology is not an important determinant of ethical judgment.

Forsyth's classification of an idealist has a lot in common with the 'ethic of caring' thesis put forward by his contemporary, Carol Gilligan (1982). She maintained that 'inflicting hurt is considered selfish and immoral in its reflection of unconcern, while the expression of care is seen as the fulfilment (sic) of moral responsibility' (Gilligan, 1982, p. 73). This thesis was a response to the work of her tutor, Kohlberg (1982) whose theory of moral development scored women as being 'less developed' than men. She felt that other studies that explored moral thought had been so heavily influenced by Kohlberg's thesis that the impact of an 'ethic of caring' had been overlooked. Gilligan responded by theorizing that women were not less developed or inferior to men; they were just different. She believed that early in life males value autonomy and females value relationship (Gilligan, 1982). She recognized the significance of gender in moral reasoning and identified a caring, compassionate dimension present only in female ethical decision-making. Men, she suggested, on the other hand, view ethical issues from a justice, rule-dominated perspective. Her thesis is consistent with gender socialization theory: a theory developed in sociology and organizational psychology literature which contends that gender identity, established at an early age, results in men and women coming to the workplace with differing ethical values and, as a consequence, making different decisions (Betz, O'Connell and Shepard, 1989; Dawson, 1995).

Forsyth et al. (1988) recognized the similarity between Forsyth's idealism/relativism taxonomy and Gilligan's (1982) 'ethic of caring'. They claimed that 'when individuals adopt an ethic of caring, they base their judgments and actions on their relationships with, and responsibilities to, other individuals. Similarly, idealistic individuals, as identified by the Ethics Position Questionnaire devised by Forsyth (1980), agree with such items as 'A person should make certain that [his or her] actions never intentionally harm another even to a small degree.' The ethic of caring may also be inversely related to relativism if individuals feel that 'caring for others is a fundamental moral principle that should be followed whenever possible' (Forsyth et al., 1988, p. 243).

Forsyth et al. (1988) produced empirical evidence to substantiate their claim that Gilligan's 'ethic of caring' was conceptually similar to the *idealism* orientation as identified in Forsyth's earlier work on individual differences in moral thought (Forsyth, 1980; 1981; 1985; Forsyth and Pope, 1984). However, they found no evidence to support the specific claim made by Gilligan (1982) that women display more of an ethic of caring than men, nor did they find gender differences in the respondents' endorsements of idealism and relativism. On the contrary, Forsyth et al.'s (1988) work on gender differences in ethical reasoning appear to provide some support for the occupational socialization theory (Smith and Rogers, 2000) or the structural approach to gender ethics, also developed in the sociology and organizational psychology literature, which suggests that different values which may have existed between the sexes in their early years gradually disappear as men and women are subject to similar training programmes, work environments and reward structures (Betz et al., 1989). This approach predicts that men and women training for and working in the same profession will exhibit the same ethical values and arrive at the same decisions (Ameen, Guffey and McMillan, 1996): a point of view that does more than Gilligan's (1982) to promote gender equality in the workplace.

Since Gilligan's (1982) pioneering work almost 30 years ago, a number of studies have visited the subject of gender influence on ethics. Indeed, according to Ford and Richardson (1994), it is the variable that is most frequently reported in empirical studies carried out on factors affecting ethical decision-making in business. These studies cover a range of functional areas, involve different populations in terms of size and type and have produced a variety of results, often quite contradictory (Borkowski and Ugras, 1998). On the one hand, Kidwell, Stevens and Bethke (1987) found that male and female managers' perceptions of ethical issues in the business world generally did not differ. Several studies involving business students' perceptions of ethical behaviour also found no significant difference between the sexes (Harris, 1989; Tsalikis and Ortiz-Buonafina, 1990; Davis and Welton, 1991). On the other hand, there is a significant body of research that has discovered differences between gender behaviour with respect to ethical dilemmas in business. In line with Gilligan (1982) and gender socialization theory, the majority of these studies have reported that women are more ethical in their attitudes/behaviour than men (Betz *et al.*, 1989; Ruegger and King, 1992; Luthar, DiBattista and Gautschi, 1997; Bass *et al.*, 1998).

The results of studies that have attempted to identify differences in the ethical perceptions of males and females in accounting are also inconclusive. While the majority of them have found that females have higher moral reasoning abilities than males (see for example, Shaub, 1994; Jones and Hiltebeitel, 1995; Ameen *et al.*, 1996; Eynon, Thorley Hill, Stevens and Clarke, 1996; Eynon, Thorley Hill and Stevens, 1997), studies by Ponemon (1990) and Stanga and Turpen (1991) found no such difference. At the other end of the gender spectrum, Marques and Azevedo-Pereira (2009), in a more recent study, reported that men are stricter than women when making ethical judgments.

In summary, the inconclusive nature of the findings with respect to the influences of ethical orientation and gender on ethical judgment in business/accounting ethics highlights the need for further research in this area. Since everyone may not adopt the same approach to identifying moral dilemmas with respect to acceptance of moral codes and degree of altruism shown, a 'one size fits all' approach to ethics instruction may be inappropriate. The auditing educator may need to be aware of differences and identify, for example, those students who are more likely to accept the absolutist position of moral code application and distinguish them from those who are not. Grouping students on the basis of ethical orientation is believed to stimulate discussion and resolution of ethical dilemmas (Radtke, 2004). Further, greater emphasis needs to be placed on ethical judgment in an auditing context since audit professionals are valued members of society who are expected to behave ethically and whose reputation has suffered a great deal of damage from recent corporate scandals. Consequently, the current study seeks to provide further insights into the impact of ethical orientation and gender on ethical judgment in a UK auditing context as a prelude to designing more effective ethical instruction at tertiary level.

Methodology

This research was conducted on a final year undergraduate auditing course in a British university. The auditing course was designed to improve, *inter alia*, students' awareness of the concepts, principles and techniques of auditing and thereby equip them (as graduates) for a career in professional auditing. The auditing course forms part of the accounting degree conferred by the university. This degree, in turn, is accredited by the main UK professional accountancy bodies. Since, on average, 85% of the accounting graduates from this university embark on a career in accountancy, this degree could be deemed vocational.

Data were collected by administering a questionnaire[2] to students enrolled on the auditing course. Section one of the research instrument included questions devised to collect data of a demographic nature such as gender, age and educational background. These data, as well as providing an interesting insight into the demographic composition of the student cohort surveyed, are believed by some researchers to provide explanatory variables with respect to ethical judgment.

Section two of the questionnaire set out the 20 statements devised by Forsyth (1980) in his EPQ. Respondents were called upon to indicate the extent of their agreement or disagreement with each of the EPQ statements using a Likert-type scale. The order of statements was made random on the questionnaire so that a pattern of related statements was less discernible and respondents would be less likely to base their Likert scale choice on what they had just selected for the previous statement.

Section three of the research instrument set out six audit scenarios. Since almost all of the available case study material in this area is US-based, and the current study was concerned with the attitudes of UK students, the researchers created their own vignettes using descriptions and terminology with which the students, who study auditing in a UK context, would be more familiar. Indeed, Cowton and Cummins (2003) point out that UK students, *ceteris paribus*, should be more responsive to case studies which are UK-based. Each vignette described an unethical act and the respondents were asked to rank the act in each of the previously unseen scenarios in terms of how unethical they perceived it to be using a six point Likert scale with 'absolutely not unethical' and 'absolutely unethical' as anchors. The scenarios cover a number of areas including concealing a major stock error; feigning a review of audit evidence; deliberately issuing an incorrect audit report; concealing a colleague's inability to undertake an audit; engaging in academic dishonesty; and falsifying a grant application and accepting a 'pay-off'. Prior to distribution, the details of these six vignettes were sent to a number of accounting academics who commented very favourably on their content and suggested a few minor changes for purposes of clarification. These suggestions were duly incorporated by the researchers.

Following the approach adopted in earlier studies (see for example Barnett *et al.*, 1994 and Marques and Azevedo-Pereira, 2009) the current study considered the relationship between the students' ethical orientation and their ethical judgement, with ethical orientation identified as the scores for idealism and relativism and ethical judgment defined by the Likert score attained in each of the scenarios. Given the conflicting nature of previous research in this area, the objective of the current study was to determine whether idealism and/or relativism have a significant impact on UK auditing students' ethical judgment. Accordingly, the following hypotheses (in null form) were stated for testing.

H_{01}: There is no significant difference in the ethical judgment of final year UK-based auditing students who are more idealistic and the ethical judgment of final year UK-based auditing students who are less idealistic.

H_{02}: There is no significant difference in the ethical judgment of final year UK-based auditing students who are more relativistic and the ethical judgment of final year UK-based auditing students who are less relativistic.

The remaining variable to be tested as a determinant for ethical judgment was gender. To this end, the following null hypothesis was formulated:

H_{03}: There is no significant difference in the ethical judgment of final year UK-based female auditing students and the ethical judgment of final year UK-based male auditing students.

Consistent with other researchers in the field of ethics (Forsyth and Nye, 1990; Barnett *et al.*, 1994; Marques and Azevedo-Pereira, 2009), to provide greater insights into the relationship between ethical orientation and ethical judgment, students were classified into one of the four ethical orientations shown in Table 1, namely, situationists, absolutists, subjectivisits or exceptionists. To test for possible significance between differences in ethical judgment and ethical orientation at this level, the following null hypothesis was formulated:

H_{04}: There is no significant difference in ethical judgment among situationalists, absolutists, subjectivisits and exceptionists.

Results and Analysis

Demographics

An analysis of demographic variables pertaining to the cohort is set out in Table 2. First, Panel A contains the breakdown of males and females. With 47% males and 53% females

Table 2. Student demographics

Panel A: Gender	n	%
Male	49	47
Female	55	53
Total	104	100
Panel B: Age	n	%
20 to 23 years	103	99
More than 23 years	1	1
Total	104	100
Panel C: Pre−university education	n	%
Britain/Ireland	101	97
Outside British Isles	3	3
Total	104	100
Panel D: Prior ethics education	n	%
Yes	10	10
No	94	90
Total	104	100

in the group, the split is fairly even. The table also reveals homogeneity with respect to two other variables, namely respondents' age and their educational background prior to starting university. Details of these two variables are set out in panels B and C respectively. This homogeneity renders age and educational background inappropriate for hypothesis testing as explanatory variables. Finally, it is clear from the data set out in Panel D that very few of the student group, namely 10%, has received any ethics education prior to studying auditing in the final semester of their final year of undergraduate study.

The data pertaining to ethical orientation were gathered from respondents' agreement or disagreement with the 20 EPQ (Forsyth, 1980) statements. Respondents' scores were totalled for the 10 statements on the idealism subscale and for the 10 statements on the relativism subscale. Higher scores achieved on both the idealism and relativism subscales indicated higher levels of idealism and relativism in the respondents. The internal consistency reliability of the EPQ instrument was measured using Cronbach's Alpha. In the current study, Cronbach's Alpha for the idealism subscale was 0.806 and 0.701 for the relativism subscale. Since a reliability coefficient of 0.70 or higher is considered 'acceptable' in most social science research situations, these results indicate that both the idealism and relativism subscales have an acceptable level of reliability.

Hypotheses H_{01} to H_{03} were tested using six linear regression tests, one for each scenario. The ethical judgment score for each of the scenarios is the dependent variable while the idealism score, the relativism score and gender serve as the independent variables. The results of the analysis are set out on Table 3. Of the three independent variables identified in the model, idealism would appear to have the greatest influence on final year undergraduate auditing students' ethical judgment. In four of the six scenarios, namely scenarios one, two, five and six, the regression coefficients for idealism are significant at conventional levels and therefore the null hypothesis H_{01} cannot be rejected. It would appear that idealism has a positive impact on ethical judgment in these four scenarios (i.e. the more idealistic an auditing student, the more ethical his or her judgment in these auditing situations). It would appear that the more idealistic auditing students believe the following actions to be more unethical than their less idealistic colleagues: concealing a major stock error; feigning a review of audit evidence; engaging in academic dishonesty; falsifying a grant application and accepting a 'pay-off'.

Table 3. Ethical judgment regression tests of final year undergraduate auditing students

Independent variables	Scenario 1 Coeff	Scenario 1 t-stat	Scenario 2 Coeff	Scenario 2 t-stat	Scenario 3 Coeff	Scenario 3 t-stat	Scenario 4 Coeff	Scenario 4 t-stat	Scenario 5 Coeff	Scenario 5 t-stat	Scenario 6 Coeff	Scenario 6 t-stat
Constant	2.770[b]	2.613	3.991[c]	4.208	5.272[c]	5.533	4.890[c]	3.771	2.227	1.949	1.865[b]	1.485
Idealism score	0.037[a]	2.021	0.045[b]	2.746	0.002	0.109	0.008	0.370	0.096[c]	4.793	0.07[b]	3.184
Relativism score	0.010	0.492	−0.021	−1.145	−0.021	−1.168	−0.021	−0.853	−0.28	−1.281	−0.008	−0.343
Gender	0.012	0.060	−0.120	−0.665	0.029	0.158	−0.174	−0.705	−0.066	−0.305	0.126	0.527
Adjusted R^2	0.015		0.071		0.014		0.016		0.213		0.097	
F-statistic	1.521		3.635a		0.538		0.446		10.268[c]		4.685[b]	
n	104		104		104		104		104		104	

[a]Statistically significant at the 0.05 level
[b]Statistically significant at the 0.01 level
[c]Statistically significant at the 0.001 level

However, in the remaining two scenarios, namely three and four, it was found that the more idealistic auditing students do not believe that the actions with respect to deliberately issuing the incorrect audit report and concealing a colleague's inability to undertake an audit to be more unethical than their less idealistic colleagues. Therefore, H_{01} cannot be rejected for these two scenarios and cannot be rejected overall. Comparing the results for idealism with those of previous studies highlights some inconsistencies. For example, Barnett *et al.* (1994; 1998) found a significant negative relationship between idealism and ethical judgment while Marques and Azevedo-Pereira (2009) reported non-significant, multi-directional relationships between idealism scores and ethical judgment. These inconsistencies might be attributed to differences in, for example, nationality and age. While the current study involves UK undergraduate accounting students, Barnett *et al.* (1998) reported on the ethical judgments of US marketing professionals while Marques and Azevedo-Pereira (2009) carried out research on Portuguese chartered accountants.

Contrary to the findings with respect to idealism, the effects of relativism on ethical judgment reported in Table 3 are very limited. In all six of the scenarios, the regression coefficients for relativism were not significant. Therefore, it would appear that there is no significant relationship between relativism scores and ethical judgment, whatever the circumstances of the scenario. Based on this result, H_{02} cannot be rejected. This finding is consistent with that reported by a number of previous studies (see for example, Barnett *et al.*, 1994; Hartikainen and Torstila, 2004; Marques and Azevedo-Pereira, 2009).

The influence of the third independent variable, namely gender, on ethical judgment is negligible. The regression coefficient for gender is multi-directional and not significant for any of the scenarios. Therefore, H_{03} cannot be rejected. The results of the test provide evidence that men and women display equal levels of ethical judgment. This finding concurs with those of a number of earlier accounting and finance based studies (see for example Stanga and Turpen, 1991; Radtke, 2000; Hartikainen and Torstila, 2004). Alternatively, it contradicts the findings of several other studies which have reported a difference in ethical judgment between the genders. Of these, the vast majority have reported that women in the field of business and accounting are more ethical than men (see, for example, Cohen, Pant and Sharp, 2001; Ruegger and King, 1992; Weeks, Moore, McKinney and Longenecker, 1999). However, in a recent study Marques and Azevedo-Pereira (2009), against their expectation, found that among accounting professionals, men evidenced stricter ethical judgments than women.

In order to provide further insights into the relationship between ethical orientation, as classified by Forsyth (1980), and ethical judgment, hypothesis H_{04} was tested. As a prelude to testing $H_{04,}$ classification into one of the four categories of ethical orientation was achieved by following the rubric suggested by Forsyth and Nye (1990) and Radtke (2004). First the median scores for idealism and relativism were ascertained. The respondents' scores were compared with the median score on both subscales to determine if they had achieved a high or low position in idealism and relativism. Respondents who scored high in both idealism and relativism were classified as situationists; those who scored high in idealism and low in relativism as absolutists; those who scored low in idealism and high in relativism as subjectivists; and finally, those who scored low in both idealism and relativism were classified as exceptionists (see Table 1). The classification, complete with gender breakdown, is set out in Table 4. A Mann-Whitney U (M-W U) test performed on these data reveals that gender difference within the quadrants is not statistically significant (the results have been included in Table 4). Therefore, it would appear that female final year auditing students do not differ significantly in their ethical orientation from their male counterparts. This finding further supports that of Forsyth *et al.* (1988) but does not conform to that of Gilligan (1982).

Table 4. Final year undergraduate students' ethical orientations

Situationists (Z = −0.767, μ = 0.443)			Absolutists (z = −0.921, μ = 0.357)		
	No.	%		No.	%
Males[a]	11	22	Males	12	25
Females[b]	16	29	Females	18	33
Total	27		Total	30	
Subjectivists (z = −1.678, μ = 0.093)			Exceptionists (z = −0.24, μ = 0.981)		
	No.	%		No.	%
Males	17	35	Males	9	18
Females	11	20	Females	10	18
Total	28		Total	19	

[a]n (males) = 49.
[b]n (females) = 55.

Table 5 summaries the mean responses for each of the six scenarios among the four different ethical orientations. The results indicate that the auditing students perceived all six scenarios to be unethical as indicated by the relatively high mean scores. The level of significance of differences in the ethical judgment among the four ethical orientations across all six scenarios was tested using a Kruskal Wallis test. The results indicate that, in all but one of the scenarios, namely scenario 5, there are no significant differences in ethical judgment with respect to the four ethical orientations. Therefore, it would appear that the judgment of an 'absolutist' is as ethical as that of a situationist or an exceptionist or a subjectivist in most of the unethical auditing situations. The only exception is scenario five which deals with academic dishonesty. In this situation, the ethical judgment of a situationist and an absolutist is significantly more ethical than the judgment of a subjectivist, in particular. This provides evidence to support Forysth's contention (1980) that absolutists, on account of their strict adherence to rules, are the harshest judges of immoral behaviour. In short, H_{04} is rejected in respect of scenario five, but cannot, however, be rejected in respect of scenarios one, two, three, four and six. Comparing these results with those reported earlier in the study in respect of the idealism and relativism subscales (see Table 3), it would appear that the effects of relativism, when combined with idealism have rendered ethical judgment to be no longer significantly different in scenarios one, two and six. However, the influence of idealism is stronger in scenario five and therefore has remained significantly different with respect to ethical orientation. Overall, the result of this test indicates that there is no significant difference between ethical orientation and

Table 5. Kruskal-Wallis test of differences in ethical judgment among the final year undergraduate auditing students for the four ethical orientations across the six audit-specific scenarios

Ethical Ideologies	Scenario1 Mean	Scenario2 Mean	Scenario3 Mean	Scenario4 Mean	Scenario5 Mean	Scenario6 Mean
Situationist	4.67	4.85	4.59	4.15	5.19	4.70
Absolutist	4.67	5.07	4.90	4.30	5.17	4.60
Subjectivist	4.25	4.68	4.50	4.21	4.00	3.96
Exceptionist	4.47	4.63	4.74	4.32	4.79	4.32
Chi-square	3.615	3.608	2.799	0.131	15.591	5.615
Sig. (P)	0.306	0.307	0.424	0.988	0.001[a]	0.132

1 = absolutely not unethical through to 6 = absolutely unethical.
[a]Statistically significant at the 0.001 level.

ethical judgment. This result calls into question Radtke's (2004) initiative of categorising students according to their ethical orientation prior to receiving ethical instruction to stimulate discussion and resolution of ethical dilemmas.

Conclusion and Discussion

This study considers the possibility of auditing students' ethical judgment being affected by two factors, namely their ethical orientation and their gender. First, with respect to ethical orientation, a significant relationship between the idealism subscale and ethical judgment was found in four of the six scenarios. However, given that two scenarios were not significant with respect to idealism, overall idealism cannot be reported as a significant predictor of ethical judgement in this study. The relationship between the other subscale of ethical orientation (i.e. relativism and ethical judgment) was also tested. The result was quite different from that with respect to idealism, in that all of the scenarios bar one produced a negative relationship between relativism and ethical judgment. Further, the relationship between relativism and ethical judgment was not significant for any of the scenarios. Therefore, ethical judgment does not appear to be stricter among auditing students who are more relativistic than those who are less so. Overall, notwithstanding some significance reported in respect of the idealism subscale, the conclusion of this study is that students' ethical judgment, in the context of auditing dilemmas, is not significantly affected by their ethical orientation.

Second, the study also tested for a significant relationship between gender and ethical judgment (see Table 3). As was the case with ethical orientation, no significant relationship was found between gender and ethical judgment among the auditing students. In reporting no significant difference in ethical judgment between the genders this study provides evidence to support the structural approach which states that different values which may have existed between the sexes in their early years gradually disappear as men and women are subject to, *inter alia*, similar training programmes (Betz *et al.*, 1989).

This result suggests that gender roles are driven by the surrounding environment and that male and female auditing students exhibit the same ethical judgment when exposed to the same educational instruction. In particular, the focus on ethics instruction within accounting education has increased significantly over the last 20 years. This increased exposure to ethics education which is the consequence of a general recognition of the need to develop professional accountants' ethical attitudes on the one hand, and the 'fall-out' from accounting/auditing scandals like Enron and Andersen on the other, may be providing an environment wherein students experience the same ethical development, irrespective of gender, to fulfil their ethical audit awareness and exhibit similar ethical judgement. The similarity, in turn, suggests that auditing courses delivered at tertiary level need not be tailored to take account of differences in ethical judgment between the genders.

When ethical orientations were also tested for significant differences between the sexes, it was found that the gender composition of the categories was not significant (see Table 4). In other words, female auditing students were just as likely as their male counterparts to display, for example, high idealism and low relativism. This finding concurs with that of Forsyth *et al.* (1988) but is at odds with that of Gilligan (1982) who put forward the view that women, on account of their caring nature, are likely to be more idealistic and therefore more ethical than men. The findings of the current study provide evidence that 'whistle blowing', as the result of adopting a strict ethical stance, is not likely to be more prevalent among female employees than among their male counterparts.

The conclusion to be drawn from these findings is that, on the whole, account need not be taken of differences in ethical orientation and gender when devising and delivering ethics instruction in auditing courses at tertiary level. First, it would appear that students who are classified according to their ethical orientation will receive little or no benefit from being grouped according to orientation. This finding calls into question Radtke's (2004) presumption that ethical orientation is a factor which impacts ethical decision-making. It renders redundant his suggestion that accounting students should be classified according to ethical orientation to stimulate discussion and promote resolution of ethical dilemmas among groups with heterogeneous ethical orientations. Second, it would appear that men and women studying auditing at tertiary level exhibit the same ethical judgment and arrive at the same decisions when faced with auditing moral dilemmas. From an educational point of view, this would suggest that ethics instruction need not be tailored to take account of differences in ethical judgment between the genders.

The focus of this research has been placed on ethics in an auditing context rather than in an accounting and/or business context because audit professionals, in particular, have the potential to make a valuable contribution to society. This potential can only be realized, however, if auditors are respected as skilled decision-makers whose opinion is free from bias and prejudice and whose judgment, above all, is perceived as being ethical. To this end, we as auditing educators are compelled to stimulate our students' moral reasoning to some degree and make them aware of the importance of sound ethical decision-making. Those involved in the current study would, in principle, agree with researchers such as Radtke (2004) that our purpose as ethics educators would be served much better if we could gain greater insights into our students' approach to ethical judgment and investigate the factors which contribute to it. In so doing, we could devise 'bespoke' ethical instruction for auditors which could influence their ability to reason morally long after the course. However, the results of the current study indicate that ethical orientation and gender are not discriminating factors which determine auditing students' ethical judgment.

Further Research

Notwithstanding the useful insights into the factors affecting ethical judgment provided by the current study, it has some limitations. First, while the findings provide evidence that there is no statistically significant relationship between ethical orientation and gender on the one hand, and ethical judgment on the other, other determinants of ethical judgment such as culture, age and religion, could be investigated in further research. These data were either not available in the current study or were insufficiently heterogeneous to permit a meaningful analysis. Second, the study was carried out in an academic context, namely on final year auditing students at a UK university and, therefore, the results may not be completely transferable to other contexts within which ethical audit instruction programmes are delivered (e.g. professional practice).Third, a further limitation is that the respondents' evaluation relates to hypothetical ethical scenarios which may not correspond with their actions in actual situations. Fourth, and finally, the research method adopted was that of a positivist nature which has inherent limitations in terms of providing the researcher with more in-depth explanations of how ethical judgments are affected by ethical orientations and gender. Further research might adopt an alternative methodology such as an interpretivist research perspective involving interviews and focus groups to gain additional insights into the factors affecting ethical judgment.

Acknowledgement

The authors wish to acknowledge the constructive and helpful comments received from the two referees in the preparation of this article.

Notes

[1]A full text of all of the APB's Ethical Standards is available at: http://www.frc.org.uk/apb/publications/ethical.cfm

[2]A copy of the questionnaire is available from either author on request.

References

Ameen, E. C., Guffey, D. M. and McMillan, J. J. (1996) Gender differences in determining the ethical sensitivity of future accounting professionals, *Journal of Business Ethics*, 15(5), pp. 591–597.

Barnett, T., Bass, K. and Brown, G. (1994) Ethical ideology and ethical judgment regarding ethical issues in business, *Journal of Business Ethics*, 13(6), pp. 469–480.

Barnett, T., Bass, K., Brown, G. and Herbert, F. (1998) Ethical ideology and the ethical judgments of marketing professionals, *Journal of Business Ethics*, 17(7), pp. 715–723.

Bass, K., Barnett, T. and Brown, G. (1998) The moral philosophy of sales managers and its influence on ethical decision making, *Journal of Personal Selling and Sales Management*, 18(2), pp. 1–17.

Betz, M., O'Connell, L. and Shepard, J. M. (1989) Gender differences in proclivity for unethical behaviour, *Journal of Business Ethics*, 8(5), pp. 321–324.

Borkowski, S. C. and Ugras, Y. J. (1998) Business students and ethics: a meta-analysis, *Journal of Business Ethics*, 17(11), pp. 1117–1127.

Cohen, J., Pant, L. and Sharp, D. (2001) An examination of differences in ethical decision making between Canadian business students and accounting professionals, *Journal of Business Ethics*, 30(4), pp. 319–336.

Cowton, C. J. and Cummins, J. (2003) Teaching business ethics in UK higher education: progress and prospects, *Teaching Business Ethics*, 7(1), pp. 37–54.

Davis, J. R. and Welton, R. E. (1991) Business ethics: business students' perceptions, *Journal of Business Ethics*, 10(6), pp. 451–463.

Dawson, L. M. (1995) Women and men, morality and ethics, *Business Horizons*, 38(4), pp. 61–69.

Eynon, G., Thorley Hill, N., Stevens, K. T. and Clarke, P. (1996) An international comparison of ethical reasoning abilities: accounting students from Ireland and the United States, *Journal of Accounting Education*, 14(4), pp. 477–492.

Eynon, G., Thorley Hill, N. and Stevens, K. T. (1997) Factors that influence the moral reasoning abilities of accountants: implications for universities and the profession, *Journal of Business Ethics*, 16(12–13), pp. 1297–1309.

Ford, R. C. and Richardson, W. D. (1994) Ethical decision making: a review of the empirical literature, *Journal of Business Ethics*, 13(3), pp. 205–221.

Forsyth, D. R. (1980) A taxonomy of ethical ideologies, *Journal of Personal and Social Psychology*, 39(1), pp. 175–184.

Forsyth, D. R. (1981) Moral judgment: the influence of ethical ideology, *Personality and Social Psychology Bulletin*, 7(2), pp. 218–223.

Forsyth, D. R. (1985) Individual differences in information processing during moral judgment, *Journal of Personal and Social Psychology*, 49(2), pp. 264–272.

Forsyth, D. R. and Pope, W. R. (1984) Ethical ideology and judgments of social psychological research, *Journal of Personal and Social Psychology*, 46(6), pp. 1365–1375.

Forsyth, D. R., Nye, J. L. and Kelley, K. (1988) Idealism, relativism, and the ethic of caring, *Journal of Psychology*, 122(3), pp. 243–248.

Forsyth, D. R. and Nye, J. L. (1990) Personal moral philosophies and moral choice, *Journal of Research in Personality*, 24(4), pp. 398–414.

Gilligan, C. (1982) *In a different voice* (Cambridge, MA, Harvard University Press).

Hartikainen, O. and Torstila, S. (2004) Job-related ethical judgment in the finance profession, *Journal of Applied Finance*, 14(1), pp. 62–76.

Harris, J. R. (1989) Ethical values and decisions processes of male and female business students, *Journal of Education for Business*, 64(5), pp. 234–238.

Hogan, R. (1973) Moral conduct and moral character: a psychological perspective, *Psychological Bulletin*, 79(4), pp. 217–232.

Jones, S. K. and Hiltebeitel, K. M. (1995) Organizational influence in a model of the moral decision process of accountants, *Journal of Business Ethics*, 14(6), pp. 417–431.

Kidwell, J. M., Stevens, R. E. and Bethke, A. L. (1987) Differences in ethical perceptions between male and female managers: myth or reality, *Journal of Business Ethics*, 6(6), pp. 489–493.

Kohlberg, L. (1982) Reply to Owen Flanagan and some comments on the Puka-Goodpaster Exchange, *Ethics*, 92(3), pp. 513–528.

Luthar, H. K., DiBattista, R. A. and Gautschi, T. (1997) Perception of what the ethical climate is and what it should be: the role of gender, academic status, and ethical education, *Journal of Business Ethics*, 16(2), pp. 205–217.

Marques, P. A. and Azevedo-Pereira, J. (2009) Ethical ideology and ethical judgments in the portuguese accounting profession, *Journal of Business Ethics*, 86(2), pp. 227–242.

Ponemon, L. (1990) Ethical judgements in accounting: a cognitive development perspective', *Critical Perspectives on Accounting*, 1(2), pp. 191–215.

Radtke, R. R. (2000) The effects of gender and setting on accountants' ethically sensitive decisions, *Journal of Business Ethics*, 24(4), pp. 299–312.

Radtke, R. R. (2004) Exposing accounting students to multiple factors affecting ethical decision making, *Issues in Accounting Education*, 19(1), pp. 73–83.

Rest, J. R. (1986) *Moral development: Advances in research and theory* (New York: Praeger).

Ruegger, D. and King, E. W. (1992) A study of the effect of age and gender upon student business ethics, *Journal of Business Ethics*, 11(3), pp. 179–186.

Schlenker, B. R. and Forsyth, D. R. (1977) On the ethics of psychological research, *Journal of Experimental Social Psychology*, 13(4), pp. 369–396.

Shaub, M. (1994) An analysis of the association of traditional demographic variable with the moral reasoning of auditing students and auditors, *Journal of Accounting Education*, 12(1), pp. 1–26.

Sharp, F. C. (1898) An objective study of some moral judgments, *American Journal of Psychology*, 9, pp. 198–234.

Smith, A. and Roger, V. (2000) Ethics-related responses to specific situation vignettes: evidence of gender-based differences and occupational socialization, *Journal of Business Ethics*, 28(1), pp. 73–86.

Stanga, K. G. and Turpen, R. A. (1991) Ethical judgements on selected accounting issues: an empirical study, *Journal of Business Ethics*, 10(10), pp. 739–747.

Tansey, R. G., Brown, G., Hyman, M. and Dawson, L. (1994) Personal moral philosophies and moral judgments of salespeople, *Journal of Personal Selling and Sales Management*, 14(1), pp. 59–76.

Tsalikis, J. and Ortiz-Buonafina, M. (1990) Ethical beliefs' differences of males and females, *Journal of Business Ethics*, 9(6), pp. 509–517.

Weeks, W., Moore, C. W., McKinney, J. A. and Longenecker, J. G. (1999) The effects of gender and career stage on ethical judgment, *Journal of Business Ethics*, 20(4), pp. 301–313.

Adding Value to Audit Education through 'Living' Cases

JULIE DRAKE

University of Huddersfield, UK

ABSTRACT   *This paper seeks to address the perceived failure of university teaching to foster critical understanding of audit practice and to identify a potential remedy. It contributes to the debate (Maltby, 2001, "Second thoughts about 'Cases in Auditing'," Accounting Education: an international journal, 10(4), 421–428) by investigating the double-faceted nature of auditing: as a sub-set of the academic discipline of accounting and as professional practice. Although case studies are helpful for students of auditing, they tend to be artificial, or at best, retrospective. This paper introduces a different type of case study for audit education using corporate failure stories from the media as an example, proposing and explaining the notion of the 'living case' in order to foster critical appraisal of audit practice. It contributes to the literature on audit education by describing how this different type of case can address both the technical activities and the social practice of audit through Kolb's (1984, Experiential Learning: Experience as the Source of Learning and Development, Englewood Cliffs, NJ: Prentice Hall) experiential learning theory and thus concludes that there is a place for the practical nature of auditing in academic study, in order to fully appreciate the social aspects.*

Introduction

The aim of this paper is to contribute to the debate on the kind of case studies that are useful in auditing education. The paper introduces the notion of a 'living case' which is a framework for analysis of a reported media story such as a financial event or crisis. It seeks to identify and explain a way forward for the auditing educator, addressing criticisms of the use of case studies in auditing, by using the media to contribute to the case study method in auditing education. Thus, the paper re-examines the problems associated with the nature of existing case studies for audit education, reviewing their limitations in the context of academic debate and use in an undergraduate auditing module. It enhances the debate through introducing the living case which is a hybrid of the case *history* (Easton, 1992) and case *study* (Milne and McConnell, 2001) with a framework to support the application of what is termed a 'living' case. The merits of the living case are evaluated using the propositions (Kolb and Kolb, 2005) for experiential learning theory (ELT). It is argued that such a case method would assist auditing educators to meet the needs of the accountancy profession and society, not only in their demand for employable graduates, but also to produce professionals with critical, broad skills that will enable the recognition of the reality and far-reaching consequences of corporate failure. Further, the model used will support the development of students' skills in abstraction and experimentation in support of the promulgation of life-long learning (Howieson, 2003) as encapsulated in the ELT model.

The aim for the pedagogy of the living case is to make it current, therefore, relevant and useful, thus avoiding a posthumous effect and a dead, life-less scenario for educator and student. It moves away from historical artefacts that are dead cases such as Enron, World-Com, and Barings, and recognizes that a freshness is required which captures events as they emerge to process a number of 'What if?' scenarios to bring an element of current affairs to help foster critical thinking. It recognizes that accounting education as a whole would be 'enhanced if the audit and assurance process is presented as part of an integrative capstone experience...with an emphasis on professional ethics, information quality, and the market-driven nature of assurance services', (Johnson, Baird, Caster, Dilla, Earley and Louwers, 2003, p. 262). Thus, in order to re-engineer the case method, one should strive through critical teaching that 'relates auditing scandals and failures to the normal course of auditing and explores the elements of corporate governance which produces corporate failure' (Maltby, 2001, p. 426). In the context of this paper corporate incidents of failure are used in the simplest and broadest form as some element that is unsuccessful or disappointing in the corporate performance or governance of an entity which, in this case, has been reported in the media. Interestingly, there has been concern in other disciplines that such financial scandals (in that they are scandalous enough for journalistic interest) might increase students' cynicism (Cagle and Bacus, 2006), perhaps fostering pessimism in students rather than a more balanced view. Cynicism is related to scepticism which, according to the principle of rigour within the Auditors' Code (Auditing Practices Board 1994), is necessary in the auditors' approach to their work. Thus an element of cynicism may well be a favourable trait for an auditor, but the educator should seek to counterbalance that cynicism and strive for healthy scepticism. Therefore, auditing case studies based on corporate and/or governance failure, documented in the media, may provide stories to address the issue of hindsight, a shift that does not ignore what has happened but does consider what might happen next and what might have worked effectively to avoid the developing financial incident. This approach concurs with the experiential learning model.

The living case thus seeks to avoid the 'surface learning' traditionally associated with accounting and audit (Lucas, 2001) and to incubate the primary stage of Kolb's experiential learning, that is the concrete experience of the learner. This stage is missing from audit courses taught in universities (Helliar, Monk and Stevenson, 2009). The aim of the living case structure is to give concrete experiences and generate observations that facilitate reflection through questions, forcing students to think about the scenario, creating abstract hypotheses and patterns in order to formulate a plan, hence abstracted experimentation. The abstracted experimentation should manifest itself both within the module (in tutorials, coursework and examination) and outside of it (in the world of work and on entering the profession). However, Kolb and Kolb (2005) contend that experiential learning theory is often 'misunderstood as a set of tools and techniques to provide learners with experiences from which they can learn', (p. 193). This implies that auditing educators would merely feed knowledge to students, which experiential learning applied in the way that the Kolb model did not intend. The living case aims to be more than a tool and technique to acquire new facts (see Table 1, for example, P3 and P4) as it aims not to be descriptive through demonstrating the techniques of auditing, which is left to the more traditional venue of the lecture theatre. Through a framework of questions the process is iterative, thus enabling student action, reflection and integration of materials in the process of learning. In order to evaluate if the living case can achieve what it sets out to do it will be analysed later in the paper against the six propositions of ELT described in Table 1.

Dilemmas for the Audit Educator

The 'living' case, it is argued, addresses the audit educators' dilemma faced with serving two masters: academia and the profession. Thus the paper argues that, on occasion and in the right context, it is legitimate to use examples of corporate failure and it becomes a useful, valid resource for the auditing educator. The latter is all the more important as, traditionally, the post- mortem of recent financial crises inevitably gravitates towards the role and skills of the modern auditor and the accountancy profession as a whole. Accountants require competencies beyond a technician role; specialist knowledge needs to be supported by generic skills as embodied by the conclusions on auditor behaviour from the Enron case and the ethical implications of the auditors' actions (Howieson, 2003). This is further supported by the International Accounting Education Standards Board (2009) recognizing that a professional accountant must possess professional knowledge, professional skills and professional values, ethics and attitudes.

The living case contributes to audit education, gives the auditing educator the opportunity to explore the richness behind a developing financial crisis before the conclusion is reported and will still be relevant whether the auditor is vindicated or not. The living case has potential to bring the double-faceted nature of auditing together as threads of the media story emerge. The framework used to analyse the living case (see Table 2) contributes to auditing education through engaging learners in case studies, away from the confines of model answers and the static cases by using ELT (see Table 1, P3). It prepares students of auditing for the world of work and the profession and, in doing so, the reality of the professional, institutional and societal response to corporate failure. Two recent corporate incidents that have been incorporated into teaching through a series of extracts

Table 1. Experiential learning theory (ELT) propositions

Proposition	Learning ...	Learning is not ...
P 1	... is a process that involves feedback	... driven by learning outcomes
P 2	... is about relearning (drawing out students' beliefs and ideas)	... about acquiring new facts
P 3	... requires logical argumentation (conflict, differences and disagreements)	... facilitated by a static environment
P 4	... is holistic: thinking; believing; perceiving; behaving	... only about cognition (knowledge acquisition)
P 5	... involves synergy between person and environment	... isolated from the environment
P 6	... is about creating knowledge (constructivist)	... presenting fixed ideas to the learner

Adapted from Kolb and Kolb (2005).

Table 2.   Framework questions

Question	Example for case A: Expect broad issues
1. What are the critical issues of the case?	Corporate Governance; Risk Management; Fraud; Negligence; Application of Company Law: Corporate Insolvency; Audit aspects
2. What audit tools and procedures are you aware of that you would have expected to eliminate the development of this incident?	See Table 4: Scientific dimension
3. What are the critical issues of the case in relation to the role of the auditor in society?	See Table 4: Social aspects

from various media sources are presented, and a framework is explained in order to analyse the emergent story. Thus, the media is used to address some of the perceived short-comings of case studies to enable a critical understanding of audit practice.

Case Studies

Contributing to Teaching in Accounting and Auditing

The potential of case studies in accounting programmes is well documented, for example: as an aid to developing generic skills (e.g. Boyce, Williams, Kelly and Yee, 2001); in developing new modules (Hassall, Lewis and Broadbent, 1998); supporting the traditional text book approach in management accounting (e.g. Stewart and Dougherty, 1993); and as a bridge between degree study and professional life through administering problem-based learning (Milne and McConnell, 2001). The use of case studies in auditing is also apparent as part of accounting programmes. Over time, auditing has come to be recognized as distinct in its role as the cornerstone of corporate governance (Higson, 2003). Thus, the traditional case study, a popular instructional aid in accounting, has also been transferred and extensively used in auditing (for example, Davies, 2000; Dennis, 2003; Drake, 1999; Helliar, Monk, Stevenson and Allison, 2007; Helliar *et al.*, 2009: Maltby, 1996; 1998: Trussel and Frazer, 2008). Further, some texts, such as Gray and Manson (2008), use short case studies to illustrate the learning points.

As auditing has become an established sub-field of the academic discipline of accounting (Ravenscroft *et al.*, 2009), it has generated accounting educator debate including the adequacy of audit teaching in undergraduate programmes and how it might improve through methods used to teach it. The use of case studies has been under the spotlight, perhaps because it is a more established method in accounting education, subsequently transferred to the sub-field of auditing. According to the Barrow Taxonomy adapted in Milne and McConnell (2001), the existing use of case studies on many undergraduate accounting course would appear to be in the form of the *case method*, a structured case presented in full prior to a tutorial at which the tutor then leads the discussion. An alternative to a case study may be what Easton (1992) describes as a *case history*: i.e. 'simply a description of what has happened, with no specific purpose in mind. A *case study*, by contrast, is, or should be, designed as a learning vehicle with specific educational objectives in mind' (p. 1).

There have been a number of shortcomings in the use of case studies in auditing as highlighted by Maltby (2001): for example, invented cases are too rigid and possibly force a single solution avoiding problem-solving; restricted access to real-life cases from the profession because of client confidentiality; the tendency to synthesize cases from multiple clients and thus distorting the picture of auditing; scandals not facilitating critical teaching as they are often presented in the context of auditing as opposed to other broader contexts such as corporate governance. However, the literature is unclear as to which auditing educators are using case studies, which are using case histories, and there are few references as to exactly how cases are being used and on what basis they are selected. This is consistent with Milne and McConnell (2001) who anticipated a continued increase in the use of case studies in accounting education yet a small literature that merely described their use and little evidence of how accounting educators actually *used* case studies. The use of cases and what they set out to do have begun to be debated in other similar subjects. For example, the business ethics literature has started to address how the use of cases helps students to understand ethics and evaluate the impact of such methods (Cagle and Bacus, 2006). For this reason, there is a need to examine more deeply how a different sort of case might have an impact and meet the needs of the sub-field of auditing within the academic discipline of accounting.

Challenges for Case Studies in Auditing: Replace or Re-engineer?

The first approach by educators has been to seek alternative approaches to the case method in auditing in order to address apparent shortfalls in the traditional case study method with little consideration of how the case method itself might be developed constructively, thus enhanced, to meet audit educators'—and their audience's—needs. Siegel, Omer and Agrawal (1997) suggested audit teaching could be improved through video simulation to take students through all the steps of experiential learning with the videotape as proxy for concrete experience. Maltby (2001) considered replacement with role-playing, or at least changing the nature of the case study, calling for the use of longer case studies due to having significant reservations about her own selection of case studies. She concludes, amongst other things, that case studies based on audit scandals are not always the most appropriate resource. However, before the method is usurped by another it is worth considering the challenge for the case study method in accounting education more broadly, as accounting is a discipline that is double-faceted; the conceptual principles of an academic discipline and practical procedures of professional practitioners, as elucidated by Ravenscroft, Rebele, St Pierre and Wilson (2008, p. 5):

> In addition to existing as an academic discipline, accounting also exists as a field of professional practice within which education and training (on a life-long basis) is of paramount importance to the public interest. This education and training should therefore be undertaken with due regard to its conceptual foundations and procedural adequacy as well as its technical content.

Thus, being double-faceted, education and training has to accommodate both the academic and the professional and, further, because it is in the public domain, it may need to serve another master as its success is judged not only by what it reports but also by how the public perceives it.

The Academic and Practical Nature of Auditing

Choices for the Auditing Educator
As a sub-set of the accounting discipline, the auditing educator has to decide what to include and how to teach auditing; the challenge is to bridge the academic and the

practical. The quality and knowledge and understanding of auditing may rely on under-standing both conceptual and practical aspects of the field. The interplay of public interest (Ravenscroft *et al.*, 2008) strikes more resonance for auditing than accounting as audit serves as a communication tool to stakeholders, a fundamental support to corporate gov-ernance, and it is certainly often perceived as the first at fault in corporate failures as the extensive literature on the expectations gap proves (for example, see: Humphrey, Moizer and Turley, 1992; Porter, 1993; Koh and Woo, 1998; Porter and Gowthorpe, 2004). The research literature has examined the underlying concepts of auditing, that is, the role of auditing and more philosophical debate (for example, Mautz and Sharaf, 1961; Humphrey, 1997). Meanwhile, on a practical level, an auditing course should have much about audit methodology and procedural steps culminating in the draft and subsequent issue of some form of audit report, in order to understand the holistic process. The approach is responsive to regulation through the issues of auditing standards and guidelines; now the national responsibility of regulators has been made somewhat easier by the globalization of audit-ing standards through the development of International Standards on Auditing (ISAs). How has the audit educator responded to the need to serve two masters, and what part has the case study played?

Audit Educator: Building Bridges with Case Studies

Traditionally the audit educator has responded to the practical dimensions of audit with the use of the case study method, perhaps not paying too much attention to how that method might help develop conceptual understanding of the audit process. Maltby (2001) refers to a way of visualizing auditing as being a scientific *activity*, which involves the auditor testing financial statement assertions through sampling and statistical techniques. Such a technical approach to an essentially practical process is reflected in the teaching of the subject, especially on professional papers and university courses seeking professional body exemption. However, for an undergraduate, such a practical approach may not meet the requirements of honours level programmes and meeting the QAA (2001) level descriptors in particular: systematic understanding of the field; conceptual understanding; appreciating uncertainty and ambiguity.

Professional bodies and training firms have also moved on in how they train their students on training contracts, effectively shifting the residual responsibility away from university teachers, justifying Maltby in questioning the style of auditing case she chose (Maltby, 1988; 1996) to construct. Maltby (2001) admitted that her own text of auditing cases was a practical response to the reaction of academics to making auditing *scientific* (see, Pentland, 1993) where auditing was presented as being subject to rigours of hypoth-esis formulation and statistical testing. This contrasts to the practicalities and reality of risk assessment and professional judgement which is embedded in International Education Standard 8 (International Federation of Accountants, 2008) and the subject of enhanced consultation (International Accounting Education Standards Board, 2010).

In order to give a flavour of real-world auditing that is not about hypothesis testing through sampling, that it is about judgement and professional decision-making dependent on the numbers and event in hand, then the case study approach seems entirely sensible. Thus, auditing cases tended to err on the practical side at undergraduate level in prep-aration for a career in the profession. However, it is important that the scientific elements of auditing and its practical nature be seen as necessary pre-cursors to understanding the social aspects of auditing, including reasons for understanding audit failure because audit itself is a process. Achieving the right combination of scientific and social aspects of audit-ing is not only important for professional body exemptions but also in order to fully appreciate and comprehend the social aspects of auditing. However, not all the cases under self-critique were a practical response (Maltby, 1996) as cases did cover broader issues—such as corporate governance, auditor liability, and fraud albeit that the questions are 'what' and 'how' based on constructed cases. Alternatively, Sherer and Turley (1997) and other auditing text authors (for example, Soltani, 2007) have moved on from practical examples to reflect current and more philosophical and conceptual issues which perhaps have contributed to the subject of auditing becoming more appropriate for honours level and perhaps worthy of undergraduate study in any depth in its own right.

Maltby (2001) further examined the dilemma for auditing educators as two-dimensional, the *scientific aspects* (that is, how audit works) and the *social practice* (that is, the critical aspects including how audit fails). It is a shame that, as a social practice, auditing is associated with corporate failure and a failure to meet stakeholders' expectations. These failures, or 'scandals' (when audit failure is exposed in the media) and perceived failure of audit to meet the expectations of users, contribute to audit from a historical perspective, that is, after the event and, such retrospect is often circumstantial. As such, the evidence of audit as a social practice based on its weaknesses is not very stimulating or fair to the audit task at hand: for educator; for student; furtherance of the profession; and confidence in the very practice of audit itself. Indeed, corporate failure does not necessarily equate to audit failure, thus one aspect of a new approach to education is that it should be forward-looking as well as retrospective; this is what happened, these are the established facts but on analysis and enquiry (see Table 1) what does the student understand about how auditing contributed to the current state of affairs and what are the implications and likely outcomes given current uncertainties? In doing so there is opportunity to evaluate failure critically before blame is assigned to parties involved and the story is concluded, or 'dead'.

Therefore, auditing cases should incorporate a critical aspect not only to meet honours degree level requirements, to foster scepticism, but also to prepare graduates for the profession, enhancing employability, and in order to fulfil the attributes of a professional (Auditing Practices Board, 1994). One could end any debate here and subsume auditing to intermediate module study but the ramifications of the audit process and the debate ensuing from subsequent corporate failure is worthy of academic debate and graduates should have a reasonable understanding of the role and purpose of auditing and the part it plays in the financial incidents. To ignore the social aspects of auditing would only serve to increase the much-debated expectations gap as more corporate failure is reported in the media and/or law courts. Thus, should the reality of corporate failure be dismissed or should it be harnessed in order to rejuvenate the case method in auditing?

Rejuvenating Case Studies: Corporate Crises in the Media

Prima facie there are good reasons to consider that corporate crises and failure stories are useful in auditing education: they are plentiful; somebody nearly always asks 'where were the auditors?' in such an event; they are real-life examples and therefore 'eye-catching' to the novice; they are often newsworthy with some scandal attached and therefore accessible. However, when scandals are presented solely in the context of auditing as opposed to the broader context, such as corporate regulation and governance, they may not facilitate critical teaching (Maltby, 2001). Corporate failure does not always result in classification as audit failure and can be useful in illustrating the point that auditors were not to blame as well as those occasions when audit failure was an issue. These failures in corporate performance and governance are a useful source from which to start thinking about living cases. However, Nelson, Ratliff, Steinhoff and Mitchell (2003) argue that, in an era of audit failure, rules-based audit courses lack the learning outcomes of critical thinking, and therefore, it is important to consider how the latter might be achieved. Nelson *et al.* (2003) suggested that a course in logic would benefit accounting and auditing students at a level beyond basic logic in order to have some impact on critical thinking skills. In the UK, at least within the confines of professional body requirements, there seems little scope for fitting a logic course into the degree curriculum that is packed with the professional exemption restrictions. Whilst it may be difficult to take a large step, by embedding logic into an undergraduate programme, it is reasonable to concern ourselves with simpler things such as how audit education could be enhanced through the value of the auditing case study method, how that method might be engineered to foster critical thinking skills, and that this may be achieved through the use of 'living cases'.

Living Cases for Experiential Learning

A *Hybrid of Case History and Case Study*
Easton (1992) labelled the case history as descriptive and simple, unlike a case study, which by contrast has a set of specific educational objectives in mind. This is a good starting point to explain the 'living case' and how it was developed: a hybrid of the case history and case study. Kreber (2001) argues that case studies, used properly, can be effective in the development of critical thinking and self-direction through fostering experiential learning. Thus, before writing off the case study method for auditing, it is important to consider how a new practice might meet that criterion. The case history implies a story, a chronicle of a series of events, which have happened. The aim with a living case is to introduce students to a breaking news story and then use emerging events, reports and differing accounts of corporate failure (see Appendix A and Appendix B). Crucially, this provides an opportunity for evaluation prior to any possible audit failure being ascribed, justifiably or not, to corporate failure, enabling the story to be reviewed as it unfolds within a number of sub-fields of the accounting discipline. Further, tasks may be set such as holding a competition to bring information to class to update the living case. This may be particularly useful in bringing the other elements of the case to life in the context of subjects studied on a degree programme avoiding a central case study subject such as 'cases in financial reporting, cases in business ethic, cases in financial reporting'. Rarely do financial failures occur as such mutually exclusive packages, sitting neatly in any one discipline.

Developing the Model for Living Case Studies: Design Context

The aim would be a case as a concrete experience, initially a case history, but the transformation to a living case comprising experiential learning will depend on how that documented evidence is used. Kreber (2001) referring to Kolb (1984) argues, 'experiential learning is fostered once instructors encourage their students to transform these abstract events through strategies that bring about reflection or though those that bring about experimentation,' (p. 221). Thus the aim is to avoid the single solution scenario to encourage experimentation from subject knowledge as new facts of the story emerge through the media, enabling a longitudinal and deeper critical analysis and understanding of the subject as the story unfolds. This also opens up opportunities for broader issues and drawing in other academic disciplines from within and outside of the accounting field. The means by which that can be achieved is currently through a framework of key questions that are transferable as potential living case stories 'break' (see Table 2). Essentially this provides an extant and emerging story to stimulate students' interest, but how does that come to be?

The 'living' case method emerged over a number of years of self- and student-evaluation regarding the content of an undergraduate auditing module and a separate professional auditing course. The living case emerged for a number of significant reasons based on the experience of the author and discussions with colleagues and students over a number of years: a natural curiosity about current corporate failure in the context of auditing; the lack of authenticity in constructed cases and subsequent student-perceived irrelevance; the rumour (by some academics and students) that auditing was difficult; the view (again by some academics and students) that auditing was boring and not as important as the discipline of which it was a sub-field of (i.e. accounting). It was also departmental policy to ask students to submit mid- module questionnaires which comprised two simple questions:

Which things worked well?

What changes would you like to take place?

These questionnaires produced a number of recurrent themes which supported the use of a varied approach to audit education and a demand for a 'reality' method (see Table 3 for questionnaire results for the two most active academic years of the living case thus far).

This type of case was informally introduced in the academic year 2007/08 and more formally the following year (with more case stories on the virtual learning environment) to a cohort of final year undergraduate students at a UK university. The cohort size was increasing (23 in 2007/08; 32 in 2008/09; 47 in 2009/10). Through teaching on both undergraduate and professional courses it was observed that what learners liked in auditing is the context, which one can assume engages them more, rather than singular themed lectures that serve to segregate what is actually a process, an audit process (Gray and Manson, 2008). A natural response was the use of current media stories used to highlight the lecture topic and the realization that the same media story was often revisited throughout the academic year to either explain a new topic, reinforce the process of auditing or put in contextual developments in the media story itself in terms of auditing, governance issues and other sub-fields of accounting issues. Prior to 2007, the inclusion of these living case examples was informal and introduced on an *ad hoc* basis as they occurred. From 2007/08 a virtual learning environment link was set up on emerging cases (starting with two only) which by 2008/09 were more developed with links added to two key cases to avoid 'case overload'. With key cases loaded on to the site it was easy to add news stories on the key cases as they emerged, and cross-reference students back to the material as the course progressed. The framework questions were not loaded up to the virtual learning environment but were used by the author as prompts when the case was mentioned in the classroom. Although apparently simple, there were early observable positive responses in class about the case and some references to the 'living case' without prompt by the tutor.

Thus it became apparent that, in an attempt to balance what Maltby (2001) later described as a *scientific* approach to auditing, that is the procedural intra-firm aspects of auditing (micro-level) and the *critical* approach that focuses on audit failures and a wider social impact of audit (macro-level) such as the expectations gap, auditor liability, audit scope and professional aspects, that students were becoming more engaged in the sub-field. The improvement in engagement was evident from the attention and interaction noted in lectures and tutorials and positive comments in the mid-module questionnaire results. Although there is no direct causation between introduction of living cases and the comments, given the many variables impacting on module satisfaction (Table 3), there does appear to be a shift in 2009/10 to students' comments on what worked well

Table 3. Mid-module questionnaire summary

2008/09	2009/10
Living case used for the first time	Living case more embedded in the virtual learning environment and tutorial discussion
What you thought worked well:	What you thought worked well:
Tutorial method is good (×4)	Group work (×9)
Group discussion method in tutorial works well (×6)	Tutorials generally (×9)
'Tutorials in small groups.'	Class discussion (×7)
'Tutorial work well with the student input—the answers [which summarise slides from actual class] are straight up onto Blackboard' (×2)	Lectures (×8)
	Tutorial clearly linked to lectures (×4)
	Good text (×2)
'Good links with exams and how to pass them.'	Tutorial and lectures being on the same day
'Interactive seminars with practice mixed up with theory helps to bring point across and gives opportunity to raise more questions to better understand. Like the seminar it is a bit different.'	Availability of coursework on Blackboard from first day
'Workshop [meaning tutorial] that allows you to put to practice what you have learned.'	'Tutorials are really helpful and useful e.g. group work. Lectures are delivered well.'
'Tutorial as group work then feed back to class' (×2)	'When lecturer expands our points and puts them in context and puts them on Blackboard.'
'Tutorial of splitting into groups and answering questions onto acetate' (×2)	'Lectures constructive because not just hand outs – required to make own notes.'
'Can relate to how it will work in practice' (×2)	'Cases used in tutorial add further to our understanding.'
'Coursework given early in the year' (×2)	'Plentiful resources on Blackboard site.'
'Textbook is easy reading.'	'Good use of real life application of auditing in the commercial world' (×3)
'Textbook ties in really well with the module and is easy to understand and useful.'	'Themes are repeated so knowledge is reinforced.'
'Lecture notes and handouts are helpful.'	
'Good lecture layout' (×2)	What changes you would like to take place:
'Good informative slides and notes as handouts.'	
What changes you would like to take place:	More standard answers (×4)
	More practical examples (×2)
'A lot of work when combined with work on other modules = stress.'	Less group work in tutorials (×1)
'Tutorial work tends to take longer than other subjects—good subject.'	

to 'context', 'cases', 'resources', 'real-life application' and, indeed, reference to a lack of standard answers which is exactly the aim of abstract experimentation in the ELT model. This is further supported by the living cases being cited in tutorial discussions, without prompt by students, and later in coursework and examinations.

Another reason for developing the living case further was some discomfort in relying on constructed cases and examples in set texts as they lacked a richness, although some were very good. Consequently, the virtual learning environment (VLE) has been developed as a mode of delivery of the living case, making it highly accessible as a gateway to link to the real world and a variety of media, including newspapers, newswires, professional body internet sites and multi-media platforms such as *You Tube*. All this in an effort to dispel the apparently tarnished view of auditing by undergraduates, as experienced by the author, and promote its relevance and utility, especially to those who were applying for training contracts with some despondency that the initial time served may well be in the audit department.

However, just as constructed cases lack authenticity, media cases, at first, may lack detail and description. But the media is the definitive source for real life events and Kaidonis (2004), reflecting on accounting education and its capacity to be transformative through the use of real -world events, does advocate sources such as newspaper clippings. Thus, media is increasingly a legitimate source to bridge the gap between theory and practice.

A further motivation was to enhance the delivery of auditing as a result of discussions and feedback by incoming undergraduate accounting students of auditing who perceived the subject as: boring because it is procedural; disliked because it is not numerical; not numerical, therefore, it is difficult; discursive and thus means argument building; lacking clarity because there may not be a right and wrong answer—it just is not numbers. However, these very issues are those that engage undergraduates in analysis, conceptual understanding and an appreciation that there is ambiguity in real-world financial incidents which necessitates the synthesis of information into an opinion (see Table 1). In the view of the author, keeping audit as procedural does not develop learning beyond delivering a concrete experience and it was clear that the ELT model could help instil skills of logical argument and place the auditor in his/her environment rather than the clinical environment of the classroom.

Thus the case study method (Maltby, 1988; 1996) had been introduced to bring variety to the forms of tutorial work. The author had observed malaise among members of the student cohort in engaging with the traditional case method even when they are interspersed between tutorial content which includes traditional examination type questions, essay type questions and research-based topics. The level of engagement varied from fully engaged (i.e. preparing full solutions to questions posed at the end of case studies) to simply having accessed the case study and brought it along to a tutorial. In the latter case, the act of having the case study seems to act as a pacifier to the students; at least having done something in bringing the case along makes them feel that they have prepared, perhaps will not receive the tutor's wrath for not preparing at all, and patiently await the cohort's contribution to flesh out their meagre effort. However, some sympathy is to be had as the available case studies are often lacking any depth, being a short story and some shortfall on 'real-life'. Of course, one solution would be more in-depth and longitudinal cases but that brings with it its own issue - such as a lack of variety, time-consuming demands, the risk of dating quickly, resource used in design, and ultimately does not resolve the limitations of a constructed case with set answers.

Using the Living Case: Analysis Framework

The living case comes alive through a series of questions presented in a framework for auditing educators which is to be used for analysing the case history, presented in a series of media reports. The framework is shown in Table 2. The media story is presented as the concrete experience. There are three stages in using the living case questions which embody ELT which have been coded in Table 1 according to the propositions (for example, P 1 being feedback). In stage 1, the critical issues are asked for, which enables the living case to be seen in the broader context. Stage 1 of the framework requires feedback to the tutor and peers in a discussion format, hence generating feedback (P1), and draws on the individual's own beliefs and ideas (P2) where the tutor can facilitate argument and debate (P3) and, in so doing, it is more than knowledge acquisition and it provides a holistic approach (P4). The holistic approach is a part of the learning process through stage 2 where the procedures and tools of audit can be reflected on and the student is placed in the environment of audit (P5). Thus, in stage 2, the procedural and scientific elements of auditing are addressed and, last but not least, in stage 3 the more social, more critical aspects. In stage 3 of the framework the critical issues are discussed and knowledge is created based on active experimentation with the issues raised through the logical argumentation. These three stages therefore foster reflective observation, examining accumulated knowledge and thus relearning, but in a new context of a media story. Other sources, in addition to the media reports, could be material from the public domain such as Audit Investigation Unit reports. Through looking for patterns and developing logical argumentation in the tutorial debate, the target is to achieve abstract conceptualization. That conceptualization is followed by the active experimentation in the solution to the framework question which is formative towards in-module assessment and externally in the analytical skills acquired for the profession.

Application to Case A

The media stories are posted on the VLE as events pan out; hence the case is 'living'. As each fragment of the story emerges the three stages can be applied accordingly: broad and critical; procedural; social. In the first instance, as the story breaks, stage 1 alone might suffice without stages 2 and 3 as a reference, to encourage the much broader view. Table 4 shows how both scientific and social aspects can be addressed by such a simple series of stories over a period of time. This kind of case aims to add to the educational value by the 'extent to which it challenges the student not only to apply but also to question the audit approaches available,' (Maltby, 2001, p. 424). Further, it normalizes the reporting of the incident rather than portraying it as a pending audit scandal. It is the media which have reported a newsworthy abnormal event but the reality is that the very occurrence allows educators to access a good story that may well have remained hidden were it not newsworthy. Sometimes even the most normal audit procedures can be reported because of the scandal associated with them, albeit in example B that the case was concluded with the subsequent jailing of the directors.

Application to Case B

The value in this media story in case B is to emphasize the far-reaching implications of perceived mundane audit procedures when they do go wrong (in this case, the impact of the stock audit failing to detect errors). This is a more mature living case than Case A, running as events unfold from when matters first hit the media headlines to the conclusion of the jailing of directors. As this case matured there would have been the broader issues similar to those documented for case A in Table 4, including, for example, corporate governance, social impact of corporate failure, and institutional regulation (e.g. whistle blowing, and adequacy of professional regulation such as

Table 4. Areas to reflect on based on example case history A

	Dimension	
	Scientific: Audit tools	Social aspects
Planning stage; members' handbook	Audit risk	Auditor independence
	Related party transactions	Long-term client-auditor relationship
	Use of specialist	Ethical: adequacy of codes
Audit evidence	Rules of reliability	Management representations—the ultimate 'get out' clause?
	Sources of evidence: value of management representations	Professional body requirements; code of conduct; members' handbook
	Audit of fair value	
	Materiality	
	Judgement	
Audit report modification options	Post balance sheet events	Role of auditors
	Scope of auditors' work	
		Limitations of current auditor remit
		Regulatory aspects
As events 'roll out'		Auditor liability and negligence
		Insurance hypothesis

professional body sanctions). Thus, a further dimension to a framework approach would be to accommodate and enable students to reflect on the professional, institutional and societal response to such media coverage, alluded to by Kaidonis (2004) in order that 'students recognize that at least more than one perspective exists,' p. 672. (See Table 5.)

Table 5. Areas to reflect on based on example case history B

	Dimension	
	Scientific: Audit tools	Social aspects
Planning stage; members' handbook	Audit risk	Auditor independence
	Related party transactions	Long-term client-auditor relationship
	Use of specialist	Ethical: adequacy of codes; over-familiarity of client
	Group audits	
Audit evidence	Rules of reliability	Management representations—the ultimate 'get out' clause?
	Sources of evidence: value of management representations	Professional body requirements; code of conduct; members' handbook
	Substantive audit of stock; trade debtors	Responsibility for detecting fraud
	Materiality	
	Corroborative evidence	
	Judgement	
Audit report modification options	Post balance sheet events	Role of auditors
		Scope of auditors' work
		Limitations of current auditor remit
		Regulatory aspects
		Responsibility of auditors in respect of illegal acts
As events 'roll out'		Auditor liability and negligence
		Insurance hypothesis
		Audit expectations by employees

Using the Living Case

Initial Impact

In the first instance the method has been used to enhance existing lectures and tutorials as part of the teaching strategy, a support to existing strategies rather than embedded as a method in its own right. Whilst Maltby (2001) suggested that the practical aspects of auditing need not be so important to undergraduate courses because the profession has developed in-house training, and indeed not all professional trainees have relevant degrees, to prepare undergraduates for auditing it appears there is still a need for the auditing educator to use the practical to put the social implications in perspective. This is embodied in ELT and the generation of propositions (see Table 1) which involve a holistic and synergistic approach towards creating knowledge and encouraging active experimentation as the end process, thereby reflecting on concrete experiences and conceptualizing through to experimentation. As the fields of corporate governance and the critique of audit and auditors has evolved over the past 20 years or so, the importance of the critical aspects of auditing for commercial awareness, employability and success in the profession may have grown. Perhaps, even more so now as auditors may find themselves defending their position, roles and responsibilities as the scope of their work comes under scrutiny. It seems that the practical nature of auditing continues to be worthy of academic study and is, indeed, a necessity for two reasons. Firstly, to accommodate Macve (2007) who suggested that university education lacks a practical edge to embed the importance of the 'real world confirmation that what we are teaching is important in practice'. Secondly there is a symbiotic relationship between the two that necessitates both elements being incorporated by audit educators. However, the challenge for educators is how the practical interfaces with the subsequent societal and critical consequences of the practical outcomes of the audit process. Using the living case as a support rather than embedding it makes it illustrative and additional to texts and published case study materials without undermining those resources and their considerable value. Indeed, the living case can enhance the validity of a lecturer's anecdotal and published evidence through a more experiential learning theory approach. As one student said of Example A, 'I thought you were making it up until I read the newspaper story on the *Blackboard* site—that's unbelievable'.

Using the Media: Bringing Multiple Rewards

One advantage of these methods in breathing life to auditing in the classroom can include the build up of various external links and documentation on the VLE. Links to developing media stories, corporate failures, scandals, publications and opinions appeared welcome by a cohort of students who were weary of the traditional illustrations of Barings, WorldCom, Enron. These popular cases are indeed time-served and *dead*, though there have been far-reaching implication of such events for accounting and auditing educators and the profession to take on board. They are so well analysed and written about that there is a risk that the using those examples and the proliferation of resources on them means that the scope for students to benefit from experiential learning may be restricted. Students may rely on such resources rather than analysing events themselves and thus failing to foster conceptual understanding and critical analysis and understanding, thereby shifting away from independent learning (see Table 1). A further benefit for the living case is that, whilst the case story is 'fresh' and the case may change, the framework used to analyse it is constant. Indeed, students can select their own 'living case' and apply the framework questions accordingly and should be encouraged to share examples with peers.

Other rewards established are the level of engagement of the student cohorts in media-born stories, perhaps reflecting the 'reality TV' and 'twitter' generation of students who are keen to follow such media. In terms of the syllabus and danger of fragmenting the procedural application of auditing, the living case approach connects lectures together, reinforcing the audit process and the lectures which are not independent events thus bringing the richness of auditing to the fore. Similarly, it also simulates how events would unfold in-house at accounting firms: to that extent it is not fictitious or constructed just as the dialogue one would hope happens across the auditing and accounting profession as corporate failures are exposed. Ultimately, the media story becomes a proxy through the framework questions and allows insight into the debates that will occur behind closed doors. One tentative measure to show whether the approach is favoured by the students, in the absence of a survey at this stage of development, is that the mid-module questionnaire results in the academic year 2009/10 do indicate that the real-world examples were being noticed by students. At this stage the experimentation with the living case is not embedded into tutorial sessions and is being used more as an additional learning resource. Indeed, it may be more fitting to embed at master's levels modules in which the reflective observation might encourage deeper learning when students have already studied auditing at undergraduate level or through the profession itself. A weakness of this current analysis of the 'living case' method is, therefore, the absence of a methodical survey of students' views due to the recent development of the method. A survey of students' views is a future intention and a clear recommendation for further research into the application of the method.

There are some drawbacks to using the media as stories emerge which can be debated in the context of ELT. The materials may seem repetitive but this can be turned around to an advantage in drawing out and analysing why the case has re-emerged in the media (i.e. what has developed). Such an analysis can assist the relearning process and help develop logical argumentation through differences between one report and another (see Table 1, P2 and P3). Thus multiple stories can revisit old themes as new themes emerge (for example, the subsequent sale description of the Gem of Tanzania in Case A media report 3 would raise questions about the substantive audit procedures for assets, including inspection and reliance on third parties). There will inevitably be differences in the quality and providence of media reports which require judgement but this variability can assist the holistic learning aspects and help develop skills of judgement. The auditor rarely features in these early stories that support the principle of the living case and helps avoid pre-conceived ideas about the auditors' impact on such corporate incidents and requires the skill of the educator using the framework in Table 2 to steer students through the emerging and creative experience of the living case.

In future there will be some fine-tuning of the approach for the method to fulfil its potential, including nomination of the case across the teaching team of the undergraduate final year to enable other 'threads' to be drawn out in other areas (e.g. Insolvency, Corporate Reporting, Business Ethics, Corporate Governance). This cross-module approach may alleviate the concerns of Maltby (2001) about the use of scandals in the context of auditing alone where they may be 'interesting as stories, but not as ways of understanding or critiquing audit,' (p. 426) by bringing out the multi-faceted nature of corporate collapse.

Closing the debate about living cases without assessing the risks would be inappropriate. Using any media means that there may be journalistic bias. Some living cases may start out as strong candidates but lose their impetus as the media become less interested or time lapses. However, the view is that the rewards outweigh such risk and that loss of impetus for those reasons may be a valuable analysis to debate in it own right in the classroom (for example, indicating a weakening in the insurance hypothesis, a strengthening of regulation as an institutional response and the witch-hunt of auditors). What is proposed is that, with the wealth of media and the current climate of accounting, auditing and general business failure, the use of the media and materials in the public domain provide an opportunity to use real-life events to try and engage the auditing undergraduate and professional students in their current studies but also in preparation for professional life. Thus, media can be used to bridge the gap between theory and practice. The media is the proxy in circumstance in which client confidentiality and professional ethics exclude case studies from the real-world based on actual events. It also addresses Maltby's (2001) concern about case studies synthesized from a variety of real scenarios from audit firms, primarily done in order to disguise them, as they rarely have a 'critical slant' and most certainly do not reflect a normal audit, regardless of its faults. Even if it were legitimate to use actual data and events, it would have to be heavily disguised to ensure professional confidentiality.

Conclusion

Stories of failure are contended to be a useful starting point to experiment with the living case, although there are other rich sources of case materials that need not involve corporate or audit failure. The audit educator's aim is to balance the practical and social aspects of auditing, and this new style of auditing case method aims to address the role of university teachers of auditing and develop the conceptual understanding (QAA, 2001) through experiential learning theory. How might the audit case study be re-engineered to a form that will serve that purpose? Corporate failure stories in the media can help through the ways in which the stories unfold as reported facts emerge and are interpreted by journalists. In effect, the living case aims to bridge audit educators' needs between the categorization of auditing as scientific activity versus a social practice (Maltby, 2001) supported by ELT. In the first instance the aim has been to introduce and give some initial evaluation of such a method and may be further enhanced in the future by some empirical investigation to investigate further embedding and refining this approach. Moreover, by explaining how cases are actually used, it is hoped this paper will encourage experimentation with this case method and further debate on the future methods of audit education, not least how the case method can be used effectively as an effective method of accounting education through a contemporary application.

References

Auditing Practices Board (1994) *The Audit Agenda—Next Steps* (London: APB).

Boyce, G., Williams, S., Kelly, A. and Yee, H. (2001) Fostering deep and elaborative learning and generic (soft) skill development: the strategic use of case studies in accounting education, *Accounting Education: an international journal*, 10(1), pp. 37–60.

Cagle, A. B. and Bacus, M. S. (2006) Case Studies of Ethics Scandals: Effect on Ethical Perceptions of Finance Students, *Journal of Business Ethics*, 64(63), pp. 213–229.

Davies, M. (2000) Using a computerized case study to teach computer auditing: the reasons, the approach and the student response, *Managerial Auditing Journal*, 15(5), pp. 247–252.

Dennis, I. (2003) OK in practice—and theory The experience of using an extended case study in auditing education: a teaching note, *Accounting Education: an international journal*, 12(4), pp. 415–426.

Drake, J. (1999) Instructional Case; the audit of Award Rosette Manufacturers Ltd, *Accounting Education: an international journal*, 8(4), pp. 363–375.

Easton, G. (1992) *Learning from Case Studies* (New York: Prentice Hall).

Gray, I. and Manson, S. (2008) *The Audit Process: ISA Edition; Principles, Practice and Cases* (London: Cengage Learning).

Hassall, T., Lewis, Broadbent, S and J. M. (1998) The use and potential abuse of case studies in accounting education, *Accounting Education: an international journal*, 7(1), pp. 37–48.

Helliar, C., Monk, E., Stevenson, L. and Allison, C. (2007) *The Development of an Audit Learning Package* (Edinburgh: Institute of Chartered Accountants of Scotland).

Helliar, C. V., Monk, E. A. and Stevenson, L. A. (2009) The Development of Trainee Auditors' Skills in Tertiary Education, *International Journal of Auditing*, 13(3), pp. 185–202.

Higson, A. (2003) *Corporate Financial Reporting: Theory and Practice* (London: Sage Publications).

Howieson, B. (2003) Accounting practice in the new millennium: Is accounting education ready to meet the challenge? *The British Accounting Review*, 35(2), pp. 69–203.

Humphrey, C. (1997) Debating Audit Expectations, in: M. Sherer and S. Turley (Eds) *Current Issues in Auditing, 3rd edition*, pp. 3–30 (London: Paul Chapman Publishing).

Humphrey, C., Moizer, P. and Turley, S. (1992) The audit expectations gap in Britain: an empirical investigation, *Accounting and Business Research*, 23(91A), pp. 395–411.

International Accounting Education Standards Board (2009) *Framework for International Education Standards for Professional Accountants* (New York: IFAC).

International Accounting Education Standard Board (2010) *A Consultation Paper for the Revision of International Education Standard 8: Competence Requirements for Audit Professional* (New York: IFAC).

International Federation of Accountants (2008) *International Education Standard 8: Competence Requirements for Audit Professional* (New York: IFAC).

Johnson, E. N., Baird, J., Caster, P., Dilla, W. N., Earley, C. E. and Louwers, T. J. (2003) Challenges to Audit Education for the 21st Century: A Survey of Curricula, Course Content, and Delivery Methods, *Issues in Accounting Education*, 18(3), pp. 241–263.

Kaidonis, M. A. (2004) Teaching and learning critical accounting using media texts as reflexive devices: conditions for transformative action or reinforcing the status quo? *Critical Perspectives on Accounting*, 15(4/5), pp. 667–673.

Koh, H. C. and Woo, E. (1998) The expectation gap in auditing, *Managerial Auditing Journal*, 13(3), pp. 147–154.

Kolb, D. A. (1984) *Experiential Learning: Experience as the Source of Learning and Development* (Englewood Cliffs, NJ, Prentice Hall).

Kolb, A. and Kolb, D. (2005) Learning Styles and Learning Spaces: Enhancing Experiential Learning in Higher Education, *Academy of Management Learning and Education*, 4(2), pp. 193–212.

Kreber, C. (2001) Learning Experientially through Case Studies? A Conceptual Analysis *Teaching in Higher Education*, 6(2), pp. 217–228.

Lucas, U. (2001) Deep and surface approaches to learning within introductory accounting: A phenomenographic study, *Accounting Education: an international journal*, 10(2), pp. 161–184.

Macve, R. (2007) Filling the education gap, *Accountancymagazine.com*, July.

Maltby, J. (1988) *Cases in Auditing* (London: Paul Chapman Publishing).

Maltby, J. (1996) *Cases in Auditing*, 2nd edition (London: Paul Chapman Publishing).

Maltby, J. (2001) Second thoughts about *'Cases in Auditing'*, *Accounting Education: an international journal*, 10(4), pp. 421–428.

Mautz, H. and Sharaf, R. (1961) *The Philosophy of Auditing* (USA: American Accounting Association).

Milne, M. J. and McConnell, P. J. (2001) Problem-based learning: a pedagogy for using case material in accounting education, *Accounting Education: an international journal*, 10(1), pp. 61–82.

Nelson, I. T., Ratliff, R. L., Steinhoff, G. and Mitchell, G. J (2003) Teaching logic to auditing students: can training in logic reduce audit judgement errors, *Journal of Accounting Education*, 21(3), pp. 215–237.

Pentland, B. (1993) Getting Comfortable with the numbers: Auditing and the micro-production of macro-order, *Accounting, Organizations and Society*, 18(7/8), pp. 595–620.

Porter, B. (1993) An empirical study of the audit expectation-performance gap, *Accounting and Business Research*, 24(93), pp. 49–68.

Porter, B. and Gowthorpe, C. (2004) *Audit expectations gap in the UK in 1999 and comparison with the gap in New Zealand in 1989 and 1999* (Edinburgh: Institute of Chartered Accountants of Scotland).

QAA (2001) *The framework for higher education qualifications in England, Wales and Northern Ireland* (U.K.: Quality Assurance Agency for Higher Education).

Ravenscroft, S. P, Rebele, J. E., St Pierre, K., Wilson, R. M. S (2008) The importance of accounting education research, *Journal of Accounting Education*, 26(4), pp. 180–187.

Sherer, M. and Turley, S. (1997) *Current Issues in Auditing*, 3rd edition (London: Paul Chapman Publishing).

Siegel, P. H, Omer, K and Agrawal, S. P. (1997) Video Simulation of an audit: An experiment in experiential learning theory, *Accounting Education: an international journal*, 6(3), pp. 217–230.

Soltani, B. (2007) *Auditing: An International Approach* (U.K.: Pearson Education).

Stewart, J. P and Dougherty, T. W. (1993) Using case studies in teaching accounting: A quasi-experimental study, *Accounting Education: an international journal*, 2(1), pp. 1–10.

Trussell, J. M. and Frazer, J. D. (2008) *Lakeside Company: Case Studies in Auditing*. 11th ed (London: Prentice Hall).

Appendix A

Case History A: A pilot living case

In March 2009, Wrekin, a medium-sized civil engineering company, went into administration in the UK. Owing a substantial amount to the Royal Bank of Scotland facilitated broad media coverage as the support by the government for that bank meant that every tax payer in the UK, theoretically, had an interest in the fallen company. A note to the 2007 accounts referred to 'the gem of Tanzania' which Wrekin had purchased at a fair value of £11m from a shareholder in exchange for interest bearing preference shares. The hunt was on to find the location of this 'valuable asset', however:

Media Report 1

"Note 13 of Wrekin's 2007 accounts states: 'The fair value of the ruby gemstone was determined by a professional valuer at the Instituto Gemmologico Italiano (sic) based in Valenza, Italy, on 31 August 2007.' Loridana Prosperi, a gemmologist at the head office of the Istituto Gemmologico Italiano in Milan, said: 'That is impossible, because we were on holiday on August 31 2007.' She said IGI never assesses the price of gemstones, only the quality—and the Valenza office does not even do that. Ms Prosperi said an £11m ruby would be equivalent to 'The Black Prince', a jewel the size of a chicken's egg in the Queen's crown. She said she would like to get a look at 'The Gem of Tanzania'. She is not the only one".

http://www.ft.com (published: 13 March 2009, 20:55).

Media Report 2
Mystery of £11m ruby on verge of solution
David Teather

"The curious case of the £11m ruby sitting on the books of a bankrupt building firm is about to be solved. Ernst & Young, administrator to Shropshire-based Wrekin Construction, has hired an independent valuer to establish the worth of the gem and expects to have an answer by the end of the week. The mysterious ruby, called variously the Star of Zanzibar and the Gem of Tanzania, was used to strengthen the balance sheet of the construction company, turning net liabilities in March 2007 to £6m net assets by the end of that year. Wrekin paid for the jewel by issuing £11m of preference shares to a company called Tamar Group, owned by David Unwin, who had recently bought Wrekin. The gem might have stayed out of sight were it not for the recession. The business ran out of money last month, the company was put into administration and its assets lined up to be sold off. The company's collapse meant the loss of 600 jobs. Initially, doubts were cast over the existence of the ruby. But a large gem, roughly the size of a cricket ball, was handed over to Ernst & Young on 20 March.

There are still questions about the ruby's value, with experts suggesting they had never seen one worth so much. According to Christie's [a leading auction house], the highest price achieved for a ruby at auction was £2.6m in 2006. According to Wrekin's last full accounts, the fair value of the ruby was 'determined by a professional valuer at the Istituto Gemmologico Italiano, based in Valenze, Italy, on 31 August 2007'. But The Istituto Gemmologico said it had never valued such a gem and it was closed on the date suggested. A laboratory manager said the institute does not assign values to gems, but only analyses them. Unwin's lawyer, Derek Miller, told the *Financial Times* last month that his client had genuinely believed the ruby would be worth £11m if it was cut into smaller gems. He said that Unwin had worked 'tirelessly' since buying Wrekin. Miller yesterday declined to comment further but said his client was 'talking fully' to the administrators. He also suggested that press reports had been littered with errors but declined to point out what they might be.

A spokesman for Ernst & Young said the gem was in safe storage. 'The gem is in the administrator's possession and is in the process of being valued at the moment.' He said the administrator was going through the process of realizing the firm's assets and recently held an auction of its plant and machinery. The *Financial Times* recently tracked down a previous owner of the gem, a South African-born businessman, Trevor Michael Hart-Jones, who said he had bought the gem for £13,000 in 2002. He sold it to the director of a foreign exchange business, Tony Howarth. Unwin bought the ruby in 2006, according to the report, in a deal valuing the gem at £300,000, and the ruby was valued at that price on the balance sheet of Tamar that year. When it filed for administration, Wrekin was due £2m from government contracts but owed more than £3.5m in VAT and tax bills, according to the administrator. It faced a number of winding-up petitions from creditors.

The business was founded in 1960 and remained in family ownership until Unwin took over in 2007."

http://www.guardian.co.uk/business/2009/apr/07/wrekin-construction-ruby (accessed 30 September 2009).

Copyright: Guardian News & Media 2009.

Media Report 3

Wrekin Ruby, the Gem of Tanzania, is put up for auction:

"The semi-mythical 'Wrekin Ruby' that caused the collapse of a Midlands construction firm has been put up for sale. The 10,700-carat, two-kilo ruby—which was valued at £11 million on the accounts of collapsed firm Wrekin Construction—later turned out to be worth a fraction of that when administrators started going through the books. Nearly 500 people lost their jobs at Wrekin Construction after the firm collapsed through lack of funds. It later turned out the inflated valuation of the ruby, known at the Gem of Tanzania, was one of the key reasons behind the collapse. And now administrators at accountants Ernst & Young have put the gem up for sale in an attempt to claw back some of the millions owed to creditors of the collapsed firm. GVA Grimley will be selling the ruby through an auction. They are asking for bids, accompanied by evidence of funding, by December 16.

The advert for the sale of the ruby describes it as a 'loose hexagonal crystal rough with co-existent green/black crystal matrix on its sides, opaque reddish purple in colour'. It weighs 2.14 kilograms and measures approximately 12.3 × 10.8 × 6.5 cm. An advertisement offering the gem for sale will also be placed in a UK Publication, *Rock-nGem Magazine* published in November; and US publication, *Coloured Stone Magazine* published in late October. Administrator Ian Best is handling the case along with colleague Tom Lukic, also of Ernst & Young. He said: 'The joint administrators are seeking to maximize realizations from the Gem of Tanzania for the benefit of the creditors. The Gem will be widely advertised in specialist publications by our agents GVA Grimley Limited and details of the sale have been circulated to all of Wrekin's creditors and appropriate media."

http://www.birminghampost.net/birmingham-business/birmingham-business-news/other-uk-business/2009/09/30/wrekin-ruby-the-gem-of-tanzania-is-put-up-for-auction-65233-248 19913/; (published and accessed 30 September 2009).
Copyright: Birmingham Post 2009.

Appendix B

Case B

Media Report 1 Top McAlpine Chiefs Go After Fraud Costs £50m

http://business.timesonline.co.uk/tol/business/industry_sectors/support_services/ article1692239.ece (accessed 30 September 2009).

Media Report 2

http://www.accountancyage.com (accessed 21 September 2009).

Attesting Adios! Airways' XBRL Filings: A Case Study on Performing Agreed-upon Procedures

STEPHANIE FAREWELL* and ROGER DEBRECENY**

*University of Arkansas at Little Rock, USA, **University of Hawai'i at Mānoa, USA

ABSTRACT   On 30 January 2009, the Securities and Exchange Commission (SEC) released Rule 33–9002. This rule phased in the required use of XBRL. The accuracy of mapping financial statement line items to the US GAAP taxonomy and the tagging of the financial statement facts are of fundamental importance to the accuracy of the XBRL instance document. Currently, there is no requirement for separate assurance on XBRL filings. However, given the significance of the information made available, firms may find it desirable to obtain attestation services. This case provides students with an agreed-upon procedures engagement plan based upon SOP 09–1 'Performing Agreed-Upon Procedures Engagements that Address the Completeness, Accuracy or Consistency of XBRL Tagged Data' released by the Auditing Standards Board in 2009. Students assume the role of an engagement manager and complete an agreed-upon procedures engagement for the quarterly financial statements of Adios! Airways Inc. The case is of general application to an international setting.

Introduction

This case seeks to expose students to the issues associated with conducting attestation on corporate reports in XBRL format. The extensible business reporting language (XBRL) is a computer-based data representation language, which allows information transfers of sophisticated business performance information in a completely unambiguous form. XBRL allows information, such as annual reports, to go from companies and other entities directly to the databases, web sites and computers of stakeholders and information consumers. In the US setting, the 2009 interactive data mandate by the SEC to require filings to its EDGAR information repository in the XBRL format for its corporate and mutual fund filers has changed the face of disclosure (SEC, 2009). XBRL is also being used in a wide variety of other settings around the world (Kernan, 2008). These include financial reporting by listed corporations in several countries including China, Japan and Korea; by small and medium enterprises in several countries including Denmark, Belgium, The Netherlands and Italy, and with corporate tax filings in both the UK and Germany. The broad international adoption of XBRL indicates the importance of XBRL for the accounting curriculum (Debreceny and Farewell, 2010a). This case addresses an important aspect of XBRL, which is the provision of attestation and assurance services on XBRL data.

In fulfilling its regulatory objectives, the SEC acts to enhance the quality of filed information. When introducing the interactive data mandate, the SEC established rules and developed methods to improve the reliability of information in XBRL format which comes to the Commission. The Commission sets out more than 200 rules in Chapter 6 of the EDGAR Filing Manual (EFM) (SEC, 2010). The Commission uses the inherent power of XBRL to validate automatically the XBRL filings against some of the EFM rules. Yet, the SEC can only do so much. The corporations and mutual funds that are filing with the Commission have the primary responsibility for ensuring that they properly meet both the SEC's technical requirements and appropriately reflect the underlying reality of the filer's business operations. Just as financial reporting is inherently complex, so is the process of filing in XBRL. An XBRL report can meet all the technical requirements of the SEC's guidance but still potentially misrepresent the filer's financial results.

Consistent with other world-wide implementations, the SEC does not require that XBRL filings be audited.[1] However, there is a significant role for voluntary attestation services by those filers that want to ensure that their filings are of the highest quality (Plumlee and Plumlee, 2008). In the USA the American Institute of Certified Public Accountants (AICPA) Auditing Standards Board's (ASB) AT section 101 'Attest Engagements' and AT section 201, 'Agreed-Upon Procedures Engagements' provides guidance on voluntary attestation services (ASB 2001a; b). In the international environment, the International Auditing and Assurance Standards Board (IAASB) provides International Standard on Related Services 4400 'Engagements to Perform Agreed-Upon Procedures regarding Financial Information' (IAASB. 2009). Agreed-upon procedures engagements are typically designed to provide management with the benefit of the assurance professional's factual findings based on testing management's assertions. The specific procedures for each engagement are tailored to the needs of the particular client. The scope of the engagement is set out in an agreement between the client and the assurance professional, hence the term 'agreed-upon procedures.' The assurance professional's report in an agreed-upon procedures engagement is restricted to those who have agreed to the procedures; hence, it is not made public.

In 2003, the ASB provided guidance for generic attestation on XBRL instance documents (ASB, 2003). Then at the same time as the SEC introduced their interactive data (XBRL) mandate, the ASB published its Statement of Position (SOP) 09–1 which guides practitioners on the conduct of an attestation engagement 'agreed-upon procedures' on the completeness, accuracy and consistency of XBRL reports, including filings with the SEC (ASB, 2009). The demand from corporations for attestation on the XBRL filings to the SEC resulted in the promulgation of SOP 09–1, which is the foundation for this case. There is similar demand for XBRL-specific agreed-upon procedures in other jurisdictions. For example, in the UK there is a need associated with the mandated tax filings to Her Majesty's Revenue and Customs (HMRC). The Institute of Chartered Accountants in England and Wales (ICAEW) assurance and audit faculty is developing agreed-upon procedures based on SOP 09–1 for the HMRC mandate (Rowden, 2010; XBRL UK, 2010). The IAASB's XBRL task force is also considering a similar, but generic, set of XBRL agreed-upon procedures guidance for a broader audience (Healy, 2010).

Case Objective

This case puts students in the shoes of the engagement manager in an 'agreed-upon procedures' engagement on the quality of the XBRL filing of Adios! Airways Inc., a fictitious US-based airline. The case builds on the SEC's mandate and the ASB's SOP 09–1 to allow students to experience the realities and complexities of attesting to the preparation of XBRL documents. The case is not dependent on an understanding of US GAAP. Any interpretation of the proper application of US GAAP would be a part of the financial statement audit and outside the scope of this case. In the agreed-upon procedures engagement the student will be coming to a statement of findings regarding the XBRL filing.

The design of the case is modular, divided into practical tasks and a research component. There are three modules which faculty can choose to implement.

The first module covers the largely technical aspects of XBRL filing under the SEC's interactive data mandate. This module consists of two tasks. In the first task students review the rendered instance document (Exhibit 9–Exhibit 11). In the second task, students review the taxonomy extensions using the mapping and extension report (Exhibit 15).

The second module addresses the management processes that underpin the preparation of the XBRL report based on client interviews (Exhibit 4) and communications with third-party providers (Exhibit 5).

The third module, which builds on the other two modules, requires students to write their findings in a report to the client, based on the framework provided in Exhibit 16Exhibit 17.

The three questions in the research component require students to examine the institutional setting for the audit of XBRL-tagged financial statements submitted to the SEC; and how companies should develop internal controls on the submission process. They are probably best suited for more advanced classes in auditing and accounting information systems as they require in-depth investigation of auditing concepts and standards and SEC filing requirements.

While this case revolves around XBRL and provides important learning outcomes for students, it has other significant benefits. First, the case provides the student with a taste of the conduct of a complete attestation engagement. An 'agreed-upon procedures' engagement covers a clearly-defined and relatively restricted set of objectives, criteria and evidence. This allows the case to provide students with the experience of conducting an attestation engagement, from the point where the engagement manager reviews the engagement and receives a partially completed set of evidence through to the writing of the report. The engagement manager must then undertake additional evidence collection using the draft XBRL instance document for Adios! Airways Inc. The manager receives the output reports (Exhibit 14, Exhibit 15) from publicly-available software tools to evaluate the quality of the instance document against an agreed-upon set of quality standards. This relatively restricted knowledge domain is a 'sand box' in which students can play. The design of the embedded errors ensures that there is not one 'correct' answer to the case.

Second, the management process component of the case exposes students to process risks and relevant management controls. This management focus reinforces the internal controls aspect of the audit course. It demonstrates the multi-dimensional nature of attestation engagements.

Third, in its full iteration, the case requires higher-order thinking. The mock engagement requires the student practitioner to evaluate the XBRL-production management process at the client, the quality of the instance document, and its relationship to the underlying traditional financial reports. The student engagement practitioners must then write up their report, using the skeleton provided by the ASB in SOP 09–1.[2] This process of evidence assessment and writing up of the report are both examples of higher-order thinking.

While this case leverages the US SEC's interactive data mandate and the ASB's SOP 09–1, it is appropriate for use in an international setting, as shown in the introductory paragraphs. The issues raised in this case are generic (i.e. not dependent on accounting choices made under US GAAP) and will apply to other XBRL implementations around the world. The general guidance for the conduct and reporting on agreed-upon procedures engagements in the US and internationally is similar. The availability of the US GAAP taxonomy and XBRL filings with the SEC make this a particularly apposite setting for a case study.

Case Background

XBRL and the SEC Interactive Data Mandate

The extensible business reporting language (XBRL) provides a foundation for organizations to report their business activities on the Internet. XBRL works by tagging facts in the business reports to a common taxonomy, or dictionary of terms. XBRL means that users of business reports, such as financial statements, can automatically extract key information from the reports without having to undertake expensive analysis and rekeying into databases. XBRL ensures that the meaning of the information is unambiguous. XBRL enhances transparency for investors and other stakeholders. In 2009, the Securities and Exchange Commission mandated that corporations and mutual funds make key filings with the Commission in XBRL.[3] Their interactive data mandate was the most important change in the disclosure environment in the USA in nearly two decades. Over a phase-in period of four years, SEC filers transition their financial filings into XBRL, for corporations and reports on risks, returns and administrative matters for mutual funds. In the initial stage of the interactive data mandate, corporate filers submitted only their financial statements fully tagged in XBRL, with the notes and additional disclosures tagged only at the level of the complete note ('block tagged'). In the second year, the program requires tagging of the full details of the individual facts in the notes and the additional disclosures.

The SEC included a number of rules and processes to ensure the quality of XBRL-tagged filings submitted to the Commission (SEC 2009; 2010). Chapter 6 of the Commission's EDGAR Filing Manual (EFM) has a series of technical reporting rules including many that are specific to XBRL (SEC, 2010). The SEC periodically updates the EFM. The Commission implements some of these rules in software validation—as the corporation files with the SEC, software checks that the report correctly meets those rules that can be checked automatically. There are many rules in the EFM that the SEC cannot validate automatically. Further, even if an instance document meets all the rules of the EFM and validates correctly, it may still be incorrect. If a corporation maps the value of the item 'Cash and Cash Equivalents' in the Statement of Financial Position to the XBRL taxonomy element 'Inventory,' the instance document will validate and meet the rules of the EFM, but still be incorrect.

Demand for Voluntary Attestation on SEC Filings

In the USA and internationally, current auditing standards do not encompass the XBRL version of the financial statements—the audit is limited to the printed report, even if most often these printed reports are transmitted across the Internet in Adobe Acrobat format. The SEC does not require audited XBRL filings (SEC, 2009). However, corporations and mutual funds filing with the SEC may voluntarily seek assurance on their XBRL filings. There are several reasons why filers might seek attestation of their XBRL filings with the SEC. First, there are the risks associated with the very nature of the XBRL reporting process itself. The XBRL filings are some of the most important disclosures that a firm makes. XBRL data is designed to be readily visible and any mistakes will quickly be evident to journalists, investors and financial analysts. It is one thing to have a fact reported on, for example, page 210 of a 300-page document. It is entirely a different situation if investors, analysts, journalists and other stakeholders can quickly pull that fact from the EDGAR XBRL filing. Apart from the responsibility which the corporation has to the SEC for correct reporting, there are considerable reputational risks at stake.

Second, there is the inherent complexity of financial reporting. There are many hundreds of facts in a standard 10-K annual financial report. These include the line items in the financial statements, text in disclosures such as accounting policies, and the numeric and monetary facts in the various notes. When a company first reports in the XBRL format, it must align each of these facts in its existing reports to the taxonomy. Second, financial accounting standards and regulations from several regulatory organizations set out a variety of standard disclosures. These disclosures provide the foundation for many of the tags in the US GAAP taxonomy.[4] There is, however, a good deal of variation between companies, even within the same industry. Often, there will not be an exact match between the financial statements and the taxonomy. The US GAAP taxonomy is a generic dictionary of accounting and business reporting concepts, albeit with many elements for different industries. A corporation is reporting the reality of their particular industry and circumstances. Lining up the corporation's own reports with the US GAAP taxonomy requires knowledge of accounting standards and various regulatory requirements. Accountants must exercise considerable judgment.

Third, there are the issues of reporting the facts in the XBRL report, known as an instance document. Have all the facts been correctly moved from the existing accounting system to the instance document?

Fourth, the US GAAP taxonomy and the SEC interactive data rules allow firms to adjust their XBRL filing to accommodate their industry-level or firm-level differences.[5] They do so by extending the US GAAP taxonomy.[6] These extensions may replace or adjust existing concepts within the taxonomy or introduce new concepts into the taxonomy. Each time a corporation extends the base taxonomy there are several issues. Is there a need to extend the element? Has the correct taxonomy been used? Is the new element included in the correct calculations and presentations?

The fifth issue is the management of the XBRL instance document business process. As with any business process, the firm must employ appropriate controls to mitigate the risks inherent in the process. In some firms, production of the XBRL instance documents takes place in the Controllers' office. In others, the information systems function will produce the instance documents on behalf of the Controller's office. Given the specialist knowledge required to produce XBRL documents, some firms will employ consultants who fully understand the requirements of the XBRL standard and the many rules set out in the SEC's EDGAR filing manual (Garbellotto, 2009a; b; c). Each of these alternatives has its own set of risks which must be subject to appropriate controls. For example, staff in the Controller's office may have excellent knowledge of the business and accounting concepts and reporting requirements but have only very limited understanding of the technical complexities of XBRL. Accountants faced with the detailed rules of the EDGAR filing manual may throw up their hands in desperation.

The Auditing Standards Board's (ASB) attestation standards on 'Agreed-upon procedures' (AT 201) govern the provision of conclusions on the reliability of submission of XBRL documents to the SEC (ASB, 2001b).[7] Given the considerable variation between corporations and the need to fine-tune the engagement, the 'agreed-upon procedures' attestation is the most appropriate form of voluntary assurance. The ASB defines an agreed-upon procedures engagement as one in which an assurance practitioner 'is engaged by a client to issue a report of findings based on specific procedures performed on subject matter. The client engages the practitioner to assist the client in evaluating subject matter or an assertion as a result of a need or needs of the client' (ASB, 2001b). The client and the assurance practitioner

> agree upon the procedures to be performed by the practitioner that the specified parties believe are appropriate. Because the needs of the specified parties may vary widely, the nature, timing, and extent of the agreed upon procedures may vary as well; consequently, the specified parties assume responsibility for the sufficiency of the procedures since they best understand their own needs. (ASB, 2001b, paragraph 3).

Auditing Standards Board Statement of Position 09–1

In 2009, the ASB issued Statement of Position (SOP) 09–1 'Performing Agreed-Upon Procedures Engagements that Address the Completeness, Accuracy or Consistency of XBRL-Tagged Data' (ASB, 2009).[8] SOP 09–1 provides XBRL-specific guidance to assurance practitioners within the context of the Board's AT 201 'Agreed-Upon Procedures Engagements.' SOP 09–1 reiterates the relative responsibilities of the client and the assurance practitioner. The major points of SOP 09–1 are:

Pre-conditions for the attestation engagement. The pre-conditions for conduct of an engagement under SOP 09–1 include the independence of the assurance practitioner, agreement on the assurance criteria and existence of written assertions on completeness, accuracy and consistency of the XBRL report ('instance document').

Agreement on procedures. As might be expected given that attestation on XBRL instance documents is undertaken under the 'Agreed-Upon Procedures Engagements' rubric it is vital that the assurance practitioner and the client do indeed agree on the procedures that the assurance provider will undertake. This agreement must be in writing.

Codifying the engagement. The SOP requires the assurance practitioner and client fully document their understanding of the engagement. This includes an exchange of letters between practitioner and client. The letters between the assurance practitioner (Grouse and Honor LLP) and the client (Adios! Airways Inc.) are made available in the body of the case.

Deciding on the procedures. The SOP notes that practitioner and client have a flexible choice of procedures. The SOP sets out typical procedures and findings in an appendix. This case embeds some of the suggested procedures, suitably adjusted. Importantly, while the SOP does not prescribe the agreed-upon procedures, it does set a floor to the procedures. The SOP notes that 'merely reading the work performed by a third party involved in the preparation of XBRL-tagged data (for example, service provider)' would be an 'inappropriate procedure.'

Report. The SOP sets out the requirements for the report prepared by the practitioner. An agreed-upon procedures engagement requires a more open-ended report than is the case with the relatively standard form of the audit report on the audit of financial statements. There are some standard parts of the report (e.g. list of procedures and identification of subject matter and criteria). The essence of the report is the listing of the agreed-upon procedures and the practitioner's findings.

Attestation on Adios! Airways Inc.'s XBRL Filings with the SEC

It is 21 October 2014. You are the manager in the XBRL practice of Grouse and Honor LLP, of New York. Exhibit 1 summarizes the individuals and their titles. You have very recently taken over responsibility for the 'agreed-upon procedures' engagement for the XBRL filings by Adios! Airways Inc. a fictional company. Your colleague Leroy Defliese, who was in charge of the engagement, has been urgently re-assigned to other engagements.

Adios! Airways Inc. is a US-based airline. The airline services the tourist markets of the Caribbean and Latin America. It is listed on the New York Stock Exchange with the code A!A and is based in Miami, FL. The auditors for Adios! Airways Inc. are Paton and Littleton LLP, headquartered in Chicago.

The first filing by Adios! Airways Inc. (A!A) in XBRL format was in 2011. The new Chair of the Adios! Airways Audit Committee, Ms. Joanne Queenan, has identified the

Adios! Airways
1. Joanne Queenan, Audit Committee Chair
2. Bernie Kester, CFO
3. Paul Spacek, Director of Financial Reporting
4. Lola Braniff, Controller

Grouse and Honor
1. Leroy Defliese, previous Manager of Adios! Airways engagement
2. Robert K. Grouse, Partner, Grouse and Honor
3. Martina Trueblood, Audit Senior
4. You, Manager, XBRL practice

Pretty Poodle
1. Danielle Beresford, Vice-President Customer Support

Paton and Littleton LLP
Adios! Airways financial statement auditors

Exhibit 1. Individuals and titles

Client: **Adios! Airways Inc.**

Contact:

Period: **Quarter ended 30 September 2014**

Manager:

Contents:

Signed Engagement Letter with Attachment	(Exhibit 3)	✓
Client Representation Letter with Attachment	(Exhibit 4)	✓
Engagement Plan (varies based on assigned tasks)		✓
Planned Procedures:		
Interview	(Exhibit 5)	✓
Confirm relationship with Pretty Poodle	(Exhibit 6)	✓
Obtain copy of 10-Q	(Exhibit 7 - Exhibit 9)	✓
Obtain rendered XBRL files	(Exhibit 10 - Exhibit 14)	✓
Obtain validation report	(Exhibit 15)	✓
Obtain mapping and extension report	(Exhibit 16)	✓
Report of Findings	(Exhibit 17)	___

Exhibit 2. Engagement file cover sheet

SEC XBRL filings as a key risk. In an effort to manage this risk the committee required the CFO, Bernie Kester, to engage an assurance practitioner to review all aspects of the XBRL filings. The Committee has instructed that the engagement be with a practitioner other than the independent auditors to mitigate any potential appearance of the lack of independence. Mr Kester reached out to other CFOs for assistance and identified Grouse and Honor LLP of New York, NY as the assurance provider. Grouse and Honor (G&H) is a relatively small firm that specializes in XBRL, SEC filings and information technology. Most of the staff in G&H hold both the CPA (Certified Public Accountant) and CISA (Certified Information Systems Auditor) qualifications.

    After discussion between A!A finance staff and Robert Grouse, partner of Grouse and Honor LLP, the two parties agreed upon a set of procedures. These procedures are set out in the Engagement Letter (see Exhibit 3) from G&H to A!A.

    When you pick up the engagement from Leroy Defliese, he passes you the engagement file. The engagement file contains all of the documents necessary to complete the engagement. The second document in the file is the Client Representation Letter with Attachment (Exhibit 4). This is followed by (Exhibit 5) the notes of an interview that Martina Trueblood, Senior at G&H conducted with Paul Spacek, Director of Financial Reporting in the A!A Controllers' Office. The interview covers the management processes of the XBRL instance document production process. Early in the engagement, it became clear that A!A outsourced the production of the XBRL documents to a Baton Rouge, LA service provider, Pretty Poodle LLC. Management of the outsourcing process is the focus of the interview.

Martina attempted several times to talk with Danielle Beresford, Vice-President of Customer Support at Pretty Poodle LLC. Martina left half a dozen messages on Danielle's voice mail. Finally, Martina put a number of questions to Danielle by email. Her email response is included as Exhibit 6. Yesterday, you received the financial statements in the 10-Q (Exhibit 7–Figure 9) and the XBRL instance document. You ran the instance document through specialist G&H software to obtain the XBRL rendered financial statements (Exhibit 10–Exhibit 12), the document information (Exhibit 13), the entity information (Exhibit 14), the validation report (Exhibit 15), and mapping and extension report (Exhibit 16).

Engagement Tasks

Your instructor will assign which of the following four tasks you are to complete.

Task 1—Review the Instance Document

Assess the instance document. Complete the procedures MA4, MA5, MA6 and MA7.

Task 2—Review the Extensions

Assess the appropriateness of extensions (procedure MA3).

Task 3—Assess the Production Process

Assess the management process and management controls over the generation of XBRL Instance Documents.

Task 4—Report

Complete the report to Adios! Airways Inc. Exhibit 16 is a skeleton of the final report. The majority of work on the report is writing up your findings on each of the procedures.

Research and Review Questions

Your instructor will specify which of the following research and review questions you are to complete.

1. Should the XBRL filing with the SEC be considered part of the financial statements and subjected to audit? What are some of the advantages and disadvantages of requiring an audit of the XBRL filing?

GROUSE and HONOR

1650, 7thAvenue
New York, NY10031
15 August 2014

Ms. JW Queenan
Chair
Audit Committee
Adios! Airways Inc.
6200 NW 18th Street
Miami, FL 33101

Dear Ms. Queenan:

This letter is to confirm our understanding of the terms and objectives of our engagement to perform certain agreed-upon procedures in assisting the Audit Committee and management of Adios! Airways Inc. to evaluate the completeness, accuracy and consistency of Adios! Airways Inc. of its XBRL filing related to the "Form 10-Q -- Quarterly report" for the quarter ended 30 September 2014. This letter also sets out the nature and limitations of the services we will provide.

We will perform the procedures set out in the Attachment to this letter. Your Audit Committee agreed to these procedures. Our responsibility is to carry out these procedures and report our findings. We will conduct our engagement in accordance with the attestation standards of the American Institute of Certified Public Accountants. The sufficiency of these procedures is solely the responsibility of the Audit Committee and management of Adios! Airways Inc. We make no representation regarding the sufficiency of the procedures for the requested report, or for any other purpose.

Management is responsible for the completeness, accuracy and consistency of the XBRL-tagged data and the information you provide to us. Management is also responsible for the design, implementation, effectiveness and monitoring of controls over the preparation and submission of Adios! Airways Inc.'s XBRL-tagged data. We make no representation regarding the completeness or accuracy of information provided to us during the engagement.

Our engagement to perform agreed-upon procedures is substantially less than an examination. The objective of an examination is the expression of a statement of findings on management's assertions regarding the XBRL-tagged data. As a result, our report under this engagement, will not express an opinion or any other form of assurance thereon.

At the completion of the agreed-upon procedures, we will issue a report which will describe the nature of the agreed-upon procedures, the procedures we carried out and our findings.

Distribution and use of our agreed-upon procedures report is restricted to the Audit Committee and management of Adios! Airways Inc.

The billing for this engagement will be in line with our normal commercial practices. Successful completion of this engagement is dependent on our access to relevant staff, contractors and advisors to Adios! Airways Inc. We expect management to facilitate access to these resources.

If this letter correctly expresses your understanding of this engagement, please sign the enclosed copy where indicated and return to us.

Sincerely,

R K Grouse

R.K. Grouse (Partner)
Attachment (1)

Agreed and accepted for and on behalf of Adios! Airways Inc.
J.W. Queenan, Chair
Audit Committee
Adios! Airways Inc.

Exhibit 3. Engagement letter

Attachment to Client Engagement Letter

Agreed-upon Procedures for Review of XBRL-tagged 10-K Annual Report for the Quarter ended 30 September 2014

Adios! Airways Inc.

We will conduct the following agreed-upon procedures as part of our review of the XBRL-tagged 10-Q Annual Report for the quarter ended 30 September 2014, as mandated by the Securities and Exchange Commission under Rule 33-9002. These agreed-upon procedures are limited solely to the core financial statements, viz: Statement of Financial Position, Statement of Operations, and Statement of Cash Flows.

Management Assertion MA1: The management process for design and preparation of the XBRL filings is robust, reliable, documented, approved at appropriate levels and incorporates apposite controls.

Attestation Procedure: We will attest to the management processes using best practices in information management relevant to the XBRL domain.

Management Assertion MA2: We have adopted the appropriate base taxonomies under the relevant SEC rule.

Attestation Procedure: We will attest to management's choice of base taxonomies.

Management Assertion MA3: We have made the correct judgments in our development of extension taxonomies to the base taxonomies. We have created extensions to the US GAAP taxonomy only when there is no appropriate element in the US GAAP taxonomy.

Attestation Procedure: We will assess the appropriateness of management's development of extension taxonomies.

Management Assertion MA4: The XBRL instance document of the financial statements for the quarter ended 30 September 2014 is consistently, accurately and correctly tagged, with the appropriate use of metadata.

Attestation Procedure: We will attest to the accuracy, consistency and correctness of XBRL tagging of the financial statements.

Management Assertion MA5: The calculations embedded in the instance document correctly represent the underlying financial data.

Attestation Procedure: We will attest to the accuracy of the calculation rollup. We will attest to the relationship of the Adios! Airways calculation linkbase to the US GAAP taxonomy linkbase.

Management Assertion MA6: The labels in the instance document accurately reflect the terms used in the quarterly financial statements in the 10-Q.

Attestation Procedure: We will compare the labels in the instance document with the financial statements in the 10-Q.

Management Assertion MA7: The presentation of elements in the instance document accurately reflects the layout of the quarterly financial statements in the 10-Q.

Attestation Procedure: We will compare the presentation of elements in the instance document with the financial statements in the 10-Q.

The criteria we will use for this engagement include, but are not limited to:

- Compliance with relevant XML and XBRL specifications and other technical standards and guidance.
- Compliance with the relevant XBRL US GAAP taxonomy.
- Compliance with the XBRL US Preparers Guide and the Securities and Exchange Commission's EDGAR filing manual.

We will apply appropriate materiality to our investigations and findings.

Exhibit 3. Continued

2. How can effective internal controls mitigate the risks inherent in the use of XBRL? Recommend a minimum of five 'best practice' internal controls which companies should follow in the production of its XBRL files.
3. Compare the implementation of XBRL by the US SEC to an international implementation of XBRL, as specified by your instructor.

Adios! Airlines Inc.

6200 NW 18th Street
Miami, FL 33101
20 October 2014

Mr. RK Grouse,
Grouse and Honor LLP
1650, 7th Avenue
New York, NY 10031
Dear Mr. Grouse,
We provide this letter in connection with performance of agreed-upon procedures to
assist the Audit Committee and Management of Adios! Airways Inc. in the evaluation of
the completeness, accuracy and consistency of our XBRL instance document which
represents the SEC Filing 10-Q for the quarter ended 30 September 2014. We confirm
that we are responsible for the XBRL instance document and our assertions on those
statements. Our assertions are shown in Attachment 1. I confirm that we are responsible
for the selection of criteria and procedures. These criteria and procedures are appropriate
for the needs of the Audit Committee and Management of Adios! Airways Inc.
We confirm the following representations which we made to you:

- We have disclosed all relevant matters related to the tagging of the financial
  statements in XBRL and the management of the tagging process.
- We attach the financial statements within the 10-Q Quarterly report.
- We include the XBRL instance document on disc.
- All of the data in the XBRL instance document has been accurately, correctly and
  consistently tagged in relation to the current XBRL US GAAP taxonomy.
- We have made appropriate extensions to the US GAAP taxonomy. I enclose a list
  of the extensions made to the current XBRL US GAAP taxonomy (see
  Attachment 2).
- We have received no communication from the SEC in respect of our previous
  XBRL filings.
- We have no knowledge of fraud or suspected fraud affecting the preparation of
  our XBRL instance document.

Sincerely,

Bernie Kester

Bernie Kester
Chief Financial Officer,

Attachments (2)

Client Representation Letter—Attachment 1
Adios! Airways Assertions in respect of the XBRL Instance Document to represent the
10-Q Report for the Quarter ended 30 September 2014
Management Assertion MA1: The management process for design and preparation of the
XBRL filings is robust, reliable, documented, approved at appropriate levels and
incorporates apposite controls.
Management Assertion MA2: We have adopted the appropriate base taxonomies under
the relevant SEC rule.
Management Assertion MA3: We have made the correct judgments in our development
of extension taxonomies to the base taxonomies. We have created extensions to the US
GAAP taxonomy only when there is no appropriate element in the US GAAP taxonomy.
Management Assertion MA4: The XBRL instance document of the financial statements
for the quarter ended 30 September 2014 is consistently, accurately and correctly tagged,
with the appropriate use of metadata.
Management Assertion MA5: The calculations embedded in the instance document
correctly represent the underlying financial data. They align appropriately with the
calculation rollup in the US GAAP XBRL taxonomy.
Management Assertion MA6: The labels in the instance document accurately reflect the
terms used in the quarterly financial statements in the 10-Q.

Exhibit 4. Representation letter

Management Assertion MA7: The presentation of elements in the instance document accurately reflects the layout of the quarterly financial statements in the 10-Q.

Client Representation Letter—Attachment 2

Adios! Airways Extension Elements

Income Statement

No extensions

Statement of Financial Position

1. Flight Equipment
2. Purchase Deposits for Flight Equipment
3. Total Other Assets
4. Air Traffic Liability

Statement of Cash Flows

1. Sale-Leaseback Transactions

Exhibit 4. continued

Interviewee: Paul Spacek (PS), Director of Financial Reporting, Controllers' Office, Adios! Airways Inc.

Interviewer: Martina Trueblood, Senior, Grouse and Honor LLP, New York Office (GH).

Date: 10 October 2014

Advised PS that the subject of the interview was to review the processes for preparation of the quarterly XBRL filings.

GH: Describe the process for preparation of the XBRL filings.

PS: We have a moderately sophisticated process, based on a set of Excel spreadsheets that we have built up over the years, for the preparation of the financial statements and the notes. However, we know nothing about XBRL and we really don't need to know. We're accountants and not computer scientists, with all these funny, techie terms like linknode, instant document, taxanatomy and so on. So, we contract out the preparation of the XBRL filings Pretty Poodle LLC in Baton Rouge, LA.

GH: First, let's make sure we are speaking the same language—I think you actually mean linkbase, instance document and taxonomy. It may not seem important but you want to make sure when you are talking to Pretty Poodle that you understand what they are telling you. The linkbases are the calculation, presentation, label, definition and reference files that document the semantic meanings in the taxonomy. The taxonomy likely refers to either the US GAAP taxonomy or the Adios! Airways Inc. extension taxonomy. And the instance document contains the Adios! Airways financial statement facts for a particular filing, for example, the 10-Q covered by this engagement.

PS: Okay, whatever.

GH: Who is Pretty Poodle? It sounds like a dog grooming service!

PS: Well you know these IT people. They all like these funny names. But Pretty Poodle is a specialist XBRL consulting practice. They are all ex-Louisiana State accounting and computing nerds.

GH: Why do you outsource?

PS: We are a relatively small company, with only a small head-office controllers' team. Our IT team is also relatively small. They say that they have no XML or XBRL expertise and don't see that it is worthwhile to develop that expertise just for our needs.

GH: What contractual arrangements do you have with Pretty Poodle LLC.?

PS: We have a standard consulting contract with them. They bill us on the hours that they spend.

GH: Do you have any other formal agreement with Pretty Poodle?

PS: Such as?

GH: For example, a non-disclosure agreement, a formal quality review process, or a supplier quality assessment.

PS: Well, this is a very small contract. It is not as though we are contracting the whole of our accounting or the financial close. All of those things would be just overkill. We only use Pretty Poodle a few times a year.

GH: This is the first time that Adios! Airways has had to file in XBRL. How did you decide on the first time adoption of XBRL?

PS: Well, we know nothing about XBRL. It is all like Klingon or high school calculus to us. Like I said, Pretty Poodle are specialists in this—XML and XBRL is all that they

Exhibit 5. Notes of interview with Paul Spacek, director of financial reporting, controllers' office.

do. So, we relied on them. The only thing that we told them when they came across to Miami for their first meeting was that the 10-Q and the 10-K were sacrosanct. My boss [Lola Braniff, Controller of Adios! Airways] had my job before she became the Controller. She's really committed to what she had done previously and didn't want a single thing changed. Besides, she thinks that the Board and shareholders and analysts and the like will get unsettled if they see changes from what we did previously. And that is what we said to Pretty Poodle. Don't change *anything*.

GH: So how did they do go about the first-time adoption?

PS: Well, we gave them a copy of an earlier 10-Q and said for them to use that as a base. Like I said, things don't change very much from quarter to quarter or year to year.

GH: And then?

PS: Well they sent a spreadsheet, with the mapping of the financial statements to the XBRL.

GH: Sorry, "the XBRL"?

PS: You know, that taxanatomy and the stuff they added for us.

GH: Oh, OK. I think you mean the US GAAP taxonomy And what happened to the mapping?

PS: Well, I reviewed it and gave my feedback.

GH: How did you review it?

PS: I checked a couple of items to see that they looked reasonable.

GH: What was in the spreadsheet?

PS: Well, it is some time ago that I reviewed it and we're really busy running the business. But, as I recall, there was a listing of the different items in the financial statements, the name in the SEC's chart of accounts. And where a new name in the chart of accounts was necessary, there was a new name and description.

GH: Chart of accounts? I'm sorry, I don't understand. I thought you said that the preparation by Pretty Poodle was based on the Excel spreadsheet financial statements?

PS: Like I said before, the US GAAP taxanatomy.

GH: Was there a formal review and sign-off process of the spreadsheet.

PS: Like I said, these guys are the experts. They're dealing with lots of other companies. When we awarded the contract, we asked them if they had any client whose XBRL filings were criticized or checked by the SEC and they're clean. We have to be guided by the experts.

GH: Did you have a formal report to the Controller or CFO?

PS: I reported to the Controller on a regular basis. The CFO has got much more important fish to fry than XBRL.

GH: But no formal sign-off?

PS: No.

GH: How did you communicate acceptance of the mapping to Pretty Poodle?

PS: I sent them an email.

GH: Could you supply a copy of the spreadsheet?

PS: Oh goodness, I get a lot of these things from different suppliers and partners and auditors and such. I don't keep every single email or spreadsheet.

GH: What happens if there is a change from the original mapping?

PS: I expect Pretty Poodle to keep me in the loop on any change from their original mappings.

GH: Were there any changes this quarter?

PS: Not that I recall. But like I said, this is a busy office.

Exhibit 5. continued

The following is the text in an email from Danielle Beresford, VP, Customer Support, Pretty Poodle Inc., in reply to an email from Martina Trueblood, Senior, Grouse and Honor LLP, New York Office.

This is in response to your request for information concerning our XBRL practice and specifically our client Adios! Airways, Inc. Our practice is limited to XBRL, the mapping and tagging of financial statements. All clients are subject to the same standard client agreement. In accordance with our standard client agreement we provide no assurance to the accuracy of the tagging or mapping because we are not privy to our client's internal accounting processes. Our process has four-steps:

(1) The client provides us with an Excel workbook containing their financial statements (i.e. 10-Q, 10-K, etc.) and a statement of their willingness to alter the presentation of the financial statement to fit the existing US GAAP taxonomy.

(2) Based on the unwillingness of the client to make any changes to their financial statements, our policy is to map the line items to the taxonomy if it is clear that there is a match. If there is not a clear match we recommend a US GAAP taxonomy element or create an extension on the mapping worksheet we return to the client for sign-off.

(3) The client reviews and signs-off on the mapping.

(4) We prepare the instance document based on the client's agreement to the mapping. The completed XBRL file is returned to the client for them to examine, validate and file as they see fit.

Please don't hesitate to follow-up if you have any other questions I can answer.

Exhibit 6. Extract of e-mail reply from Danielle Beresford, VP, Customer Support, Pretty Poodle LLC

Case Learning Objectives and Implementation Guidance

Learning Objectives

The use of XBRL for financial reporting to the SEC and other regulators world-wide represents a major change in the disclosure environment. XBRL increases the transparency of financial information. Given the increase in transparency, firms are likely to identify this as an area of reporting risk. To manage that risk the audit committee may seek attestation services on the XBRL filing and the process surrounding the production of the XBRL filing (Boritz and No 2009; Plumlee and Plumlee, 2008). The case is designed to encompass several key learning points:

1. the underlying issues that might be encountered in XBRL filings;
2. the output reports of publicly available validation tools;
3. agreed-upon procedures engagements; and
4. SOP 09–1 for the conduct of XBRL engagements.

Passenger revenues—mainline	6014
Passenger revenues—regional affiliates	692
Total passenger revenue	$6707
Cargo revenues	279
Other operating revenues[a]	445
Total operating revenues	$7431
Wages, salaries and benefits expense	$2439
Contract carrier arrangements—regional affiliates	777
Aircraft fuel expense	1166
Depreciation and amortization	534
Other rentals and landing fees	473
Maintenance, materials and repairs expense	416
Aircraft rental expense	340
Commissions to agents	334
Food service expense	328
Other operating expenses	1165
Asset impairment charge, other	426
Total operating expenses	$8397
Operating income (loss)	(966)
Interest income	95
Interest expense	182
Gain on sale of other investments	39
Miscellaneous-net	3
Total other income (expense)	$(45)
Earnings (loss) from continuing operations	$(1011)
Income tax provision (benefit)	−377
Net earnings (loss)	$(634)
Weighted average shares outstanding—basic	22,694,100
Weighted average shares outstanding—diluted	23,781,500
Shares outstanding	20,050,000
Net earnings (loss) per share—basic	(27.94)
Net earnings (loss) per share—diluted	(26.66)

[a]Includes baggage fees, preferred seating charges, and live customer service booking fees

Exhibit 7. Income statement, extracted from 10-Q filing (in millions of dollars)

The skills developed in this case are transferable to other agreed-upon procedures engagements. However, the multi-dimensional skill set extends beyond agreed-upon procedures engagements. The case adds to the limited but growing stock of teaching cases on IT auditing and assurance. Many of the students in the classes who will use this case will become general auditors. These auditors have difficulty with IT and in adapting to new technologies including XBRL (Curtis, Jenkins, Bedard and Deis, 2009). The case enhances higher-order thinking skills through the evaluation of evidence (Hassall and Milne, 2004; Wynn-Williams, Whiting and Adler, 2008). The ability to evaluate evidence is important in accounting education, generically and to all assurance engagements, specifically. The case enhances IT literacy skills, with its detailed consideration of the implications for accounting of an important Web-based technology (Jackson and Durkee 2008). Further, communication skills are developed by writing up the results of findings to the client's audit committee.

Learner Proficiencies

The requisite skills for learners to use this case are:

1. an understanding of the agreed-upon procedures engagement; and

Cash and cash equivalents	1284
Short-term investments, net	4289
Receivables, net	2026
Deferred income tax assets	1248
Other current assets	767
Total current assets	9614
Flight equipment	19,721
Purchase deposits for flight equipment	1233
Other equipment and property	2957
Equipment under capital lease-flight equipment	2345
Equipment and property, net	26,256
Route acquisition costs	1904
Goodwill	1911
Other assets	5713
Total other assets	9529
Total assets	$45,399
Accounts payable	2478
Accrued salaries and wages	986
Accrued liabilities	1975
Air traffic liability	4084
Payable to affiliates, net	97
Current maturities of long-term debt	573
Current obligations under capital leases	280
Total current liabilities	10,473
Long-term debt, less current maturities	9653
Obligations under capital leases, less current maturities	2063
Deferred income tax liability	2166
Postretirement benefits	4521
Other liabilities and deferred credits	7947
Total liabilities	36,824
Ordinary capital	2005
Additional paid-in capital ordinary capital	2408
Accumulated other comprehensive income (loss)	−215
Retained earnings	4377
Total stockholders' equity	8575
Total liabilities and stockholders' equity	$45,399

Exhibit 8. Statement of financial position, extracted from 10-Q filing (in millions of dollars)

2. an understanding of the mapping and tagging process of financial statement line items to a particular XBRL taxonomy.

The requisite skills may have been covered in previous courses. If the requisite skills have not been covered in previous courses, it will be necessary for the students to complete other XBRL assignments or case studies to develop those skills (e.g. Debreceny and Farewell, 2010b; White, 2009; SEC, 2010).

Case Materials

The case materials provide students with background on XBRL and the SEC interactive data mandate. The instructor controls the attestation program through the specific tasks assigned. The case materials include all engagement materials necessary to complete the engagement. The materials include the engagement file cover sheet; signed engagement letter with attachments; client representation letter with attachments; client interview; third-party communications; rendered XBRL files; mapping and extension

Net earnings (loss)	(634)
Depreciation	426
Amortization	107
Provision for asset impairment	425
Deferred income taxes	(282)
Gain on sale of other investments	(39)
Change in receivables	43
Change in inventories	(20)
Change in accounts payable and accrued liabilities	154
Change in air traffic liability	(117)
Other change in assets and liabilities, net	85
Net cash from operating activities	148
Capital expenditures	(1377)
Net (increase) decrease in short-term investments	(555)
Acquisition of Auf Wiedersehen Air	(1261)
Proceeds from sale of equipment and property	(157)
Proceeds from sale of other investments	8
Other cash flow from investing activities	8
Net cash from investing activities	(3022)
Proceeds from issuance of long-term debt	2860
Proceeds from short-term line of credit	836
Sale-leaseback transactions	598
Funds transferred to affiliates	(105)
Payments of long-term debt and capital lease obligations	(178)
Net cash from financing activities	4011
Net increase (decrease) in cash	1137
Cash at beginning of period	146
Cash at end of period	1283

Exhibit 9. Statement of cash flow, extracted from 10-Q filing (in millions of dollars)

reports; and validation reports. All engagement materials are available as an electronic file from the authors to facilitate distribution.

Case Administration

We estimate that reviewing the materials, performing the agreed-upon procedures and writing up the results of findings would take students 10–12 h as indicated on the engagement time budget. Depending on the role of the case and the time available in your course, it is possible to assign the three modules individually or collectively. The three modules are:

1. complete tasks 1 and 2, reviewing the instance document and extension taxonomy;
2. evaluate the internal controls surrounding the XBRL production process; and
3. writing up the results of findings.

For example, the modules could be assigned in the following configurations:

1. module 1;
2. module 2;
3. modules 1 and 3; and
4. modules 1, 2 and 3.

The case is intended to be completed as an individual assignment, but it could be assigned to groups.

Statement of Income (Including Gross Margin) (USD $) In Millions, except Share data	3 Months Ended Sep. 30, 2014
Operating Income (Loss) [Abstract]	
Total Passenger Revenue	$ 6,706
Cargo Revenue	279
Other Operating Revenues	445
Total Operating Revenues	7,431
Affiliate Costs	776
Fuel Costs	1,166
Depreciation and Amortization	534
Aircraft Rental and Landing Fees	812
Maintenance, Materials, and Repairs Expense	416
Commissions to Agents	334
Food Sevice Expense	328
Other Operating Expenses	1,165
Asset Impairment Charge, Other	426
Wages, Salaries, and Benefits Expense	2,439
Total Operating Expenses	8,397
Operating Income (Loss)	(966)
Nonoperating Income (Expense) [Abstract]	
Interest Income	95
Interest Expense	182
Gain on Sale of Other Investments	39
Miscellaneous Net	3
Total Other Income (Expense)	(45)
Income (Loss) from Continuing Operations before Equity Method Investments, Income Taxes, Extraordinary Items, Cumulative Effects of Changes in Accounting Principles, Noncontrolling Interest	(1,011)
Income Tax Expense (Benefit) [Abstract]	
Income Tax Provision (Benefit)	(377)
Net Earnings (Loss)	$ (634)
Earnings Per Share, Basic [Abstract]	
Earnings Per Share, Basic	(27.93678)
Earnings Per Share, Basic, Other Disclosures [Abstract]	
Weighted Average Shares Outstanding - Basic	22,694,100
Earnings Per Share, Diluted [Abstract]	
Earnings Per Share, Diluted	(26.65938)
Earnings Per Share, Diluted, Other Disclosures [Abstract]	
Weighted Average Shares Outstanding - Diluted	23,781,500
Shares Outstanding	20,050,000

Exhibit 10. XBRL rendered income statement

Statement of Financial Position, Classified (USD $) In Millions	Sep. 30, 2014
Cash and Cash Equivalents, at Carrying Value [Abstract]	
Cash	$ 1,284
Short-term Investments [Abstract]	
Short-term Investments, Net	4,289
Receivables, Net, Current [Abstract]	
Receivables, Net	2,026
Deferred Income Tax Assets	1,248
Other Current Assets	767
Total Current Assets	9,614
Flight Equipment	19,721
Purchase Deposits for Flight Equipment	1,233
Other Equipment and Property	2,957
Capital Leased Assets, Gross, Total	2,345
Equipment and Property Net	26,256
Route Acquisition Costs	1,904
Goodwill	1,911
Other Assets	5,713
Total Other Assets	9,529
Assets, Total	45,399
Liabilities, Current [Abstract]	
Accounts Payable	2,478
Accrued Salaries and Wages	986
Accrued Liabilities	1,975
Air Traffic Liability	4,084
Payable to Affiliates, Net	97
Current Maturities of Long-term Debt	573
Current Obligations Under Capital Leases	280
Total Current Liabilities	10,473
Long-term Debt, Excluding Current Maturities [Abstract]	
Long-term Debt, Less Current Maturities	9,653
Capital Lease Obligations, Noncurrent	2,063
Deferred Income Tax Liability	2,166
Postretirement Benefits	4,521
Other Liabilities and Deferred Credits	7,947
Total Liabilities	36,824
Ordinary Capital	2,005
Additional Paid in Capital Ordinary Capital	2,408
Accumulated Other Comprehensive Income (Loss)	(215)
Retained Earnings	4,377
Stockholders' Equity	8,575
Total Liabilities and Stockholders' Equity	$ 45,399

Exhibit 11. XBRL rendered statement of financial position

Statement of Cash Flows (USD $) In Millions	3 Months Ended Sep. 30, 2014
Net Cash Provided by (Used in) Operating Activities [Abstract]	
Net Earnings (Loss)	$ (634)
Depreciation	426
Amortization	107
Provision for asset impairment	425
Deferred Income Taxes	(282)
Gain on Sale of Other Investments	(39)
Change in Receivables	43
Change in Inventories	(20)
Change in Accounts Payable and Accrued Liabilities	154
Change in Air Traffic Liability	(117)
Other Change in Assets and Liabilities, Net	85
Net Cash Provided by (Used in) Operating Activities	148
Net Cash Provided by (Used in) Investing Activities [Abstract]	
Payments to Acquire Property, Plant, and Equipment	1,377
Proceeds from Sale of Property, Plant, and Equipment	156
Net (Increase) Decrease in Short-Term Investments	(555)
Proceeds from Sale of Other Investments	8
Payments to Acquire Businesses, Net of Cash Acquired	1,261
Other Cash Flow From Investing Activities	(8)
Net Cash Provided by (Used in) Investing Activities	(3,022)
Net Cash Provided by (Used in) Financing Activities [Abstract]	
Proceeds from Issuance of Long-term Debt	2,860
Proceeds from Short-Term Line of Credit	836
Sale-Leaseback Transactions	598
Funds Transferred to Affiliates	(105)
Payments of Long-term Debt and Capital Lease Obligations	178
Net Cash Provided by (Used in) Financing Activities, Total	4,011
Cash and Cash Equivalents, Period Increase (Decrease)	$ 1,137

Exhibit 12. XBRL rendered statement of cash flows

Document Information	3Months Ended
	Sep. 30, 2014
Document Information [Line Items]	
Document Type	10-Q
Amendment Flag	false
Document Period End Date	2014-09-30

Exhibit 13. XBRL rendered document information

Entity Information (USD $)	3Months Ended
	Sep. 30, 2014
Entity Information [Line Items]	
Entity Registrant Name	Adios Airways, Inc.
Entity Central Index Key	0000123456
Current Fiscal Year End Date	--12-31
Entity Well-known Seasoned Issuer	Yes
Entity Voluntary Filers	No
Entity Current Reporting Status	Yes
Entity Filer Category	Large Accelerated Filer
Entity Public Float	$ 153,276,142
Entity Listings [Line Items]	
Entity Common Stock, Shares Outstanding	20,050,000

Exhibit 14. XBRL rendered entity information

Experiential Use

This case is currently a component of workshops for faculty and has been used in CPE training for accounting professionals. Discussions with faculty and accounting professionals following these workshops indicated that the attestation case solidified their understanding of the impact of mapping and tagging choices on the instance document.

In an academic setting, the case can be used in Auditing or Advanced Auditing. In the Auditing courses, this case would be covered in the course modules on evidence collection and assessment. The case could also be used in Accounting Information Systems or Advanced Accounting Information Systems if the students have sufficient prior exposure to audit concepts.

Conclusion

In this teaching case, students assume the role of engagement manager for an agreed-upon procedures engagement for the fictitious airline Adios! Airways Inc. The students will encounter errors and warnings similar to those that will be encountered by real-world filers as they comply with the SEC's mandate for interactive data. The embedded errors were developed as a result of the typical errors and warnings encountered with actual SEC filings and the authors' direct experiences. Since this is not an attestation engagement in which an opinion is expressed, it is helpful to

adios-20140930.xml
Result: Success
Completion Time: 2009-07-21 04:04:08:6590092

INCONSISTENCY: Calculation
Report: *124000-Statement – Statement of Income (Including Gross Margin)* (http://xbrl.us/us-gaap/role/statement/StatementOfIncome)
Total: Operating Expenses (us-gaap:OperatingExpenses)

- Result: Documented value 8397000000 does not match calculated value 8398000000
  Addends:
  - Asset Impairment Charge, Other (us-gaap:AssetImpairmentCharges) value: 426000000
  - Other Operating Expenses (us-gaap:OtherCostAndExpenseOperating) value: 1165000000
  - Food Service Expense (us-gaap:FoodAndBeverageCostOfSales) value: 328000000
  - Commissions to Agents (us-gaap:SalesCommissionsAndFees) value: 334000000
  - Affiliate Costs (us-gaap:AffiliateCosts) value: 777000000
  - Maintenance, Materials, and Repairs Expense (us-gaap: MaintenanceCosts) value: 416000000
  - Aircraft Rental and Landing Fees (us-gaap:AircraftRentalAndLandingFees) value: 813000000
  - Fuel Costs (us-gaap:FuelCosts) value: 1166000000
  - Wages, Salaries, and Benefits Expense (us-gaap:LaborAndRelatedExpense) value: 2439000000
  - Depreciation and Amortization (us-gaap:CostOfServicesDepreciationAndAmortization) value: 534000000

INCONSISTENCY: Calculation
Report: *12400 – Statement – Statement of Income (Including Gross Margin)* (http://xbrl.us/us-gaap/role/statement/StatementOfIncome)
Total: Nonoperating Income (Expense) (us-gaap:NonoperatingIncomeExpense)

- Result: Documented value -45000000 does not match calculated value -84000000
  Addends:
  - Miscellaneous Net (us-gaap:OtherNonoperatingIncome) value: 3000000
  - Interest Income (us-gaap:InvestmentIncomeInterest) value: 95000000
  - Interest Expense (us-gaap:InterestExpense) value; 182000000

INCONSISTENCY: Calculation
Report: *104000 – Statement – Statement of Financial Position, Classified* (http://xbrl.us/us-gaap/role/statement/StatementOfFinancialPositionClassified)
Total Assets, Current (AssetsCurrent)

- Result: Documented value 9,614,320,000 does not match calculated value 4,041,000,000
  Addends:
  - Receivables, Net (ReceivablesNetCurrent) value: 2,026,000,000
  - Deferred Income Tax Assets (DeferredTaxAssetsNetCurrent) value: 1,248,000,000
  - Other Current Assets (OtherAssetsCurrent) value: 767,000,000

INCONSISTENCY: Calculation
Report: *104000 – Statement – Statement of Financial Position, Classified* (http://xbrl.us/us-gaap/role/statement/StatementOfFinancialPositionClassified)
Total Liabilities, (Liabilities)

- Result: Documented value 36,823,920,000 does not match calculated value 10,473,000,000
  Addends:
  - Liabilities, Current (Liabilities Current) value: 10,473,000,000

INCONSISTENCY: Calculation
Report: *104000 – Statement – Statement of Financial Position, Classified* (http://xbrl.us/us-gaap/role/statement/StatementOfFinancialPositionClassified)
Total: Total Other Assets (TotalOtherAssets)

- Result: Documented value 9,528,690,000 does not match calculated value 9,528,000,000
  Addends:
  - Route Acquisition Costs (FiniteLivedContractualRightsGross) value: 1,904,000,000
  - OtherAssets, Noncurrent (OtherAssetsNoncurrent) value: 5,713,000,000
  - Goodwill (Goodwill) value: 1,911,000,000

INCONSISTENCY: Calculation
Report: *152200 – Statement – Statement of Cash Flows* (http://xbrl.us/us-gaap/role/statement/statementOfCashFlowsIndirect)
Total: Net Cash Provided by (Used in) Investing Activities (us-gaap: NetCashProvidedByUsedInInvestingActivities)

- Result: Documented value -3022000000 does not match calculated value -3020000000
  Addends:
  - Payments to Acquire Property, Plant, and Equipment (us-gaap:PaymentsToAcquirePropertyPlantAndEquipment) value: 1377000000
  - Proceeds from Sale of Property, Plant, and Equipment (us-gaap:ProceedsFromSaleOfPropertyPlantAndEquipment) value: 157000000
  - Net (Increase) Decrease in Short-Term Investments (us-gaap:ProceedsFromSaleMaturityAndCollectionsOfInvestments) value:-555000000
  - Payments to Acquire Businesses, Net of Cash Acquired (us-gaap:PaymentsToAcquireBusinessesNetOfCashAcquired) value: 1261000000
  - Other Cash Flow From Investing Activities (us-gaap:PaymentsForProceedsFromOtherInvestingActivities) value: -8000000
  - Proceeds from Sale of Other Investments (us-gaap:ProceedsFromSaleAndMaturityOfOtherInvestments) value: 8000000

INCONSISTENCY: Calculation
Report: *152200 – Statement – Statement of Cash Flows* (http://xbrl.us/us-gaap/role/statement/statementOfCashFlowsIndirect)
Total: Net Cash Provided by (Used in) Operating Activities (us-gaap: NetCashProvidedByUsedInIOperatingActivities)

- Result: Documented value 148000000 does not match calculated value -385000000
  Addends:
  - Net Earnings (Loss) (us-gaap:ProfitLoss) value: -634000000
  - Provision for asset impairment (us-gaap:OtherAssetImpairmentCharges) value: 425000000
  - Deferred Income Taxes (us-gaap:DeferredIncomeTaxExpenseBenefit) value: -282000000
  - Gain on Sale of Other Investments (us-gaap:GainLossOnSaleOfOtherInvestments) value: -39000000
  - Change in Receivables (us-gaap:IncreaseDecreaseInReceivable) value: 43000000
  - Change in Inventories (us-gaap:IncreaseDecreaseInInventories) value: -20000000
  - Change in Accounts Payable and Accrued Liabilities (us-gaap:IncreaseDecreaseInAccountsPayableAndAccruedLiabilities) value:154000000
  - Change in Air Traffic Liability (us-gaap:IncreaseDecreaseInCustomerAdvances) value: -117000000
  - Other Change in Assets and Liabilities, Net (us-gaap:IncreaseDecreaseInOtherOperatingCapitalNet) value: 85000000

Exhibit 15. Validation report

124000 - Statement - Statement of Income (Including Gross Margin)

Element	Period	Period	Unit	Extended?	Scenario(s)	Segment(s)
Label: Total Passenger Revenue ID: us-gaap_PassengerRevenue	7/1/2014 - 9/30/2014	7/1/2013 - 9/30/2013	USD	No		
Definition: A transportation (plane, train, ship) carrier's fare revenue recognized in the period from carrying passengers between destinations.						
Label: Cargo Revenue ID: us-gaap_CargoAndFreightRevenue	7/1/2014 - 9/30/2014	7/1/2013 - 9/30/2013	USD	No		
Definition: Revenue from transporting cargo and freight between locations.						
Label: Other Operating Revenues ID: us-gaap_SalesRevenueServicesNet	7/1/2014 - 9/30/2014	7/1/2013 - 9/30/2013	USD	No		
Definition: Aggregate revenue during the period from services rendered in the normal course of business, after deducting allowances and discounts.						
Label: Total Operating Revenues ID: us-gaap_Revenues	7/1/2014 - 9/30/2014	7/1/2013 - 9/30/2013	USD	No		
Definition: Aggregate revenue recognized during the period (derived from goods sold, services rendered, insurance premiums, or other activities that constitute an entity's earning process). For financial services companies, also includes investment and interest income, and sales and trading gains.						
Label: Affiliate Costs ID: us-gaap_AffiliateCosts	7/1/2014 - 9/30/2014	7/1/2013 - 9/30/2013	USD	No		
Definition: Costs associated with revenues arising from an entity that is an affiliate of the reporting entity by means of direct or indirect ownership.						
Label: Fuel Costs ID: us-gaap_FuelCosts	7/1/2014 - 9/30/2014	7/1/2013 - 9/30/2013	USD	No		
Definition: Fuel costs incurred that are directly related to goods produced and sold and services rendered during the reporting period.						
Label: Depreciation and Amortization ID: us-gaap_CostOfServicesDepreciationAndAmortization	7/1/2014 - 9/30/2014	7/1/2013 - 9/30/2013	USD	No		
Definition: Depreciation of property, plant and equipment directly related to services rendered by an entity during the reporting period.						
Label: Aircraft Rental and Landing Fees ID: us-gaap_AircraftRentalAndLandingFees	7/1/2014 - 9/30/2014	7/1/2013 - 9/30/2013	USD	No		
Definition: Direct costs related to generating revenue from aircraft rental.						
Label: Maintenance, Materials, and Repairs Expense ID: us-gaap_MaintenanceCosts	7/1/2014 - 9/30/2014	7/1/2013 - 9/30/2013	USD	No		
Definition: Costs incurred and are directly related to generating maintenance revenues. Also includes cost of maintenance on client contracts.						
Label: Commissions to Agents ID: us-gaap_SalesCommissionsAndFees	7/1/2014 - 9/30/2014	7/1/2013 - 9/30/2013	USD	No		
Definition: Primarily represents commissions incurred in the period based upon the sale by commissioned employees or third parties of the entity's goods or services, and fees for sales assistance or product enhancements performed by third parties (such as a distributor or value added reseller).						
Label: Food Service Expense ID: us-gaap_FoodAndBeverageCostOfSales	7/1/2014 - 9/30/2014	7/1/2013 - 9/30/2013	USD	No		
Definition: The cost related to generating revenue from the sale of food (prepared and cooked-to-order foodstuffs, as well as snack items) and beverages (bottled or on-tap alcoholic beverages, as well as nonalcoholic beverages like carbonated drinks, juices, energy/sports drinks, water, coffee, and tea).						
Label: Other Operating Expenses ID: us-gaap_OtherCostAndExpenseOperating	7/1/2014 - 9/30/2014	7/1/2013 - 9/30/2013	USD	No		
Definition: The total amount of other operating cost and expense items that are associated with the entity's normal revenue producing operation.						
Label: Asset Impairment Charge, Other ID: us-gaap_AssetImpairmentCharges	7/1/2014 - 9/30/2014	7/1/2013 - 9/30/2013	USD	No		
Definition: The charge against earnings resulting from the aggregate write down of all assets from their carrying value to their fair value.						
Label: Wages, Salaries, and Benefits Expense ID: us-gaap_LaborAndRelatedExpense	7/1/2014 - 9/30/2014	7/1/2013 - 9/30/2013	USD	No		
Definition: The aggregate amount of expenditures for salaries, wages, profit sharing and incentive compensation, and other employee benefits, including share-based compensation, and pension and other postretirement benefit expense.						
Label: Total Operating Expenses ID: us-gaap_OperatingExpenses	7/1/2014 - 9/30/2014	7/1/2013 - 9/30/2013	USD	No		
Definition: Generally recurring costs associated with normal operations except for the portion of these expenses which can be clearly related to production and included in cost of sales or services. Includes selling, general and administrative expense.						
Label: Operating Income (Loss) ID: us-gaap_OperatingIncomeLoss	7/1/2014 - 9/30/2014	7/1/2013 - 9/30/2013	USD	No		
Definition: The net result for the period of deducting operating expenses from operating revenues.						
Label: Interest Income ID: us-gaap_InvestmentIncomeInterest	7/1/2014 - 9/30/2014	7/1/2013 - 9/30/2013	USD	No		
Definition: Income derived from investments in debt securities and on cash and cash equivalents the earnings of which reflect the time value of money or transactions in which the payments are for the use or forbearance of money.						
Label: Interest Expense ID: us-gaap_InterestExpense	7/1/2014 - 9/30/2014	7/1/2013 - 9/30/2013	USD	No		
Definition: The cost of borrowed funds accounted for as interest that was charged against earnings during the period.						
Label: Gain on Sale of Other Investments ID: us-gaap_GainLossOnSaleOfOtherInvestments	7/1/2014 - 9/30/2014	7/1/2013 - 9/30/2013	USD	No		
Definition: The difference between the book value and the sale price of other nonspecific investments. This element is used when other, more specific, elements are not appropriate. This element refers to the gain (loss) included in earnings.						
Label: Miscellaneous Net ID: us-gaap_OtherNonoperatingIncome	7/1/2014 - 9/30/2014		USD	No		
Definition: The aggregate amount of other income amounts resulting from ancillary business-related activities (that is, excluding major activities considered part of the normal operations of the business) also known as other nonoperating income recognized for the period. Such amounts may include: (a) dividends, (b) interest on securities, (c) profits on securities (net of losses), and (d) miscellaneous other income items.						

Exhibit 16. 2013–2014 Mapping and extension report

follow-up the case with an in-class discussion on the nature of the errors discovered and the impact of such errors on the XBRL documents. By completing the case, students enhance their knowledge of the structure and the elements that make-up the US GAAP taxonomy, build experience in publicly-available XBRL validation tools and refine higher-order thinking skills through the evaluation of evidence and the write-up of findings.

Label: Total Other Income (Expense)	7/1/2014 -	7/1/2013 -	USD	No			
ID: us-gaap_NonoperatingIncomeExpense	9/30/2014	9/30/2013					
Definition: The aggregate amount of income (expense) from ancillary business-related activities (that is to say, excluding major activities considered part of the normal operations of the business).							
Label: Income (Loss) from Continuing Operations before Equity Method Investments, Income Taxes, Extraordinary Items, Cumulative Effects of Changes in Accounting Principles, Noncontrolling Interest	7/1/2014 -	7/1/2013 -	USD	No			
ID: us-gaap_IncomeLossFromContinuingOperationsBeforeIncomeTaxesMinorityInterestAnd-IncomeLossFromEquityMethodInvestments	9/30/2014	9/30/2013					
Definition: Sum of operating profit and nonoperating income (expense) before income (loss) from equity method investments, income taxes, extraordinary items, cumulative effects of changes in accounting principles, and noncontrolling interest.							
Label: Income Tax Provision (Benefit)	7/1/2014 -	7/1/2013 -	USD	No			
ID: us-gaap_IncomeTaxExpenseBenefit	9/30/2014	9/30/2013					
Definition: The sum of the current income tax expense (benefit) and the deferred income tax expense (benefit) pertaining to continuing operations.							
Label: Net Earnings (Loss)	7/1/2014 -	7/1/2013 -	USD	No			
ID: us-gaap_NetIncomeLoss	9/30/2014	9/30/2013					
Definition: The portion of consolidated profit or loss for the period, net of income taxes, which is attributable to the parent. If the entity does not present consolidated financial statements, the amount of profit or loss for the period, net of income taxes.							
Label: Earnings Per Share, Basic	7/1/2014 -	7/1/2013 -	USD	No			
ID: us-gaap_EarningsPerShareBasic	9/30/2014	9/30/2013					
Definition: The amount of net income or loss for the period per each share of common stock outstanding during the reporting period.							
Label: Weighted Average Shares Outstanding - Basic	7/1/2014 -	7/1/2013 -	shares	No			
ID: us-gaap_WeightedAverageNumberOfSharesOutstandingBasic	9/30/2014	9/30/2013					
Definition: Number of [basic] shares, after adjustment for contingently issuable shares and other shares not deemed outstanding, determined by relating the portion of time within a reporting period that common shares have been outstanding to the total time in that period.							
Label: Earnings Per Share, Diluted	7/1/2014 -	7/1/2013 -	USD	No			
ID: us-gaap_EarningsPerShareDiluted	9/30/2014	9/30/2013					
Definition: The amount of net income or loss for the period per each share of common stock and dilutive common stock equivalents outstanding during the reporting period.							
Label: Weighted Average Shares Outstanding - Diluted	7/1/2014 -	7/1/2013 -	shares	No			
ID: us-gaap_WeightedAverageNumberOfDilutedSharesOutstanding	9/30/2014	9/30/2013					
Definition: The average number of shares issued and outstanding that are used in calculating diluted EPS, determined based on the timing of issuance of shares in the period.							
Label: Shares Outstanding	9/30/2014	9/30/2013	shares	No			
ID: us-gaap_CommonStockSharesOutstanding							
Definition: Total number of shares of common stock held by shareholders. May be all or portion of the number of common shares authorized. These shares represent the ownership interest of the common shareholders. Excludes common shares repurchased by the entity and held as Treasury shares. Shares outstanding equals shares issued minus shares held in treasury. Does not include common shares that have been repurchased.							

104000 - Statement - Statement of Financial Position, Classified

Element	Period	Period	Unit	Extended?	Scenario(s)	Segment(s)
Label: Cash	9/30/2014	9/30/2013	USD	No		
ID: us-gaap_Cash						
Definition: Unrestricted cash available for day-to-day operating needs.						
Label: Short-term Investments, Net	9/30/2014	9/30/2013	USD	No		
ID: us-gaap_ShortTermInvestments						
Definition: Investments which are intended to be sold in the short term (usually less than one year or the normal operating cycle, whichever is longer) including trading securities, available-for-sale securities, held-to-maturity securities, and other short-term investments not otherwise listed in the existing taxonomy.						
Label: Receivables, Net	9/30/2014	9/30/2013	USD	No		
ID: us-gaap_ReceivablesNetCurrent						
Definition: The total amount due to the entity within one year of the balance sheet date (or one operating cycle, if longer) from outside sources, including trade accounts receivable, notes and loans receivable, as well as any other types of receivables, net of allowances established for the purpose of reducing such receivables to an amount that approximates their net realizable value.						
Label: Deferred Income Tax Assets	9/30/2014	9/30/2013	USD	No		
ID: us-gaap_DeferredTaxAssetsNetCurrent						
Definition: The current portion of the aggregate tax effects as of the balance sheet date of all future tax deductions arising from temporary differences between tax basis and generally accepted accounting principles basis recognition of assets, liabilities, revenues and expenses, which can only be deducted for tax purposes when permitted under enacted tax laws; after deducting the allocated valuation allowance, if any, to reduce such amount to net realizable value. Deferred tax liabilities and assets shall be classified as current or noncurrent based on the classification of the related asset or liability for financial reporting. A deferred tax liability or asset that is not related to an asset or liability for financial reporting, including deferred tax assets related to carryforwards, shall be classified according to the expected reversal date of the temporary difference. An unrecognized tax benefit that is directly related to a position taken in a tax year that results in a net operating loss carryforward should be presented as a reduction of the related deferred tax asset.						
Label: Other Current Assets	9/30/2014	9/30/2013	USD	No		
ID: us-gaap_OtherAssetsCurrent						
Definition: Aggregate carrying amount, as of the balance sheet date, of current assets not separately presented elsewhere in the balance sheet. Current assets are expected to be realized or consumed within one year (or the normal operating cycle, if longer).						
Label: Total Current Assets	9/30/2014	9/30/2013	USD	No		
ID: us-gaap_AssetsCurrent						
Definition: Sum of the carrying amounts as of the balance sheet date of all assets that are expected to be realized in cash, sold, or consumed within one year (or the normal operating cycle, if longer). Assets are probable future economic benefits obtained or controlled by an entity as a result of past transactions or events.						
Label: Flight Equipment	9/30/2014	9/30/2013	USD	Yes		
ID: adios_FlightEquipment						
Definition: Net value of flight equipment owned on balance sheet date.						
Label: Purchase Deposits for Flight Equipment	9/30/2014	9/30/2013	USD	Yes		
ID: adios_PurchaseDepositsForFlightEquipment						
Definition: Deposits made when flight equipment has been ordered.						

Exhibit 16. continued

Teaching Notes

Teaching Notes for adopters are available from the authors.

Label: Other Equipment and Property	9/30/2014	9/30/2013	USD	No
ID: us-gaap_PropertyPlantAndEquipmentOther				
Definition: This element represents capitalized assets classified as property, plant and equipment not otherwise defined in the taxonomy.				
Label: Capital Leased Assets, Gross, Total	9/30/2014	9/30/2013	USD	No
ID: us-gaap_CapitalLeasedAssetsGross				
Definition: The total gross amount of assets subject to a lease meeting the criteria for capitalization.				
Label: Equipment and Property Net	9/30/2014	9/30/2013	USD	No
ID: us-gaap_PropertyPlantAndEquipmentNet				
Definition: Tangible assets that are held by an entity for use in the production or supply of goods and services, for rental to others, or for administrative purposes and that are expected to provide economic benefit for more than one year; net of accumulated depreciation. Examples include land, buildings, and production equipment.				
Label: Route Acquisition Costs	9/30/2014	9/30/2013	USD	No
ID: us-gaap_FiniteLivedContractualRightsGross				
Definition: Gross carrying amount before accumulated amortization as of the balance sheet date of an intangible asset that arises from a contractual arrangement with a third party (not including franchise rights and license agreements).				
Label: Goodwill	9/30/2014	9/30/2013	USD	No
ID: us-gaap_Goodwill				
Definition: Carrying amount as of the balance sheet date, which is the cumulative amount paid, adjusted for any amortization recognized prior to adoption of FAS 142 and for any impairment charges, in excess of the fair value of net assets acquired in one or more business combination transactions.				
Label: Other Assets	9/30/2014	9/30/2013	USD	No
ID: us-gaap_OtherAssetsNoncurrent				
Definition: Aggregate carrying amount, as of the balance sheet date, of noncurrent assets not separately disclosed in the balance sheet due to materiality considerations. Noncurrent assets are expected to be realized or consumed after one year (or the normal operating cycle, if longer).				
Label: Total Other Assets	9/30/2014	9/30/2013	USD	Yes
ID: adios_TotalOtherAssets				
Definition: The total value of assets not classified as current or as property and equipment.				
Label: Assets, Total	9/30/2014	9/30/2013	USD	No
ID: us-gaap_Assets				
Definition: Sum of the carrying amounts as of the balance sheet date of all assets that are recognized. Assets are probable future economic benefits obtained or controlled by an entity as a result of past transactions or events.				
Label: Accounts Payable	9/30/2014	9/30/2013	USD	No
ID: us-gaap_AccountsPayableCurrent				
Definition: Carrying value as of the balance sheet date of liabilities incurred (and for which invoices have typically been received) and payable to vendors for goods and services received that are used in an entity's business. Used to reflect the current portion of the liabilities (due within one year or within the normal operating cycle if longer).				
Label: Accrued Salaries and Wages	9/30/2014	9/30/2013	USD	No
ID: us-gaap_EmployeeRelatedLiabilitiesCurrent				
Definition: Total of the carrying values as of the balance sheet date of obligations incurred through that date and payable for obligations related to services received from employees, such as accrued salaries and bonuses, payroll taxes and fringe benefits. Used to reflect the current portion of the liabilities (due within one year or within the normal operating cycle if longer).				
Label: Accrued Liabilities	9/30/2014	9/30/2013	USD	No
ID: us-gaap_AccruedLiabilitiesCurrent				
Definition: Carrying value as of the balance sheet date of obligations incurred and payable, pertaining to costs that are statutory in nature, are incurred on contractual obligations, or accumulate over time and for which invoices have not yet been received or will not be rendered. Examples include taxes, interest, rent and utilities. Used to reflect the current portion of the liabilities (due within one year or within the normal operating cycle if longer).				
Label: Air Traffic Liability	9/30/2014	9/30/2013	USD	Yes
ID: adios_AirTrafficLiability				
Definition: The sum of advanced payments received from customers for future air travel and the expected liability which arises from frequent flier programs.				
Label: Payable to Affiliates, Net	9/30/2014	9/30/2013	USD	No
ID: us-gaap_DueToRelatedPartiesCurrent				
Definition: Carrying amount as of the balance sheet date of obligations due all related parties. For classified balance sheets, represents the current portion of such liabilities (due within one year or within the normal operating cycle if longer).				
Label: Current Maturities of Long-term Debt	9/30/2014	9/30/2013	USD	No
ID: us-gaap_LongTermDebtCurrent				
Definition: Total of the portions of the carrying amounts as of the balance sheet date of long-term debt, which may include notes payable, bonds payable, debentures, mortgage loans, and commercial paper, which are scheduled to be repaid within one year or the normal operating cycle, if longer, and after deducting unamortized discount or premiums, if any.				
Label: Current Obligations Under Capital Leases	9/30/2014	9/30/2013	USD	No
ID: us-gaap_CapitalLeaseObligationsCurrent				
Definition: Amount equal to the present value (the principal) at the beginning of the lease term of minimum lease payments during the lease term (excluding that portion of the payments representing executory costs such as insurance, maintenance, and taxes to be paid by the lessor, together with any profit thereon) net of payments or other amounts applied to the principal, through the balance sheet date and due to be paid within one year (or one operating cycle, if longer) of the balance sheet date.				
Label: Total Current Liabilities	9/30/2014	9/30/2013	USD	No
ID: us-gaap_LiabilitiesCurrent				
Definition: Total obligations incurred as part of normal operations that are expected to be paid during the following twelve months or within one business cycle, if longer.				
Label: Long-term Debt, Less Current Maturities	9/30/2014	9/30/2013	USD	No
ID: us-gaap_LongTermDebtNoncurrent				
Definition: Sum of the carrying values as of the balance sheet date of all long-term debt, which is debt initially having maturities due after one year from the balance sheet date or beyond the operating cycle, if longer, but excluding the portions thereof scheduled to be repaid within one year (current maturities) or the normal operating cycle, if longer, and after deducting unamortized discount or premiums, if any.				
Label: Capital Lease Obligations, Noncurrent	9/30/2014	9/30/2013	USD	No
ID: us-gaap_CapitalLeaseObligationsNoncurrent				
Definition: Amount equal to the present value (the principal) at the beginning of the lease term of minimum lease payments during the lease term (excluding that portion of the payments representing executory costs such as insurance, maintenance, and taxes to be paid by the lessor, together with any profit thereon) net of payments or other amounts applied to the principal, through the balance sheet date and due to be paid more than one year (or one operating cycle, if longer) after the balance sheet date.				
Label: Deferred Income Tax Liability	9/30/2014	9/30/2013	USD	No
ID: us-gaap_DeferredTaxLiabilitiesNoncurrent				
Definition: Represents the noncurrent portion of deferred tax liabilities, which result from applying the applicable tax rate to net taxable temporary differences pertaining to each jurisdiction to which the entity is obligated to pay income tax. A noncurrent taxable temporary difference is a difference between the tax basis and the carrying amount of a noncurrent asset or liability in the financial statements prepared in accordance with generally accepted accounting principles. In a classified statement of financial position, an enterprise shall separate deferred tax liabilities and assets into a current amount and a noncurrent amount. Deferred tax liabilities and assets shall be classified as current or noncurrent based on the classification of the related asset or liability for financial reporting. A deferred tax liability or asset that is not related to an asset or liability for financial reporting, including deferred tax assets related to carryforwards, shall be classified according to the expected reversal date of the temporary difference.				
Label: Postretirement Benefits	9/30/2014	9/30/2013	USD	No
ID: us-gaap_PensionAndOtherPostretirementDefinedBenefitPlans-LiabilitiesNoncurrent				
Definition: This represents the noncurrent liability for underfunded plans recognized in the balance sheet that is associated with the defined benefit pension plans and other postretirement defined benefit plans.				

Exhibit 16. continued

Acknowledgements

The authors thank Karen van Peursem, Guest Editor, and two anonymous referees for guidance which improved the quality of the paper.

Label: Other Deferred Credits, Noncurrent		9/30/2013		USD	No	
ID: us-gaap_OtherDeferredCreditsNoncurrent						
Definition: Carrying amount as of the balance sheet date of unearned revenue or income not otherwise specified in the taxonomy which is expected to be taken into income after one year or beyond the normal operating cycle, if longer.						
Label: Other Liabilities and Deferred Credits		9/30/2014		USD	No	
ID: us-gaap_OtherLiabilitiesNoncurrent						
Definition: Aggregate carrying amount, as of the balance sheet date, of noncurrent obligations not separately disclosed in the balance sheet due to materiality considerations. Noncurrent liabilities are expected to be paid after one year (or the normal operating cycle, if longer).						
Label: Total Liabilities		9/30/2014	9/30/2013	USD	No	
ID: us-gaap_Liabilities						
Definition: Sum of the carrying amounts as of the balance sheet date of all liabilities that are recognized. Liabilities are probable future sacrifices of economic benefits arising from present obligations of an entity to transfer assets or provide services to other entities in the future.						
Label: Ordinary Capital		9/30/2014	9/30/2013	USD	No	
ID: us-gaap_CommonStockValue						
Definition: Dollar value of issued common stock whether issued at par value, no par or stated value. This item includes treasury stock repurchased by the entity. Note: elements for number of common shares, par value and other disclosure concepts are in another section within stockholders' equity.						
Label: Additional Paid in Capital Ordinary Capital		9/30/2014	9/30/2013	USD	No	
ID: us-gaap_AdditionalPaidInCapitalCommonStock						
Definition: Value received from shareholders in common stock-related transactions that are in excess of par value or stated value and amounts received from other stock-related transactions. Includes only common stock transactions (excludes preferred stock transactions). May be called contributed capital, capital in excess of par, capital surplus, or paid-in capital.						
Label: Accumulated Other Comprehensive Income (Loss)		9/30/2014	9/30/2013	USD	No	
ID: us-gaap_AccumulatedOtherComprehensiveIncomeLossNetOfTax						
Definition: Accumulated change in equity from transactions and other events and circumstances from non-owner sources, net of tax effect, at fiscal year-end. Excludes Net Income (Loss), and accumulated changes in equity from transactions resulting from investments by owners and distributions to owners. Includes foreign currency translation items, certain pension adjustments, and unrealized gains and losses on certain investments in debt and equity securities as well as changes in the fair value of derivatives related to the effective portion of a designated cash flow hedge.						
Label: Retained Earnings		9/30/2014	9/30/2013	USD	No	
ID: us-gaap_RetainedEarningsAccumulatedDeficit						
Definition: The cumulative amount of the reporting entity's undistributed earnings or deficit.						
Label: Stockholders' Equity		9/30/2014	9/30/2013	USD	No	
ID: us-gaap_StockholdersEquity						
Definition: Total of all Stockholders' Equity (deficit) items, net of receivables from officers, directors, owners, and affiliates of the entity which are attributable to the parent. The amount of the economic entity's stockholders' equity attributable to the parent excludes the amount of stockholders' equity which is allocable to that ownership interest in subsidiary equity which is not attributable to the parent (noncontrolling interest, minority interest). This excludes temporary equity and is sometimes called permanent equity.						
Label: Total Liabilities and Stockholders' Equity		9/30/2014	9/30/2013	USD	No	
ID: us-gaap_LiabilitiesAndStockholdersEquity						
Definition: Total of all Liabilities and Stockholders' Equity items.						

152200 - Statement - Statement of Cash Flows

Element	Period	Period	Unit	Extended?	Scenario(s)	Segment(s)
Label: Net Earnings (Loss)	7/1/2014 - 9/30/2014	7/1/2013 - 9/30/2013	USD	No		
ID: us-gaap_ProfitLoss						
Definition: The consolidated profit or loss for the period, net of income taxes, including the portion attributable to the noncontrolling interest.						
Label: Depreciation	7/1/2014 - 9/30/2014	7/1/2013 - 9/30/2013	USD	No		
ID: us-gaap_CostOfServicesDepreciation						
Definition: The expense recognized in the current period that allocates the cost of a tangible asset used in providing revenue generating services over the asset's useful life.						
Label: Amortization	7/1/2014 - 9/30/2014	7/1/2013 - 9/30/2013	USD	No		
ID: us-gaap_CostOfServicesAmortization						
Definition: The amount of expense recognized in the current period that reflects the allocation of the costs of intangible assets over the expected benefit period of such assets. This element applies only to intangible assets used in the delivery of services.						
Label: Provision for asset impairment	7/1/2014 - 9/30/2014	7/1/2013 - 9/30/2013	USD	No		
ID: us-gaap_OtherAssetImpairmentCharges						
Definition: The charge against earnings resulting from the write down of long lived assets other than goodwill due to the difference between the carrying value and lower fair value.						
Label: Deferred Income Taxes	7/1/2014 - 9/30/2014	7/1/2013 - 9/30/2013	USD	No		
ID: us-gaap_DeferredIncomeTaxExpenseBenefit						
Definition: The component of income tax expense for the period representing the net change in the entity's deferred tax assets and liabilities pertaining to continuing operations.						
Label: Gain on Sale of Other Investments	7/1/2014 - 9/30/2014	7/1/2013 - 9/30/2013	USD	No		
ID: us-gaap_GainLossOnSaleOfOtherInvestments						
Definition: The difference between the book value and the sale price of other nonspecific investments. This element is used when other, more specific, elements are not appropriate. This element refers to the gain (loss) included in earnings.						
Label: Change in Receivables	7/1/2014 - 9/30/2014	7/1/2013 - 9/30/2013	USD	No		
ID: us-gaap_IncreaseDecreaseInReceivables						
Definition: The net change during the reporting period in the total amount due within one year (or one operating cycle) from all parties, associated with underlying transactions that are classified as operating activities.						
Label: Change in Inventories	7/1/2014 - 9/30/2014	7/1/2013 - 9/30/2013	USD	No		
ID: us-gaap_IncreaseDecreaseInInventories						
Definition: The net change during the reporting period in the aggregate value of all inventory held by the reporting entity, associated with underlying transactions that are classified as operating activities.						
Label: Change in Accounts Payable and Accrued Liabilities	7/1/2014 - 9/30/2014	7/1/2013 - 9/30/2013	USD	No		
ID: us-gaap_IncreaseDecreaseInAccountsPayableAndAccruedLiabilities						
Definition: The net change during the reporting period in the aggregate amount of obligations and expenses incurred but not paid.						
Label: Change in Air Traffic Liability	7/1/2014 - 9/30/2014	7/1/2013 - 9/30/2013	USD	No		
ID: us-gaap_IncreaseDecreaseInCustomerAdvances						

Exhibit 16. continued

Label / ID	Period 1	Period 2	Currency	Extension
Label: Other Change in Assets and Liabilities, Net **ID:** us-gaap_IncreaseDecreaseInOtherOperatingCapitalNet	7/1/2014 - 9/30/2014	7/1/2013 - 9/30/2013	USD	No
Definition: For entities with classified balance sheets, the net change during the reporting period in the value of other assets or liabilities used in operating activities, that are not otherwise defined in the taxonomy. For entities with unclassified balance sheets, the net change during the reporting period in the value of all other assets or liabilities used in operating activities.				
Label: Net Cash Provided by (Used in) Operating Activities **ID:** us-gaap_NetCashProvidedByUsedInOperatingActivities	7/1/2014 - 9/30/2014	7/1/2013 - 9/30/2013	USD	No
Definition: The net cash from (used in) all of the entity's operating activities, including those of discontinued operations, of the reporting entity. Operating activities generally involve producing and delivering goods and providing services. Operating activity cash flows include transactions, adjustments, and changes in value that are not defined as investing or financing activities.				
Label: Payments to Acquire Property, Plant, and Equipment **ID:** us-gaap_PaymentsToAcquirePropertyPlantAndEquipment	7/1/2014 - 9/30/2014	7/1/2013 - 9/30/2013	USD	No
Definition: The cash outflow associated with the acquisition of long-lived, physical assets that are used in the normal conduct of business to produce goods and services and not intended for resale; includes cash outflows to pay for construction of self-constructed assets.				
Label: Proceeds from Sale of Property, Plant, and Equipment **ID:** us-gaap_ProceedsFromSaleOfPropertyPlantAndEquipment	7/1/2014 - 9/30/2014	7/1/2013 - 9/30/2013	USD	No
Definition: The cash inflow from the sale of long-lived, physical assets that are used in the normal conduct of business to produce goods and services and not intended for resale.				
Label: Net (Increase) Decrease in Short-Term Investments **ID:** us-gaap_ProceedsFromSaleMaturityAndCollectionsOfInvestments	7/1/2014 - 9/30/2014	7/1/2013 - 9/30/2013	USD	No
Definition: The cash inflow associated with the sale, maturity and collection of all investments such as debt, security and so forth during the period.				
Label: Proceeds from Sale of Other Investments **ID:** us-gaap_ProceedsFromSaleAndMaturityOfOtherInvestments	7/1/2014 - 9/30/2014	7/1/2013 - 9/30/2013	USD	No
Definition: The cash inflow associated with the sale and maturity (principal being due) of other investments, prepayment and call (request of early payment) of other investments not otherwise defined in the taxonomy.				
Label: Payments to Acquire Businesses, Net of Cash Acquired **ID:** us-gaap_PaymentsToAcquireBusinessesNetOfCashAcquired	7/1/2014 - 9/30/2014	7/1/2013 - 9/30/2013	USD	No
Definition: The cash outflow associated with the acquisition of a business, net of the cash acquired from the purchase.				
Label: Other Cash Flow From Investing Activities **ID:** us-gaap_PaymentsForProceedsFromOtherInvestingActivities	7/1/2014 - 9/30/2014	7/1/2013 - 9/30/2013	USD	No
Definition: The net cash outflow (inflow) from other investing activities. This element is used when there is not a more specific and appropriate element in the taxonomy.				
Label: Net Cash Provided by (Used in) Investing Activities **ID:** us-gaap_NetCashProvidedByUsedInInvestingActivities	7/1/2014 - 9/30/2014	7/1/2013 - 9/30/2013	USD	No
Definition: The net cash inflow (outflow) from investing activity.				
Label: Proceeds from Issuance of Long-term Debt **ID:** us-gaap_ProceedsFromIssuanceOfLongTermDebt	7/1/2014 - 9/30/2014	7/1/2013 - 9/30/2013	USD	No
Definition: The cash inflow from a debt initially having maturity due after one year or beyond the operating cycle, if longer.				
Label: Proceeds from Short-Term Line of Credit **ID:** us-gaap_ProceedsFromLinesOfCredit	7/1/2014 - 9/30/2014	7/1/2013 - 9/30/2013	USD	No
Definition: The cash inflow from a contractual arrangement with the lender, including letter of credit, standby letter of credit and revolving credit arrangements, under which borrowings can be made up to a specific amount at any point in time with either short term or long term maturity that is collateralized (backed by pledge, mortgage or other lien in the entity's assets).				
Label: Sale-Leaseback Transactions **ID:** adios_SaleLeasebackTransactions	7/1/2014 - 9/30/2014	7/1/2013 - 9/30/2013	USD	Yes
Definition: The cashflow from the sale and leaseback of property plant and equipment.				
Label: Funds Transferred to Affiliates **ID:** us-gaap_ProceedsFromRepaymentsOfRelatedPartyDebt	7/1/2014 - 9/30/2014	7/1/2013 - 9/30/2013	USD	No
Definition: The net cash inflow (outflow) from the proceeds and repayments made on the borrowing from related party where one party can exercise control or significant influence over another party; including affiliates, owners or officers and their immediate families, pension trusts, and such forth.				
Label: Payments of Long-term Debt and Capital Lease Obligations **ID:** us-gaap_RepaymentsOfLongTermDebtAndCapitalSecurities	7/1/2014 - 9/30/2014	7/1/2013 - 9/30/2013	USD	No
Definition: The cash outflow associated with security instrument that either represents a creditor or an ownership relationship with the holder of the investment security with a maturity of beyond one year or normal operating cycle, if longer. The nature of such security interests included herein may consist of debt securities, long-term capital lease obligations, and capital securities.				
Label: Net Cash Provided by (Used in) Financing Activities, Total **ID:** us-gaap_NetCashProvidedByUsedInFinancingActivities	7/1/2014 - 9/30/2014	7/1/2013 - 9/30/2013	USD	No
Definition: The net cash inflow (outflow) from financing activity for the period.				
Label: Cash and Cash Equivalents, Period Increase (Decrease) **ID:** us-gaap_CashAndCashEquivalentsPeriodIncreaseDecrease	7/1/2014 - 9/30/2014	7/1/2013 - 9/30/2013	USD	No
Definition: The net change between the beginning and ending balance of cash and cash equivalents.				

Exhibit 16. continued

Notes

[1]The Public Company Accounting Oversight Board (PCAOB) is silent on XBRL other than a 2005 staff 'Questions and Answers' paper on the then SEC voluntary filings program (PCAOB, 2005). The Q&A saw that auditors might issue an opinion under the Board's interim Attestation Standards. The Board's 2009–2013 Strategic Plan notes that 'in the future, the SEC may require some companies' filings to include auditor attestation reports on XBRL data. Such changes would likely require the PCAOB to establish specific standards for such engagements and to include such engagements in its inspections and other oversight activities (PCAOB, 2009).

[2]International Standard on Related Services 4400 'Engagements to Perform Agreed-Upon Procedures Regarding Financial Information' provides a similar illustrative report for factual findings of a generic nature (IAASB, 2009).

[3]XBRL is used in a wide variety of settings internationally (Kernan, 2008). International implementations of XBRL include: financial reporting by listed corporations in China, Japan and Korea; financial reporting by small and medium enterprises (SMEs) in Denmark, Belgium, The Netherlands and Italy; and corporate tax filings in the UK and Germany.

Independent Accountant's Report on Applying Agreed-Upon Procedures

Evaluation of the completeness, accuracy and consistency of Adios!

Airways Inc. XBRL Filing

[Recipient]

[Describe the procedures undertaken in the engagement]

This agreed-upon procedures engagement was performed in accordance with the attestation standards of the American Institute of Certified Public Accountants. The sufficiency of these procedures is solely the responsibility of [insert organization]. Consequently, we make no representation regarding the sufficiency of the procedures described in the Attachment either for the purpose for which this report was requested or for any other purpose.

[Describe limitations to the engagement]

[Describe who report is intended for]

[Signature] [CPA Firm] [Date]

Attachment

Procedure	Finding
Set out procedure	**Describe your findings on each of the procedures**

Exhibit 17. Report skeleton

[4]There are other taxonomies that are approved by XBRL International including the CN Listed Company Information Disclosure based on Chinese GAAP or acknowledged (e.g. International Financial Reporting Standards Taxonomy 2009).

[5]However, the SEC suggests that firms create extensions only when appropriate elements do not exist in the US GAAP taxonomy.

[6]Whether or not extensions are allowed depends on the implementation. For example, the Netherlands does not allow extensions.

[7]The IAASB provides similar guidance in International Standard on Related Services 4400 'Engagements to Perform Agreed-Upon Procedures Regarding Financial Information' (IAASB, 2009).

[8]The IAASB is considering issuing XBRL specific guidance for the conduct of agreed-upon procedures engagements (Healy, 2010).

References

ASB (2001a) *AT Section 101-Attest Engagements* (New York: Auditing Standards Board, American Institute of CPAs).

ASB (2001b) *AT Section 201-Agreed-Upon Procedures Engagements* (New York: Auditing Standards Board, American Institute of CPAs).

ASB (2003) *AT Section 9101: Attest Engagements—Interpretations of Section 101* (New York: Auditing Standards Board, American Institute of CPAs).

ASB (2009) *Statement of Position 09–1: Performing Agreed-Upon Procedures Engagements that Address the Completeness, Accuracy or Consistency of XBRL-tagged Data* (New York: Auditing Standards Board, American Institute of CPAs).

Boritz, J. E. and No, W. G. (2009) Assurance on XBRL-related documents: the case of United Technologies Corporation, *Journal of Information Systems*, 23(2), pp. 49–78.

Curtis, M. B., Jenkins, J. G., Bedard, J. C. and Deis, D. R. (2009) Auditors' training and proficiency in information systems: a research synthesis, *Journal of Information Systems*, 23(1), pp. 79–96.

Debreceny, R. and Farewell, S. (2010a) XBRL in the accounting curriculum, *Issues in Accounting Education*, 25(3), pp. 379–403.

Debreceny, R. S. and Farewell, S. M. (2010b) Adios! Airways: a case study on mapping financial statements to the US GAAP XBRL taxonomy, *Issues in Accounting Education*, 25(3), pp. 465–488.

Garbellotto, G. (2009a) XBRL implementation strategies: the bolt-on approach, *Strategic Finance*, 90(11), pp. 56–57.

Garbellotto, G. (2009b) XBRL implementation strategies: the built-in approach, *Strategic Finance*, 91(2), pp. 56–57.

Garbellotto, G. (2009c) XBRL implementation strategies: the deeply embedded approach, *Strategic Finance*, 91(5), pp. 56–61.

Hassall, T. and Milne, M. J. (2004) Using case studies in accounting education, *Accounting Education: an international journal*, 13(2), pp. 135–138.

Healy, K. (2010) IAASB to take up Agreed upon Procedures for XBRL. (Personal communication), New York: International Auditing and Assurance Standards Board. 29 April 2010).

IAASB (2009) International standard on related services 4400—engagements to perform agreed-upon procedures regarding financial information, *in: Handbook of International Standards on Auditing and Quality Control*, pp. 370–379 (New York: International Auditing and Assurance Standards Board, International Federation of Accountants).

Jackson, S. and Durkee, D. (2008) Incorporating information literacy into the accounting curriculum, *Accounting Education: an international journal*, 17(1), pp. 83–97.

Kernan, K. (2008) XBRL Around the world, *Journal of Accountancy*, 206(4), pp. 62–66.

PCAOB (2005) Staff questions and answers attest engagements regarding XBRL financial information furnished under the XBRL voluntary financial reporting program on the EDGAR system, Available at http://pcaobus.org/Standards/QandA/05-25-2005.pdf (accessed 17 August 2011).

PCAOB (2009) Public Company Accounting Oversight Board Strategic Plan, 2009–2013. Available at http://pcaobus.org/About/Ops/Documents/Strategic%20plans/2010-2014.pdf (accessed 17 Aughust 2011).

Plumlee, R. D. and Plumlee, M. A. (2008) Assurance on XBRL for financial reporting, *Accounting Horizons*, 22(3), pp. 353–368.

Rowden, J. (2010) ICAEW Audit and Assurance Faculty developing guidance on Agreed Upon Procedures for Tax Filings (Personal communication.) London, 29 April 2010.

SEC (2009) Interactive Data to Improve Financial Reporting. Available at http://www.sec.gov/rules/final/2009/33-9002.pdf (accessed 17 August 2011).

SEC (2010) *EDGAR Filer Manual (Volume II) EDGAR Filing*. 14th ed (Washington, DC, Securities and Exchange Commission).

White, C. E. (2009) *The Guide & Workbook for Understanding XBRL*. 3rd ed (Newark, DE, SkipWhite.com).

Wynn-Williams, K., Whiting, R. H. and Adler, R. W. (2008) The influence of business case studies on learning styles: an empirical investigation, *Accounting Education: an international journal*, 17(2), pp. 113–128.

XBRL UK (2010) XBRL Projects in the UK. Available ar http://www.xbrl.org/uk/Projects/ (accessed 17 August 2011).

TEACHING RESOURCE

J&K Fitness Supply Company: Auditing Inventory

PAUL M. CLIKEMAN

University of Richmond, USA

ABSTRACT   *This case provides auditing students with an opportunity to perform substantive tests of inventory using realistic-looking source documents. The learning objectives are to help students understand: (1) the procedures auditors perform in order to test inventory; (2) the source documents used in auditing inventory; and (3) the types of misstatements that might occur in inventory. Student feedback indicates the case is successful in meeting all three learning objectives.*

Introduction

Approximately 20 years ago, accounting practitioners (Arthur Andersen *et al.*, 1989) and a blue ribbon committee of accounting educators (Accounting Education Change Commission, 1990) recommended greater use of active learning techniques in undergraduate accounting education. Active learning techniques include case studies, role playing, simulations (Tate and Grein, 2009), games (Cook and Hazelwood, 2002), and student-authored mini-cases (Chu and Libby, 2010). Albrecht and Sack (2000) urged accounting educators to reduce their reliance on the lecture, and devote more time to written communication assignments and cases dealing with uncertainty.

Although simple skills can be learned through passive teaching methods such as lectures and assigned readings, complex tasks require active learning techniques (Bonner, 1999). Auditing is a complex task. Auditors must understand the client's operations, assess risk, gather evidence, and evaluate the materiality of misstatements. Pricewaterhouse-Coopers (2003) identified 'fostering students' ability to solve problems in complex business environments where the best answer is difficult to identify' as one of three areas in which accounting education needs improvement. To prepare students for the complexity of participating in audits, many auditing instructors assign case studies (AAA, 2003). Watson, Apostolou, Hassell and Webber (2007) list 22 auditing-related instructional cases published in accounting education journals from 2003 to 2005, more than the number of cases related to other functional areas such as financial accounting, managerial accounting, and taxation.

First-year auditors are frequently assigned to examine accounting records and supporting documents, yet few teaching cases provide sufficient materials to help students learn these skills. Notable exceptions are Miller and Savage (2009) who provide a set of customer orders, sales invoices, and shipping documents for a fictitious computer company which students use to perform tests of sales transactions, and Dee and Durtschi (2010) who provide more than 20 pages of accounting records and supporting documents for a fictitious minor league baseball team so students can practice looking for fraud. The J&K Fitness Supply Company case contributes to the auditing education literature by providing a comprehensive set of accounting records and supporting documents for a fictitious wholesaling company that students can use to perform substantive tests of inventory.

Learning Objectives

This case is designed to:

1. help students understand the procedures which auditors use to test inventory;
2. familiarize students with source documents commonly encountered when testing inventory; and
3. demonstrate the types of misstatements that might occur in inventory.

After completing the case, students should be able to perform substantive audit procedures commonly used to test inventory. The case requires students to test inventory quantities by comparing them to the inventory count tags, verify unit costs by tracing them to vendor invoices, test mathematical accuracy through recomputation, and search for obsolete products by reviewing the perpetual inventory records.

In addition, after completing the case, students should be familiar with source documents (e.g. count tags, vendor invoices) and records (e.g. tag control listing, perpetual inventory files) commonly encountered when testing inventory. Inspection of records and documents is one of the primary means of obtaining audit evidence (AICPA, 2006). Unfortunately, auditing textbooks rarely provide opportunities for students to examine sets of source documents. Some auditing instructors supplement their textbook by assigning an audit practice set such as Paul (2007), Morris and Jones (2009), or Hoyle, Trussel and Frazer (2007). However, commercially-published practice sets are expensive and may be too lengthy for instructors who wish to assign only a brief exercise. This case provides a set of realistic-looking source documents supporting a small company's inventory balance. The source documents are provided in electronic format thus allowing instructors to alter them in order to prevent students from relying on solutions from prior semesters.

After completing this case, students should understand the types of misstatements that might occur in inventory. The case materials contain four types of misstatements. The first misstatement is an arithmetic error in which the extended cost of an item on the inventory summary does not equal the number of units multiplied by the unit price. The second misstatement occurs when the quantity of one product on the inventory summary exceeds the number of items listed on the associated count tag. Two pricing errors exist in which the unit costs on the inventory summary do not agree with the prices shown on the vendor invoices. The last issue deals with slow-moving inventory. The perpetual inventory records indicate that the year-end supply of one product exceeds three times the previous year's sales. Students should identify this item as a potentially obsolete product. The Teaching Notes contain suggestions for other misstatements that may be seeded in the source documents if desired.

Case Effectiveness

This case was developed during autumn 2008 for an undergraduate auditing class at a selective, private American university. The auditing class is required for students majoring in accounting, and is usually taken in the fourth year. Most students are approximately 21 years old, and have little, if any, auditing experience.

Based on feedback from students in 2008, the case was revised to provide more explicit instructions about the audit procedures to be performed. A second instructor at the same institution assigned the case to his undergraduate auditing students during autumn 2009, and the case (as reproduced below) was assigned for a third time in autumn 2010. Students who completed the case during 2009 and 2010 were asked five questions to assess the case's effectiveness. The questions focused on whether the case helped the students to understand the procedures which auditors use to test inventory, whether the case helped students understand the types of misstatements that might occur in inventory, and whether the case should be assigned in future semesters. Twenty-four students from a cohort of 26 students in 2009 and 71 students from a cohort of 72 students in 2010 provided feedback about the assignment's effectiveness. The students' responses are presented in Table 1. More than 80% of the students in each semester indicated that the case was a valuable learning experience and recommended that it be used in the future.

Students had the opportunity to provide written comments.

One student, discussing what he learned about inventory audit procedures, wrote that the case: '… helped [me] better understand the procedures by using them rather than reading about what needs to be done.'

Another student wrote that he: '… would be comfortable auditing inventory now.'

Commenting about the source documents, a student wrote that she: '… enjoyed seeing how the documents fit together, almost like a puzzle, to paint a picture of the inventory account.'

Table 1. Students' assessment of the case assignment

The J&K inventory assignment:		Number of students selecting each response				
		Strongly disagree	Disagree	Neutral	Agree	Strongly agree
Helped me understand the procedures	2009	0	2	2	12	8
auditors use to test inventory.	2010	1	0	2	34	34
Helped me understand the documents	2009	2	0	0	9	13
used in testing inventory.	2010	1	0	1	31	38
Helped me understand the types of	2009	1	0	1	10	12
misstatements that might occur in inventory.	2010	1	0	4	40	26
Was a valuable learning experience.	2009	1	1	2	9	11
	2010	1	0	2	41	27
Should be used in future semesters.	2009	2	0	1	4	17
	2010	1	0	3	33	34

Regarding the misstatements seeded in the case, a student wrote that the assignment: '... was useful in gaining hands-on experience with audit procedures and the types of errors and misstatements that might occur in inventory.'

Many students praised the realism of the case, including one who wrote: 'This assignment was a very valuable learning tool and helped give me a realistic perspective of how auditing actually works. I was able to think like an auditor. It should certainly be used in future semesters.'

Unfortunately, the students who disliked the case provided few comments about what they did not like. One student criticized the case for being difficult to understand. Another student said the misstatements were too easy to find. Based on experience from three semesters, two suggestions should minimize potential problems which students might encounter in completing the assignment. First, it may be helpful to demonstrate how to display two files side-by-side on the computer screen. The case requires students to trace information in one Excel file to another file. Students who were unfamiliar with how to display two files simultaneously complained about the difficulty of switching back and forth between files. Second, instructors should review the textbook coverage of inventory audit procedures very thoroughly before assigning this case. The case provides a good opportunity for students to practice performing inventory audit procedures, but assumes that students already have a basic understanding of the procedures to be performed.

The Case

Background Information

J&K Fitness Supply Company was founded in 1993 by John and Kathryn Miles. The company acts as a wholesaler of fitness equipment; buying treadmills, exercise bikes, and elliptical trainers from manufacturers and distributing them to sporting goods stores and other retailers.

J&K occupies 800 square meters of rented warehouse space in an industrial park. John handles the company's sales. He visits customers monthly to describe new products, answer questions, and take sales orders. John's wife Kathryn handles all the administrative duties. Kathryn prepares sales invoices, opens mail, deposits cash receipts, pays bills, and keeps all the accounting records on a personal computer using a commercial accounting software package.

The only paid employee is Steve Park who works in the warehouse. Steve uses a forklift to unload incoming equipment from delivery trucks and store the items in their proper locations. When sales are made, Steve uses the forklift to pull desired items from their shelves and load them onto outgoing delivery trucks. J&K contracts with freight companies to deliver products to customers.

You are a first-year auditor with the public accounting firm Harris & Tate. Your firm has audited J&K since 1999. Although J&K is a relatively small partnership owned by John and Kathryn Miles, an annual audit is required by the finance company that issued J&K's revolving line of credit. J&K's inventory is pledged as security for the line of credit. J&K's 2010 financial statements are given in Table 2.

Tests of Inventory

J&K distributes 12 models of treadmills, 10 models of exercise bikes, and seven models of elliptical trainers produced by three manufacturers—Arrow, New Health, and Olympia.

Table 2. J&K Fitness Supply Company Financial Statements (All figures in US$)

Balance sheet				Income statement	
31 December 2010				Year ended 31 December 2010	
Cash	280 104	Accts payable	587 500	Sales	3 268 285
Accts receivable	533 240	Accrued liabilities	6115	Cost of goods sold	2 924 055
Bad debt allowance	(39 800)	Revolving credit	275 980	Gross margin	344 230
Inventory	374 410	Total liabilities	869 595	Rent	48 000
Other assets	4825			Wages	30 100
Prop. & equipment	44 175	Owners' equity	306 232	Depreciation	6050
Acc. depreciation	(21 127)			Other expenses	51 865
Total assets	1 175 827	Total liab. & OE	1 175 827	Net income	208 215

You were present on 31 December 2010 when J&K conducted its annual physical inventory count. Steve Park's brother Ben was hired for one day to help with the count. John and Ben counted the exercise bikes and elliptical trainers. Kathryn and Steve counted the treadmills. The counts were recorded on pre-numbered two-part count tags. You test-counted 10 items noting no differences between the numbers of items on hand and the quantities recorded on the count tags. The inventory appeared to be in good condition except for one Arrow model #8600ES1 treadmill, which had fallen off the forklift and been badly damaged; John promised to exclude the damaged item from the final inventory summary. After all items had been counted, John collected the count tags and made a schedule listing the numbers of the 'used' and 'unused' tags. You made a copy of the tag control schedule for your work papers.

Your audit manager has assigned you to perform the following audit procedures to test J&K's 31 December 2010 inventory balance:

- Obtain a copy of J&K's 31 December 2010 inventory summary (J&K Inventory Summary.xls).
  - Agree or reconcile the inventory summary total to the inventory balance on J&K's 31 December 2010 balance sheet.
  - Test the mathematical accuracy of the inventory summary by recomputing the extensions and total.
- Test the quantities on the inventory summary by tracing them to the inventory count tags (Inventory Count Tags.doc). Determine that all count tags listed on the inventory summary are classified as 'used' on the tag control listing (Tag Control Listing.xls).
- Trace the 10 test counts (Auditor Test Counts.xls) to the inventory summary.
- Test the unit prices on the inventory summary by comparing them to the appropriate vendor invoices (Arrow Invoices.doc; New Health Invoices.doc; Olympia Invoices.doc).
- Trace the quantities on the inventory summary to the perpetual inventory records (Perpetual Inventory Records.xls). Review the perpetual inventory records for evidence of obsolete or slow-moving items.

Case Requirements

Prepare a memorandum describing any misstatements or suspected misstatements you discovered while auditing J&K's 31 December 2010 inventory records.

Teaching Notes

Use of Case

This case is designed for use in undergraduate auditing courses after students have studied substantive audit procedures for inventory. Students need to be familiar with procedures to test inventory quantities and unit prices. The case should be distributed to students with instructions to perform the necessary audit procedures outside of class and prepare a written memorandum describing known or suspected misstatements in inventory. Students report spending approximately two hours performing the audit procedures and preparing the memo. On the day the memorandum is due, approximately 20–30 min are required to discuss the solution.

Suggested Solution

1 Inventory summary.   Obtain a copy of J&K's 31 December 2010 inventory summary. Agree or reconcile the total to the inventory balance on J&K's balance sheet. Test the mathematical accuracy of the inventory summary.

A copy of J&K's 31 December 2010 inventory summary (J&K Inventory Summary.xls) is presented in Appendix A. The $374 410 total on the inventory summary agrees with the Inventory balance on J&K's balance sheet. However, when students add the total costs of the individual inventory items, they should discover that the sum equals $378 410. There is a footing error in the inventory summary. In addition, when students recompute the extensions, they should discover that the total cost of the New Health model 9.0e elliptical trainer (Tag 112) is incorrect. The total cost of 32 units at $475 each should be $15 200 rather than the $17 200 listed on the inventory summary.

Note to instructors: Some students print the inventory summary and then use a hand calculator to test the mathematical accuracy. One reason the inventory summary is provided as an electronic spreadsheet instead of being printed in the case materials is to encourage students to practice their computer skills. Students can save several minutes by recomputing the extensions and summarization through Excel rather than by hand.

2 Inventory count tags.   Test the quantities on the inventory summary by tracing them to the inventory count tags (Inventory Count Tags.doc).

A sample inventory count tag is presented in Appendix B. Students should discover that the inventory summary reports 37 units of the Olympia model 990X treadmill, but the inventory count tag (Tag 130) indicates only 34 units. As students perform subsequent procedures, they should discover that the perpetual inventory records also indicate 34 units. It appears that the quantity on the inventory summary is overstated by 3 units. All count tags listed on the inventory summary are classified as 'used' on the tag control listing.

Note: Some students have difficulty distinguishing tests of existence from tests of completeness. Instructors may wish to emphasize that selecting items from the inventory summary and tracing them to the count tags is a test of existence.

3 Test counts.   Trace the 10 test counts (Auditor Test Counts.xls) to the inventory summary.

Students should find that all 10 items test counted during the physical inventory observation agree with the inventory summary.

Note: Instructors may wish to remind students that tracing the auditor's test counts to the inventory summary is a test of completeness. The auditor is determining that items which the auditor observed in the client's warehouse on 31 December 2010 are properly included on the inventory summary.

4 Unit prices. Test the unit prices on the inventory summary by tracing them to the appropriate vendor invoices (Arrow Invoices.doc; New Health Invoices.doc; Olympia Invoices.doc).

Students should discover two pricing errors during this procedure. The New Health model 6100 recumbent bike (Tag 106) is valued at $125 per unit on the inventory summary but the most recent New Health invoice indicates a unit price of $175. The Arrow model 9500 treadmill (Tag 121) is valued at $900 per unit on the inventory summary but the most recent Arrow invoice indicates a unit price of $800. Students should multiply the correct unit prices by the quantities on hand to determine that the total cost of the bikes is understated by $1750 [35 × ($175 − $125)] while the total cost of the treadmills is overstated by $4500 45 × ($900 − $800).

5 Perpetual inventory records. Trace the quantities on the inventory summary to the perpetual inventory records (Perpetual Inventory Records.xls). Review the perpetual inventory records for evidence of obsolete or slow-moving items.

The perpetual inventory schedule is presented in Appendix C. Students should discover that the quantities listed on the inventory summary agree with the ending quantities on the perpetual inventory schedule with the exception of the Olympia model 990X treadmill (Tag 130) discussed above. When students review the purchases and sales of each item, they should notice that only six units of the Olympia model 450UR upright bike (Tag 107) were sold during 2010 and 21 units remain in inventory. No Olympia model 450UR bikes were purchased during 2010, meaning that all the units in inventory are more than one year old. Students should identify this item in their memorandums as a potentially obsolete product.

Possible Extensions

The files of supporting documents containing the seeded misstatements described in the case assignment are available at http://jkfitnesscase.blogspot.com. Instructors may download the files for distribution to their students. In addition, the web site contains a second 'clean' set of files in which all the supporting documents agree with each other and with J&K's financial statements. Instructors may use the second set of files to create their own variations of the case. This flexibility permits instructors to choose the number and type of misstatements they want the case to contain and prevents students from relying on solutions from prior semesters.

In addition to changing the location of the extension, pricing, and quantity errors, instructors may introduce different types of misstatements. Instructors who want to raise the issue of fraud might consider adding some large book-to-physical adjustments to the perpetual inventory records suggesting that inventory has been stolen from the warehouse. Alternatively, instructors might add a fictitious inventory item to the inventory summary and assign it a tag number that does not appear on the tag control listing suggesting that the count tag was forged after the completion of the physical count.

Concluding Comments

PricewaterhouseCoopers (2003) and Albrecht and Sack (2000) state that future accountants must learn to solve complex, unstructured problems and communicate their solutions clearly and concisely. The J&K Fitness Supply Company case provides accounting students an opportunity to practice both skills. Students must examine a realistic-looking set of accounting records and source documents to locate four types of inventory misstatements, and must document their findings in a written memorandum. Students report that the case is effective in helping them understand the substantive procedures which auditors perform to test inventory, the documents used in testing inventory, and the types of misstatements that might occur in inventory.

References

Accounting Education Change Commission (1990) *Objectives of Education for Accountants: Position Statement Number One.* Available at http://aaahq.org/AECC/ (accessed 11 November 2009).

Albrecht, W. S. and Sack, R. J. (2000) *Accounting Education: Charting the Course through a Perilous Future* (Sarasota, FL, American Accounting Association).

American Accounting Association (AAA) Auditing Section Education Committee (2003) Challenges to audit education for the 21st century: a survey of curricula, course content, and delivery methods, *Issues in Accounting Education*, 18(3), pp. 241–263.

American Institute of Certified Public Accountants (2006) *Audit Evidence.* Statement on Auditing Standards No. 106 (New York: AICPA).

Arthur Andersen & Co., Arthur Young, Coopers & Lybrand, Deloitte Haskins & Sells, Ernst & Whinney, Peat Marwick Main & Co., Price Waterhouse and Touche Ross (1989) *Perspectives on Education: Capabilities for Success in the Accounting Profession* (White Paper) (New York: Arthur Andersen & Co., Arthur Young, Coopers & Lybrand, Deloitte Haskins & Sells, Ernst & Whinney, Peat Marwick Main & Co., Price Waterhouse and Touche Ross)

Bonner, S. E. (1999) Choosing teaching methods based on learning objectives: an integrative framework, *Issues in Accounting Education*, 14(1), pp. 11–39.

Chu, L. and Libby, T. (2010) Writing mini-cases: an active learning assignment, *Issues in Accounting Education*, 25(2), pp. 245–265.

Cook, E. D. and Hazelwood, A. C. (2002) An active learning strategy for the classroom—'who wants to win . . . some mini chips ahoy?' *Journal of Accounting Education*, 20(4), pp. 297–306.

Dee, C. C. and Durtschi, C. (2010) Return of the Tallahassee bean counters: a case in forensic accounting, *Issues in Accounting Education*, 25(2), pp. 279–321.

Hoyle, J. B., Trussel, J. and Frazer, J. D. (2007) *Lakeside Company: Case Studies in Auditing*, 11th edition (Englewood Cliffs, NJ, Prentice Hall).

Miller, C. R. and Savage, A. (2009) Vouch and trace: a revenue recognition audit simulation, *Issues in Accounting Education*, 24(1), pp. 93–103.

Morris, J. M. and Jones, A. III (2009) *Short Audit Case: The Valley Publishing Company.* 11th ed (Okemos, MI, Armond Dalton Publishers Inc.).

Paul, J. W. (2007) *Peach Blossom Cologne Company: Short Audit Case.* 4th ed (New York, NY, McGraw-Hill Irwin).

PricewaterhouseCoopers (2003) *Educating for the Public Trust* (New York: PricewaterhouseCoopers).

Tate, S. L. and Grein, B. M. (2009) That's the way the cookie crumbles: an attribute sampling application, *Accounting Education: an international journal*, 18(2), pp. 159–181.

Watson, S. F., Apostolou, B., Hassell, J. M. and Webber, S. A. (2007) Accounting education literature review (2003–2005), *Journal of Accounting Education*, 25(1), pp. 1–58.

Appendix A

Inventory Summary

Table A1.

Inventory summary

Tag no.	Manufacturer	Model	Description	Quantity	Unit cost	Total cost
Bikes						
101	Arrow	RB310	Recumbent bike	45	200	9000
102	Arrow	RT300	Upright bike	34	150	5100
103	New Health	6500	Recumbent bike	41	175	7175
104	New Health	5100	Upright bike	47	190	8930
105	New Health	5500	Upright bike	42	140	5880
106	New Health	6100	Recumbent bike	35	125	4375
107	Olympia	450UR	Upright bike	21	150	3150
108	Olympia	GT120	Recumbent bike	31	200	6200
109	Olympia	GT85X	Upright bike	44	100	4400
110	Olympia	GT95X	Recumbent bike	38	150	5700
Ellipticals						
111	Arrow	RL1500	Elliptical	46	500	23 000
112	New Health	9.0e	Elliptical trainer	32	475	17 200
113	Olympia	850	Spacesaver elliptical	48	250	12 000
114	Olympia	830	Stride select elliptical	34	175	5950
115	Olympia	330	Elliptical	34	150	5100
116	Olympia	400	Razor elliptical	34	200	6800
117	Olympia	925	Spacesaver elliptical	44	300	13 200
Treadmills						
120	Arrow	8600ES	Treadmill	38	450	17 100
121	Arrow	9500	Treadmill	45	900	40 500
122	Arrow	Vista	Treadmill—TV	38	600	22 800
123	New Health	1800	Treadmill	48	650	31 200
124	New Health	1600	Treadmill	44	500	22 000
125	Olympia	755	Crosstrainer	45	400	18 000
126	Olympia	810TR	Treadmill	50	400	20 000
127	Olympia	Crosswalk	Treadmill	45	300	13 500
128	Olympia	425	Treadmill	30	250	7500
129	Olympia	540	Treadmill	44	250	11 000
130	Olympia	990X	Treadmill	37	450	16 650
131	Olympia	860	Treadmill	30	500	15 000
Total cost =						374 410

Appendix B

Sample Inventory Count Tag

Appendix C

Perpetual Inventory Records

Table A2.

Manufacturer	Model	Beginning	Purchases	Sales	Adjustments	Ending
Arrow	RB310	28	360	343		45
Arrow	RT300	45	275	286		34
New Health	6500	47	330	336		41
New Health	5100	41	375	369		47
New Health	5500	45	335	338		42
New Health	6100	26	280	271		35
Olympia	450UR	27	0	6		21
Olympia	GT120	48	250	267		31
Olympia	GT85X	48	350	354		44
Olympia	GT95X	37	305	304		38
Arrow	RL1500	34	370	358		46
New Health	9.0e	39	255	262		32
Olympia	850	47	385	384		48
Olympia	830	36	270	272		34
Olympia	330	40	275	281		34
Olympia	400	47	245	258		34
Olympia	925	29	370	355		44
Arrow	8600ES	38	300	299	−1	38
Arrow	9500	25	360	340		45
Arrow	Vista	48	305	315		38
New Health	1800	31	385	368		48
New Health	1600	47	350	353		44
Olympia	755	30	360	345		45
Olympia	810TR	47	400	397		50
Olympia	Crosswalk	35	360	348	−2	45
Olympia	425	26	240	236		30
Olympia	540	42	355	353		44
Olympia	990X	42	270	278		34
Olympia	860	33	240	243		30

Index

Page numbers in *Italics* represent tables.
Page numbers in **Bold** represent figures.

www.routledge.com/9780415685559

Related titles from Routledge

Teaching IFRS

Edited by Richard M.S. Wilson and Ralph W. Adler

The increasing pace of global conformance towards the adoption of International Financial Reporting Standards (IFRS) highlights the need for accounting students as well as accounting practitioners to be conversant with IFRS. *Teaching IFRS* offers expert descriptions of, and insights into, the IFRS convergence process from a teaching and learning perspective. Hence this book is both timely and likely to have considerable impact in providing guidance for those who teach financial reporting around the world.

Drawing upon the experiences of those who have sought to introduce IFRS-related classroom innovations and the associated student outcomes achieved therefrom, the book offers suggestions about how to design and deliver courses dealing with IFRS and catalogues extensive listings of IFRS-related teaching resources to support those courses.

This book was originally published as a special issue of *Accounting Education: an international journal*.

January 2012: 246 x 174: 192pp
Hb: 978-0-415-68555-9
£80 / $125

For more information and to order a copy visit
www.routledge.com/9780415685559

Available from all good bookshops

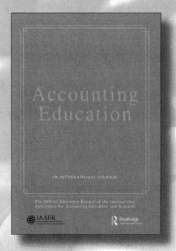